TEACHING LATIN
IN THE MODERN WORLD

p. 21

(The Proceedings of the Workshop on the
Teaching of Latin in the Modern World,
conducted at The Catholic University of America,
June 12 to 23, 1959.)

Edited by
MARTIN R. P. McGUIRE, Ph.D.

THE CATHOLIC UNIVERSITY OF AMERICA PRESS
Washington 17, D. C.
1960

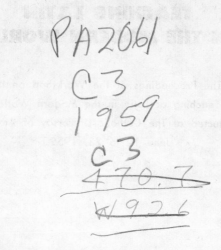
Copyright 1960

The Catholic University of America Press, Inc.

FOREWORD

New methods of presenting Latin at the high
school and college levels have been advocated or put
into practice in recent years, changes in the objectives and content of Latin programs have been suggested or carried out, audio-visual aids for Latin instruction have multiplied at a phenomenal rate, and
there has been much discussion of Latin literature in
translation, especially at the college level. But it has
long been evident that all is not well with Latin. For
some years, there has been much confusion among
Latin teachers about objectives and methods, and they
have been seeking help in their difficulties. Accordingly, when Dr. Deferrari, Director of Workshops at
Catholic University, asked me, in July, 1958, to
prepare and direct a Latin workshop in June, 1959, I
gladly accepted his invitation.

The program for the Latin workshop was worked
out in consultation with him, and the announcement,
bearing the title, On the Teaching of Latin in the
Modern World, was published early in 1959. The
workshop was intended to deal comprehensively, but,
at the same time, as concretely as possible with all
phases of Latin instruction in our Catholic high
schools and colleges. The themes of the morning
conferences and evening lectures were chosen de-
signedly to accompany and supplement the work of the
seminars, and the lecturers, as well as the seminar
directors, were selected for their special competence.

The response to the announcement of the Latin
workshop was most enthusiastic. In fact, the total
enrollment of some 160 members was about three
times larger than we had anticipated. It became
necessary, therefore, to provide for three sections of
Seminar 1, and to add Sister M. Aquinata and Sister
Claire Helene as directors of the two new sections.
Furthermore, we discovered that about a fourth of
those signifying their intention of participating in the
workshop were teachers at the high school or college
level in minor seminaries. Accordingly, we set up

iii

two additional seminars, one at the high school level
and one at the college level, to meet the special needs
of minor seminary teachers. In spite of the lateness
in date, we were able, fortunately, to secure Father
Hermigild Dressler, O. F. M. , and Father Simon P.
Wood, C. P. , to direct the new seminars.

Parts I and II of the Proceedings of the Latin
Workshop contain the full texts of all the papers given
in the morning conferences and the reports of the
seminars. The reports are sufficiently detailed to
give some concrete idea of the critical and construc-
tive approach to problems that characterized the work
of the seminars throughout. Sister M. Melchior's
report on visual aids furnishes not only valuable
guidance in the use of such aids, but also indicates
where audio-visual materials may be obtained. The
four Appendices contain respectively: the outlines,
with accompanying select bibliographies, of the
evening lectures which I gave on certain aspects of
Roman Civilization; a suggested syllabus for a four-
year high school Latin course; a translation of the
letter on the teaching of Latin sent to local Ordinaries
by the Sacred Congregation for Seminaries and Universities in 1958; and, finally, a list of the participants
in the Latin workshop.

The Proceedings should thus be of considerable
value and interest not only to the participants in the
Latin workshop, but also to Latin teachers and educational administrators everywhere. However, they
furnish only a partial and rather matter-of-fact account of what was said and done. The give-and-take
of animated seminar discussion, the use of books and
materials, the fruitful exchange of ideas in informal
conversations outside of regular meetings, the new
enthusiasms awakened in a large group of experienced
and beginning teachers, the equally stimulating effects of the Latin workshop on its directors, these
are vital and precious things of which the Proceedings
can at best give but an inkling or faint echo.

I should like to express my sincere thanks to the
lecturers and seminar directors for the enthusiasm
and effectiveness with which they carried out their
assignments. I should like to express my sincere
thanks likewise to Dr. Deferrari, Director of Workshops at Catholic University, to Miss Rita Watrin,

Assistant to the Director of Workshops, and to Mrs.
Virginia Miller, for their invaluable help in making
the Latin workshop function so smoothly and effectively. I wish to thank also the Staff of the Mullen
Library, and, in particular, Mr. Joseph Popecki
for the aid given to Sister M. Melchior in the operation of certain types of projection equipment. The
warm thanks of all are extended to Monsignor Patrick
W. Skehan, Professor of Semitic and Egyptian
Languages and Literatures, for his splendid illustrated lecture on the discovery and study of the Dead
Sea Scrolls. His lecture was the highlight of the
seminar sessions on visual aids. Finally, I wish to
thank Miss Mary Anderson for the assistance she gave
in preparing and distributing the outlines of my
evening lectures.

Martin R. P. McGuire

TABLE OF CONTENTS

PART II
SUMMARIES OF SEMINARS

directed by Josephine P. Bree, Ph.D.,
Professor of Classics, Albertus Magnus
College, New Haven, Connecticut.

PART III
APPENDICES

PART I

PRESENTATION OF MAIN TOPICS

THE PLACE OF LATIN IN OUR MODERN CURRICULUM

by

Herbert Musurillo, S.J.

There are many serious fallacies abroad in the field of American education, some of which are due to the inroads of modern progressivism, others to the frankly utilitarian spirit of our age. It is, of course, always dangerous to generalize. More factual surveys are needed, of the sort that Father Walter M. Abbott gave us in his America article, "Danger: Too Little Latin."[1] Abbott speaks of an "effective, if not intentional, sabotage of America's humanistic scholarship."[2] A reaction is now setting in. But though the battle lines are drawn, it is hard to flush out a definite enemy: for the humanistic educators of today have as their opponent a long-standing, deep-seated distrust of the liberal arts which has been ingrained, I think, in a vast body of American thinking as far back as the days of the Puritans and the Pioneers. The typical Ugly American -- to borrow the title of a recent book -- is a charming, two-fisted, self-reliant rebel whose interests have long been geared to the practical and to his immediate environment.

And yet despite this pragmatic trend in American culture, there has been, I think, a constant growth in the desire of our young people to read and think for themselves -- and here lies the future strength of the nation. We must therefore encourage our students to be suspicious of the purely utilitarian; we must show them how important it is to preserve the primacy of our humanistic goals -- the primacy of literature, philosophy and theology -- if we are ever to become a truly educated and cultured people.

As educators who are deeply interested in Greco-Roman civilization, which is the fountainhead of Western humanism, we have become anxious over what appears to be the gradual abandonment of the

3

Classical curriculum in many of our best schools as a
concession to the pressure of the times. At the
moment we are passing through a very painful period
of reappraisal and self-scrutiny; and the end is not
yet. But I think that our greatest mistake is that we
have cast ourselves in the role of delinquent parents,
asking: How have I failed? We have given in to
feelings of defeat and self-depreciation, obsessed with
the fear that we have somehow been wrong -- as
though every move made by modern educational
theorists is necessarily the right one, and all bucking
of the popular tide is necessarily wrong. I strongly
protest against that widespread and wrong-headed
notion of democracy that makes a capital sin of non-
conformity and constantly urges us to think with the
crowd. To this we should reply in the words of
Horace:[3]

> Quodsi me populus Romanus forte roget cur
> non, ut porticibus, sic iudiciis fruar isdem,
> nec sequar aut fugiam quae diligit ipse vel odit --

> If the Roman mob should ask me why,
> Though I enjoy their public porches, I do not
> Enjoy their tastes, I shall reply...:
> You are a many-headed monster -- whose
>   judgement
> Am I to take, what point of view?

So it is that in the face of the many-headed Hydra of
American education some at least have chosen to think
for themselves.

But to come more directly to our immediate concern, it is not the aim of our present discussion to
attack the Ugly American, but rather to explore a
little more deeply the place of the Classical languages
in our high school and college curriculum, and this
perhaps not so much to bring forth any new ideas as to
reassure ourselves of the value of the old ones.

Men and women have studied Latin and Greek and
all the allied disciplines because, to put it simply,
they have been deeply interested in the spiritual
tradition that has in large part created our Western
democratic culture. But this truth should not occasion
misunderstanding. Of the widely varied -- and indeed,

sometimes cafeteria-style -- programmes in our high
schools and colleges it may be said, as Augustine once
said, speaking of God's creatures, that all subjects in
themselves are good; evil comes only from imperfec-
tion and deficiency. The Classical subjects have no
absolute claim on goodness -- though sometimes to
hear some Classicists talk one would think so. There
is no strict need that all should follow a Classical
curriculum. Indeed, many great men and women,
many saints and scientists, and many worldly-wise
businessmen, did not. But the truth of the matter is
that without it we can never fully understand the
source, the meaning, and the direction of our Christian
heritage. Somewhere, in some small segment of its
population, humanity must forever keep in contact with
its historical, literary, and philosophical roots, with
what Karl Jaspers has called the Axial Period of human
thought, [4] at least insofar as it affected the growth of
modern Western civilization. For, whether we like
it or not, our character, temperament, and very
thinking have been moulded within the framework of
the Indo-European tradition. In the heroes and myths
of Greece and Rome even our children find a kinship
they do not share with the tales of India and Japan.
Plato, Aristotle, and Cicero taught the West philosophy, and Homer, Vergil, and Horace taught us the
meaning of poetry. Classical sculpture gave us our
canons of art; and Greco-Roman modes, mediated
through the liturgy and Gregorian chant, taught us the
pleasures of music. Even our theology is not completely immune from Classical influence: for we must
always recall that the Word of God was manifested to
us within the context of the Greco-Roman world; and
that it was not Hindu or Confucian, but Greco-Roman
philosophy that helped to guide and support the growth
of Christian theology. There is a clear and intelligible
bond that links Plato, Cicero, and Thomas Aquinas. [5]

But things that are worth while are often difficult
and complicated; they may take many years and a certain maturity to appreciate them. The advantages of a
Classical education are indeed subtle, and the way to
success demands constant study and application. The
result is that the typical American youngster, who
naturally dislikes learning foreign languages and has
been accustomed to seek the easy way out, can hardly

be expected to elect the Classics program. And the
matter is complicated by over-solicitous parents who
want their offspring to learn practical things, or else
be able to move from the ordinary parochial or public
school training into the highest regions of space
rocketry and astrophysics. Thus the Classical curriculum on the high school and college level has become
the whipping boy for those who are pushing scientific
training, for those who dislike linguistic or literary
disciplines, and, finally for those who would water
down any tough, muscular educational program on the
plea that every youngster, no matter how ill-equipped,
must be subjected to the same useless, colorless
courses.

But on the other side of the ledger it must be admitted that many students on the high school as well as
college level, have been repelled by our Latin and
Greek offerings simply because the courses were dull
and unimaginative. It may be that many teachers of
the Classics tend to be a conservative lot, wedded to
tradition, slow to follow trends in modern literature,
stressing in their classes agreement and conformity.
I have heard students say that in their Latin classes
there was never any possibility of discussion, never
an occasion for disagreeing either with the teacher or
other students; all seemed so fixed, rigid -- dead.
And yet what is so exciting about modern thought and
literature is that there is so much room for original
thinking, disagreement, discussion and spontaneity.
This, I fear, is something of the picture our young
people have of the typical Classical curriculum, and it
is one which we must seriously examine.

How can it be that the Classical tradition, which
has inspired such original thinking in men like Aquinas,
Goethe, Hegel, and in modern philosophers like
Heidegger and Jaspers, could ever be considered
stodgy, unexciting, dead? How is it that the literature
and thought, which have been archetypal and normative
for writers and thinkers for so many centuries, should
suddenly be considered old-fashioned and dull? As
R. R. Bolgar has analyzed it in his outstanding book,
The Classical Heritage,[6] the source of our difficulty
lies in the climate of the age, an atmosphere which is
quite beyond the control of the individual student or
teacher; and here, Bolgar suggests, the forces at

work are dominated by what he calls "the ethics of fragmentation," a view of life which subordinates the individual to the specific needs of the economic machine.

> If we come to see [says Bolgar] that the ethics of fragmentation are threatening to replace the ethics of Humanism, the educational trends of our time will become easier to understand. The traditional Arts curriculum still -- in spite of the defects foisted upon it by the current love of specialisation -- inculcates a view of life which respects individual integration of human experience.[7]

It is this sort of knowledge, Bolgar continues, which is now being pushed aside in favor of a scientific and technical training, of the sort that makes no ethical demands upon the total human personality. It is this sort of escape which is typical of our age.

Indeed, to Bolgar's position I shall add one further point. The pressure of Russian Communism has subtly been driving us into the same view of education as the Marxists have always held. For now, by slow strangulation, the liberal arts are being moved out for those subjects which best serve the interests of the State and, indeed, of the war machine. Russia is forcing the Western nations to think precisely the same way about education as she does: courses that lead to the further development of government scientists are at a premium. Government grants encourage this folly, and college administrators and the public at large are slowly being moulded to this point of view. That splendid heterogeneity that once marked American and English education is being crushed. The liberal arts programs -- and the Classics in particular -- are the first to be sacrificed on the altar of Fear, and we are gradually becoming temple-servants of the high priest, economic determinism. Or are we? If we once become aware of the enemy and adopt a positive, aggressive attitude, there may still be hope for the future.

Though the chief cause of the present situation is, as I have suggested, quite beyond the control of our students or our faculties, this is not to justify

slovenliness in our presentation of the Classical
curriculum: good teaching is still within our province. Indeed, I feel that the only hope for the sur-
vival of the Classical languages -- beyond the narrow
limits of a small scholarly minority -- will come from
a far-reaching reappraisal and revision of our teaching
methods.

It is true not only of Latin and Greek. In this age
of easily accessible libraries and cheaply purchased
books, the teacher must justify his existence. On the
high school level at least, there is never any excuse
for the teacher who is dull. Discipline, course
organization, objective marking -- yes. But when
young people are being introduced for the first time to
an area of knowledge, we teachers, if we would
achieve success, must be interesting. Further, as
the student becomes more mature and moves towards
college, the teacher -- especially if he or she is
poorly prepared -- becomes harder and harder to
justify. If the student can comprehend the subject
quicker and more clearly from a book, a college
outline, or a set of notes, we are wasting our time
preparing and paying a staff of teachers. Thus,
whether we are teaching Latin or anything else we
must never lose sight of the fact that true education,
paideia in Werner Jaeger's sense, is never merely
information, merely the communication of facts,
merely the reading or translation of a text. It is
something far more subtle and profound: it is the
stimulation of a sound and independent growth of the
individual person, within the limited area of our
subject matter, and within the cultural context of our
age. The central focus of the educational process is
therefore internal and spiritual, personal and individual -- and not strictly measurable in quantitative
terms. Indeed, there must always be a polarity
between the inner awareness of the student and the
concrete, quantitative norms by which it must be
judged. We must make sure that our students have
not only mastered the facts of the particular subject,
but have also grasped its ultimate significance, so far
as their talents and vision allow.

What I shall now say is perhaps a commonplace:
but it is always useful to remind ourselves that in the
teaching of Latin -- and, indeed, of any language --

grammar, vocabulary, and translation are only means
to an end. If the ultimate achievement of our students
is simply to give back a rote translation, then we have
failed as teachers. The aim of Classical studies is
not to create translation machines. Again, I need not
stress, before this audience, the value of Latin -- and
of Greek -- in conveying to the student a sense of
grammatical structure and linguistic form. Yet perhaps in the past there has been too much emphasis,
especially with the more mature students, of the
philology and bare mechanics of the language. For
younger students, however, there is no substitute for
solid grammar training, despite what some of the
proponents of the oral-aural methods would have us
believe. At the same time grammar is not an end in
itself, but only a halfway house on the road to comprehension and insight. A grave disservice was done to
Latin by some of the old schoolmasters who felt that
the ferule and Latin grammar were the divinely
appointed instruments of vengeance in the task of
ridding their charges of the remains of original sin.
In England at least the story used to be told that many
a Classical scholar had the Latin conjugations im-
printed on every bone in his body. But I trust that
this mistake is not being made in America; in fact, we
are probably going to the other extreme in our use of
electronic devices and audio-visual aids to make
grammar more palatable. But if our aim is comprehension, and not the mere memorization and repetition
of half understood phrases, then grammar -- or call it
what you will -- cannot be by-passed. And any system which professes to do so is, to my mind at least,
doing an ultimate disservice to the cause of Latin
studies.

It is most important that we never lose sight of
the original reason why our Classical authors were
chosen and retained in the humanistic curriculum, as
for example, Vergil, Catullus and Horace, Livy,
Tacitus, Caesar, Sallust, and Cicero. They were not
chosen -- as I fear my students sometimes think -- to
give employment to down-at-the-heel textual critics
or philologians. It is clear that they owe their place
of honor in the liberal arts curriculum to their importance in world literature and world history. Indeed, as a confirmation of this you will find in those

indispensable bibliographical tools, like Nairn,
McGuire, and Marouzeau, which are first discovered
with a profound shock by the college student, that the
longest lists of articles or monographs will usually
be found within the areas of greatest interest, and, to
put it simply, in connection with the authors that are
the most fascinating to teach and to discuss -- such as
Homer, Vergil, Tacitus, Livy, and so on. I stress
this point because there seems to be a fallacy current
among our high school and college students that
Classical scholars have only taken up their work as a
kind of penitential atonement for sin, and that all their
waking moments are spent counting peculiar forms. and
Hence, while keeping always within the comprehension
of our students, we must always try to explain to them
the literary importance of the texts we read. This
seems so obvious as not to need restatement; we must
show them how the stories we are taking are good
stories; why Caesar and Livy are considered good
historians; what makes Horace, Vergil, and Catullus
truly great poets. In this way too we will help the
young student to take his first steps in analytic and
independent thinking; and we will open his mind to new
avenues of development. We will suggest some of the
problems involved in writing history, and particularly
in the area of Roman history. We will introduce him
to the peculiar narrative viewpoint of Caesar, for
example, or Sallust, or Livy. When our text is a
poem, we must help the student to analyze it, so far
as possible, in the manner of modern literary
criticism, stressing such norms as theme, imagery,
dramatic setting, and thus open up some of the endless
riches that are to be found in the study of ancient
poetry. In this area the Classical scholar must keep
abreast, so far as he can, of the more recent develop-
ments in the field of poetic and dramatic analysis --
just as he must keep up with the changes in English
and American idiom. In short, the teacher of Latin
must not justify a charge that has, I fear, been
leveled in the past, that he has cut himself off from
the modern world. Rather, by appreciating what is
best in modern literature, the drama, the novel, we
can best introduce our young people to what was best
in the literature which stood at the origin of all
Western creativity.

In this context it may be well to air an objection which some of my students have raised in criticism of their Latin courses. In the Classics classes, it is said, everything seems so cut-and-dried; there seem to be no further avenues to be explored; one must always give back to the teacher what he or she has dictated in class or what can be found in the text book; [there is never any room in Classics for imagination or spontaneity.] Now these are objections which deserve our serious consideration. It is surely true that, because many areas of Classical studies have been so thoroughly worked over, and because Latin grammar usually seems to our grammarless students of today as rigid and unimpregnable as the Iron Curtain, the false impression is given currency that Latin studies and, worse still, the men and women who are engaged in them are inflexible and unimaginative. In this respect, Classical languages have suffered from a poor press and unjustifiably bad public relations. In any case, we must do our best to destroy this false impression. First of all, with younger students, [while demanding good, idiomatic English, we must not always insist on our own verbatim translations or interpretations; indeed, we should encourage variety in the writing or construing of Latin, provided alternate versions are all correct. The more attentive we become to the wide divergences that exist among good Latin authors, and the more deeply we are aware of the varied richness of English or American prose, the more exciting even the process of translation will prove. Sometimes as an experiment, I have my students translate a text in the manner of, say, Damon Runyon, Evelyn Waugh, Newman, Dickens, a well-known TV commentator. There is enormous variety in the levels of good English; and the students soon learn that there is no such thing as the one right translation, and that the one lesson that languages teach us is that some things cannot be translated at all. In any case, we must, so far as our subject allows, encourage our students to cultivate an independent and individual grasp of the text, based, .as it must always be, on thorough study coupled with personal insight and reflection.

I am afraid that in the area of the actual college and high school curriculum there are not many

changes that can practically be made. We must still
spend at least one solid semester and perhaps more on
a thoroughgoing grounding in grammar. As the ability
to read develops towards second term, there is a
wide variety of texts we have to choose from, including
the new Latin Psalter, simple hymns from the Missal
and the Breviary, like Dies Irae and Adoro te devote.
Some of the Renascence and later Latin scholars have
composed fine, interesting texts for high school level
Latin: among these should be mentioned the Abbé
Lhomond's charming De viris illustribus urbis
Romae, and his adaptation of the Vulgate, Epitome
historiae sacrae.[8] There is also the English Classics
master Francis Ritchie's delightful creation, Fabulae
faciles, including the fairyland world of the Argonauts.
For the rest I can only counsel more saturation reading, and a wider variety of authors than is sometimes
found in our high school programs. What has happened
to all those fine authors that used to be staple in our
Latin curriculum? I refer especially to the fables of
Phaedrus in simple iambic verse, to which we might
add some of Avianus, especially his thirty-third, The
Goose That Laid the Golden Eggs; there is nothing so
charming until we come to the French classical
fabulist, the anti-clerical La Fontaine. There is also
a simple mediaeval prose paraphrase of Aesop, which
may be used in first or second year Latin, but it is
not quite as good. We should not forget the sayings
excerpted from Publius Syrus; some of these are
delightful, especially the more amusing ones about
women. You may recall Aut amat aut odit mulier;
nihil est tertium, which might be paraphrased "With a
woman everything is either black or white." I am
sure this is untrue, but it is good Latin! Or perhaps:
Muliebris lacrima condimentum est malitiae, "When
a woman's tears are the seasoning, beware of the
main dish." Professor Waldo E. Sweet in his experimental book on structural Latin[9] makes good use of
some of Syrus' proverbs, along with some others of
less Classical Latinity.

In many schools the Latin program has become too
closely identified with Cicero and Caesar -- authors
that in the hands of some teachers can become hopelessly dull. In addition to some of the perceptive
biographies of Cornelius Nepos -- the Atticus, for

example, the Cato, and some of the Greek generals --
let us not forget Quintus Curtius Rufus' fascinating
history of Alexander the Great, especially the section
dealing with India; it is Livian prose used to tell an
exciting story. Then for our more mature girls and
boys there is the Vigil of Venus with its sprightly
symbols of spring and young love, and even perhaps
the smoky atmosphere of the pseudo-Vergilian Syrian
Dancing Girl (Copa), moving to the primitive melody
of some Roman tavern song.

I assume as the students move into the third and
fourth year of Latin, the curriculum will remain very
much as it has been, with Vergil, Horace, Catullus,
and Cicero. All good Latin teachers are aware of the
danger of reading too much Cicero, especially the
orations: too much of any author, no matter how good,
can become boring for the restless student of today.
And surely there is no need to spend an entire
semester on one speech, say the Pro Milone; Cicero
should be read with care but, with those who are
adequately prepared, briskly and rapidly. For the
college student especially, I cannot recommend too
highly some selections from the Annales and the
minor works of Tacitus, Sallust's Catiline, the
Phormio of Terence, at least in a cut version. Here
is not the place to discuss the question of Christian
Latin; but for supplementary reading all students
would enjoy selections from the Goliardic poets,
some of the narrative portions of Augustine's Confessions, some poems of Prudentius, and perhaps an
entire Latin play of that talented nun of Gandersheim,
Hroswitha. But, of course, the question of how much
Latin is to be read will depend on the quality of our
students from year to year. The curriculum, in any
case, must be arranged to avoid all appearance of
dullness or lack of variety. Catalogue descriptions
of our courses should stress the importance of our
authors from a cultural or literary point of view.
Our Latin classes should be known for their atmosphere of encouragement and stimulation of new,
interesting points of view.

To aid in this end I should suggest that, when we
find we have a particularly good group of students,
who have been well trained in their fundamentals, we
might abandon the usual classroom procedure and

adopt the project-method. Taking a specific topic,
author, or area of ancient history, we may break up
boys and girls into smaller discussion groups
responsible for different areas. For example, in
discussing the conspiracy of Catiline, one group may
be assigned whole or part of Sallust's Catiline; another,
some or all of Cicero's Orations on the conspiracy;
still others may be asked to gather further information
or modern parallels. The final results of the project
are to be left to the students themselves to assess.
The speeches of Cicero are in the nature of a vivid
on-the-scene report of the action; Cicero is, of
course, biased, but no more than a modern columnist
or statesman would be with a position to defend. The
subtlety of Sallust's retrospective portrait is that it
has many levels of meaning: there is, first of all,
the allegedly historical; secondly, there is the
suggestion that Sallust is projecting in the young
Catiline some of his own disillusioning experience as
a youth in the big city; and, lastly, in Catiline we see
a kind of symbolic portrait of Rome's slow degeneration under the domination of the nobiles, according to
the laws of history which Sallust puts forward in the
course of his work. The students themselves must
weigh the validity of Sallust's historic analysis; they
will decide how far the activities of Catiline and his
companions can be paralleled in the lives of modern
delinquents and lawbreakers. And they, too, can
make an attempt to judge the legality and prudence of
Cicero's procedure. The conspiracy is one of the
best documented events in ancient history; to examine
it closely would be a fine experiment in the meaning
and importance of Classical-historical studies. If
our curriculum allows, we may attempt many
similar seminars in related areas of poetry, history,
the drama, and oratory. And though we shall always
aim at a definite goal, the exact nature of the outcome
should be left, so far as possible, to the application
and ingenuity of the students themselves.

In our re-examination of our Classical program,
one final point remains to be considered, the use of
audio-visual aids. Every teacher should become
acquainted with the range of material -- slides,
films, records and tapes -- available within the area
of his particular class authors and subjects. They are

absolutely indispensable when we are concerned with
concrete details of ancient life and culture, art,
architecture, music, and so on. In discussing
painting, sculpture, crafts, some aids are essential.
But in the teaching of history, literature, and the
more abstract areas of ancient thought, their use is
quite limited, and indeed they are perhaps better
dispensed with in dealing with the more mature student. Audio-visual aids should not be made -- as I
fear they sometimes are -- an end in themselves; if
unwisely used they can consume costly time, and if
not accurately geared to a course they can cause
distraction and confusion. In the successful use of
tapes, slides, etc., the aptitude of the individual
teacher as well as the receptivity of a particular
student must always be carefully considered. Hence,
though they should always be available, teachers may
be encouraged but should never be forced to use them.

This leads me to the very thorny, controversial
subject of the aural-oral methods of teaching Latin
with emphasis on the tape-recorder. Every new
method must prove its worth; and the truth is that we
have not yet had enough time to evaluate the results of
this experiment. I have expressed my own skepticism
on more than one occasion. As a means of repetition
and an extension of the teacher's voice, or as an added
motivation for extra study and application, tapes are
most valuable. But that they should be the center of a
complete revision of our methodology in the teaching
of ancient languages is still the source of heated
debate.[10] The excessive and even exclusive use of the
oral-aural method in the teaching of Latin seems, to
my mind, based on a number of misconceptions. In
the first place, we must beware of a false analogy
between modern and ancient languages, and the
different motives a person might have for learning
them. The cardinal principle of many of the electronic
methods, that all languages are fundamentally oral,
however true, need have no influence on the reasons
I may have for learning, as, for instance, I may learn
Russian or Greek or Latin solely to be able to read it.
In such a case, for me to learn to repeat Russian or
Latin phrases from a recording might interfere with
my particular language goal. There is no doubt that
short of living in a country the electronic method of

learning to speak a modern language is surely indispensable. Secondly, with some oral-aural Latin
systems I have seen, there seems to be an inadequate
grasp of the place of grammar in the comprehension of
a language. Call it what you will, and teach it as you
will, grammar is merely a means to enable the
student to understand the language symbols of a foreign
tongue. In modern languages, especially in speaking,
there is sometimes little need for formal knowledge of
grammar so long as the sounds we use achieve their
purpose, get their job done in the daily context of
living. But there is no such opportunity -- or present
need -- for the creation of such a concrete communication context in the case of ancient languages. Hence,
I fear that the skimping of grammar in the case of the
Classical languages -- and the same holds true, I
suggest, of Hebrew, Sanskrit, Akkadian, etc. -- will
only result in shoddy comprehension, which will have
to be remedied if the student wishes to study the
language seriously later on. But the truth of the
matter is that the various methods are still experimental, and we cannot make a definitive judgement
until all the results are in. But until we are sure,
I can only warn teachers of the Classical languages not
to make any far-reaching changes in their methods of
teaching fundamentals, for what may be a useful experiment in the field of linguistics may perform a
disservice to the cause of Latin studies, and the
effects may be felt in this country for many generations to come. In this matter, I should prefer to be
considered a Cassandra now than have to weep for the
death of Agamemnon when it is too late.

In conclusion, we must continue to remind ourselves of the very serious reasons which compel our
loyalty to that system of liberal education which
emphasizes the study of the Classical languages. I
have suggested the importance of insisting on a
healthy pluralism in the heavy, utilitarian atmosphere
of American education. I have stressed the importance
of the Classical languages as the source and fountainhead of our Western traditions in literature, art, and
philosophy; renewed contact with our literary and
philosophical origins has always in the past been a
fruitful stimulus to creativity, and should continue to
be so for our students today. Last of all, I need not

emphasize the important symbolism that the study of
Latin has presented from the first centuries of the
existence of the Church in Western Europe. It is no
mystery that these studies should be dear to the heart
of those of us who belong to the Latin rite, whose
liturgy, whose philosophy and theology have always
been given their primary expression in the Latin
tongue.

But apart from all of these ties which bind us to
Latin, we must constantly remind ourselves as well
as our students that Christianity is a religion that is
deeply, passionately attached to the past. And this
attachment is far from being merely static and
passive. Indeed, for us the past is ever present in
our Christian mysteries -- just as our present
constantly melts into the future, in an atmosphere of
constant vigilance, waiting for the future glory of God
to be revealed. For we Christians are merely the
band of those faithful ones whom Christ left on earth
to celebrate the Memorial of His Passion, praying and
watching for His Final Coming. For us now history
has meaning: God in becoming Man has once for all
removed the ambiguity of history; and the fulness of
time in which the Word was manifested presented a
unique synthesis of Greco-Roman and Judaic currents
of thought and culture. As Christians we shall never
cease to find that period of the world full of mystery
and fascination. For our younger students, the
Classical languages still present the soundest introduction to the sources of Western literature and
thought and hence, I think, to the cultural meaning of
Christianity. Though a goal difficult of attainment,
we should still strive to keep this link with the past
amid the confusing maelstrom of American education.
We shall not be able to maintain Latin in our present-
day curriculum unless we somehow communicate it
to the modern mind in the modern idiom. But, above
all, we cannot communicate it unless we ourselves
have studied its values and appreciate them pro-
foundly.

FOOTNOTES

[1]*America* 100 (Jan., 1959) 422-424.

[2]Ibid., 424.

[3]Epistulae 1.1.70-75.

[4]See especially his Ursprung und Ziel der Geschichte (3rd ed. Munich 1951). What Jaspers has called the Achse der Weltgeschichte, the axis or pivot, as it were, occurred between the year 800 and 200 B.C.: during this period, in Jaspers' view, developed man's habit of philosophical awareness of the world, of himself, and of the Transcendent.

[5]See my survey article, "Some Influences of Pagan Antiquity on Christian Thought," Folia 7 (1953) 11-19, with the bibliography there cited. An interesting link between ancient thought and Catholic philosophy is demonstrated by E. K. Rand, Cicero in the Court-room of St. Thomas (Marquette University Press 1946). Ernst Robert Curtius has attempted to show another sort of continuity in his European Literature and the Latin Middle Ages. Translated by W. R. Trask (New York 1953), but he falls into the fallacy of emphasizing an often purely rhetorical, superficial heritage.

[6]The Classical Heritage and Its Beneficiaries (Cambridge [England] 1958).

[7]Ibid., 392. See the entire discussion, 380 ff.

[8]The diligent French priest, Charles-François Lhomond (1727-94) was for a long time a teacher at the College d' Inville, at Paris, and it was for his students here that he composed his useful series of simplified Latin texts. Too often in modern textbooks the Abbé's excellent style is modified and proper credit is not given to his pioneering work. It is ironic that within a few years of his death France would produce the Abbé Gaume, who was as violent an opponent of Classical learning as Lhomond was its devoted patron.

[9]Waldo E. Sweet, Latin: A Structural Approach (Ann Arbor 1957).

[10]See, for example, "The Georgetown Latin Project: A Symposium," Jesuit Educational Quarterly 20 (March 1958) 199-210, in which the present writer collaborated with W. M. A. Grimaldi, S.J., in pointing out some of the difficulties connected with the oral-aural methods.

GREEK AND ITS IMPORTANCE FOR THE TEACHER OF LATIN

by

Right Reverend James M. Campbell

A TRIO OF LEARNED FOOTNOTES ON THE TITLE

Any red-blooded Ph.D. suffers from a compulsion to indite footnotes, and the very title assigned to this paper -- "Greek and Its Importance For The Latin Teacher" -- affords him at least three plausible opportunities to indulge his addiction promptly. The footnotes could run somewhat as follows:

Footnote 1. The title just read to you leaves the proper adjective "Greek" most improperly naked of a noun. Since we are first of all teachers of a language, our first impulse on realizing the adjective's predicament is to rush in to the rescue with raiment consisting of the definite article as prefix and the noun "language" as affix -- "The Greek Language And Its Importance ...." It is too long after the Risorgimento, however, to thus cabin the adjective. In our day, whether we like it or not, the noun "civilization" inevitably takes over the ellipsis. The resultant phrase means ancient Greek civilization as it expressed itself in the ancient language and literature, to be sure, but also in architecture and art; in religion and philosophy; in law, politics, and governmental structures; in mathematics, science, and even technology; in the artifactitious memorials of what was once everyday life. It includes within its province everything available, and still to become available, literary and non-literary, in whole or in fragments, from Homer down to at least St. Gregory of Nazianzus -- to use authors as a basis of reference -- in the Greek motherland and in the colonies across the seas, in all the known dialectical variants in which traces of it abide, in all the non-Greek peoples and

19

languages in whom or which it was carried. This
oecumenical monstrosity is summoned up here at the
outset in acknowledgement of its claim to passing
attention and in order to get rid of it. For we need an
over-look a bit more manageable, something a bit
more commensurate with the possibilities of flesh and
blood and brains and with the historical realities of the
transmission of the Greek achievement, to say nothing
of the realities which condition the life of the Latin
teacher for whom Greek -- language, literature,
civilization -- cannot be a major commitment.

No human being, majoring throughout a long
maturity in what the word Greek connotes today and
dowered with extraordinary health and mind and leisure
and drive could do more than master a fraction of a
heritage, which, if reduced for the moment to the
item of literature only, was reckoned by Hermann
Diels some fifty years ago, on the score of bulk
alone, to be at least ten times as great as its Latin
counterpart.[1] Four centuries after Dr. Faustus, two
centuries after the last of the polymaths, and a half-
century after the calculus of Diels, no one stoops to
conquer this bulk by selling his soul to the Devil.
Rather he comes sensibly to terms with it. He
finally proceeds to do what all of his contemporaries
who have studied Greek perseveringly and comprehensively have finally had to do -- he picks and
chooses for individual cultivation this and that from
here and there in the oceanic vastness of surviving
Hellenism. He takes home to himself Dr. Johnson's
dictum into a context which the latter could not have
foreseen, "Greek, Sir, is like lace: every man gets
as much of it as he can."[2]

The teacher of Latin in our day does not aspire to
be a polymath nor even a major in Greek. But if he
is faithful to his office, he tries to grow steadily in
mastery of the Latin language and of Latin literature
-- pre-Classical, Classical, post-Classical -- in
such measure as conditions afford him opportunity,
and of Roman civilization as an illuminator of them.
And soon he finds himself confronted by the challenge
of the Greek language and Greek literature, and by the
pageant of a civilization which is Greco-Roman rather
than Roman, and begins to glimpse the professional
importance of the prefix to him in this widely-used

and awkward-sounding adjective.

The resulting problem of conscience is not as dismaying in practice, however, as at first sight it may seem to be. Fortunately, he has not only the pronouncement of Dr. Johnson to console him. He has also the example of the Romans themselves. "When in Rome, do as the Romans do" may be a dubious norm when transplanted to the field of conduct, but "when in Latin literature do as the Romans did" will serve well enough as a rough, initial rule-of-thumb in getting at the prefix of the Greco-Roman hyphenate, provided that he remember that the "Romans" thus invoked as a model were not always Romans even in the hospitable extension of the word which imperial policy came to foster, that some of these "Romans" chose to write in Greek, that much that was written in Latin was not written in Rome, and that a literature in Greek continued to be produced with little or no discernible regard for contemporary literature in Latin. Even thus alerted, he will not learn much to the point -- at least not directly to the point -- from Roman-firsters like Helleno-phobic Cato who made such noisy professions of his hatred of everything Greek, despite all that his Roman agriculture owed to Greek procedures, nor from the scanty traces of avant-garde Hellenophiles who postured on the edges of the Scipionic Circle. But the Romans and adopted Romans, the Latins and adopted Latins, who created through a process of creative borrowing the literature which is read in modern Latin classes did so in heavy and open and selective dependence, humbly and honestly, on Greek predecessors and contemporaries. The teacher of Latin who must budget his time and energy can begin with their example, can try to emphasize what they emphasized in the extant Greek deposit and ignore what they ignored, although they were not always impeccable in what they chose to borrow and imitate and although many of the originals on which they leaned are no longer at our command except in fragments. The Latin authors will thus be better understood for immediate classroom purposes, even though the dimensions of the Greek achievement are not. And time and opportunity may lead to better things.

Footnote 2. If page 10 of this Workshop's brochure be submitted to a little Textkritik, the alert observer discovers after a scrutiny sufficiently prolonged that the phrase "in the Atomic Age," which gave such a glow of contemporaneity to the title of the preceding paper, has been denied to the title of this morning, though nothing could be more indigenously Greek in etymology or thought than the word "atomic."[3] Whatever may have moved the Director of this Workshop to thus deny to Greek its moment of modernity (and he a Ph.D. in Greek), let us assume that he was recalling the mournful fact that regardless of its claims to cultural priority, regardless of any questions about originality and dependence and how much, Ancient Greek -- language, literature, civilization -- with the rarest exceptions in the history of post-Roman pedagogy, has been ancillary to ancient Latin, a minor to the Latin major; often a very minor minor, when it has been conceded a place at all.

John Stuart Mill tells us in his Autobiography[4] that he began to study Latin when he was eight; that his father inducted him into Greek, probably, when he was three -- at a time, one may speculate scatologically, when the future author of Utilitarianism and On Liberty, may have been as insouciant about household conventions as the baby Orestes in the narrative of the reminiscent Nurse in the Libation-Bearers.[5] But regardless of the stage of his domestication when he began to study Greek, Mill concedes that the course of his education was eccentric; eccentric, we may add, at a time when there was more elbow-room for Greek and Latin in curricula than is usually the case today.

In our crowded age the degree of Ph.D. in Greek is awarded now and then, and its recipient may or may not qualify thereby as one of Karen Horney's neurotic personalities of our time,[6] but often enough he is an odd bird in any man's language, as he has certainly been a rare bird even in periods much more hospitable to Greek and Latin studies than is the usual case now. He serves to remind us once more that the formal study of Greek by and large in the story of Western education has existed chiefly by grace of Latin, and that in a workshop devoted to the teaching of Latin, Greek must inevitably be considered in that subordinate role, despite its major role as a cultural

carrier in the cultural life of the West. This is not as
it should be, but this is how things are, and have
usually been, else the topic of this paper would be a
redundancy and as much of a nuisance in its way as
the adjective Greek is semantically a nuisance, when
not nailed fast by a noun.

Footnote 3. Since about the middle of the nineteenth
century, when the ancient quarrel between the protagonists of background and the protagonists of language
was finally laid to rest, we have been trying to study
language and literature with what we hope is appropriate attention to the background of which language and
literature are an expression. And in the practical
dilemma which faces us because of the impossible
vastness of the Greek heritage we are grateful to
Dr. Johnson for his aphorism and are not above
quoting it a bit out of context in self-defense. We are
rather glad that Latin authors were selective, if not
always faultlessly selective, in their appropriations.
At times we may be tempted to be glad that so much
of the Hellenistic literature from which the Romans
borrowed survives in so fragmentary a state that we,
as teachers of Latin, are absolved by the attritions
of the centuries from what would otherwise be a
formidable professional obligation. We have another
and less dubious consolation, however. I refer to the
fact that much which is valuable in Hellenism comes
to us and is, consciously or unconsciously, a part of
us from non-Roman and pre-Roman and post-Roman
as well as Roman and Greco-Roman sources; that the
Greek impact on other peoples antedated among the
Romans themselves the Roman conquest of Greek-
speaking lands and met them in their imperial
progress among non-Greek-speaking peoples; that
what we call Roman Hellenism is, at least in its
floruit, only a comparatively late example of
oecumenical Hellenic influence; that there have been
other roads from Hellenism to us than the road which
leads through Rome, though this is admittedly the
chief highway through which Hellenism has been
funnelled to the West. We cannot do better than to
touch upon so intricate and treacherous a topic in
the time at our disposal, but we can suspect something of its dimensions as we recall in some detail

certain representative facts about the transmission of
Hellenism.

THE TRANSMISSION OF HELLENISM

The story of the transmission of Hellenism is a
triumphant example of what the historians sometimes
call "the tangled skein of causality." In this Workshop
our first concern is with the Greco-Roman strand in
such a skein, but we enlarge our appreciation of it, if
we recollect some of the other strands though which
Hellenism has travelled and recall some of the
generalizations which their common traits suggest.
It is well to approach them, however, fortified by a
few caveats.

Caveat 1. As teachers of an ancient language we can
be victims as well as beneficiaries of the Risorgimento, of artists and scholars who had very firm
notions about what they wanted of the civilization
which they professed to be recapturing. The rhetoric
of their pronouncements and the aggregate of their
action can be reduced to one common denominator.
They were interested primarily in beautiful form -- in
language, painting, sculpture, architecture, and they
cultivated and ignored accordingly. Only much later,
if Boccacio and Lorenzo Valla be excepted, and in
countries beyond the Alps, did the background of
beautiful form begin to enjoy serious attention.
Meanwhile these Italian pioneers, through their pre-
occupations and predilections, fastened on historiography the habit of viewing Greek literature and
Latin literature as each culminating in a golden age
followed by a silver age and by nothing else worth a
moment's attention. Historiography has finally sur-
mounted this handicap, and so has philology; but the
victory has been so recent that as teachers of
Classics of a golden or silver hue, we can revert to
something like the misconceptions of the Risorgimento,
if we do not watch out. In considering the torturous
question of transmission, we need to recall this
recurrent danger.

Caveat 2. As teachers of an ancient and highly inflected language we are so taken with mastering it

ourselves and in trying to seduce others into some
mastery of it that it is all too easy for us to think of
transmission solely in terms of a language -- in this
case the Greek language -- despite the fact that
language, to say nothing of the Greek language, was,
and is, only one of the channels through which Hellenism has had, and still has, its impact on the world.
We need to remind ourselves that Greek agriculture,
the Greek city-state, Greek commercial practices,
and Hellenistic military science have had admirers
and imitators in other civilizations independently of,
as well as through, the medium of published works.
And Greek art, in effortless emancipation from any
language, with a lingua franca of its own, reaching
regions as far apart as Britain and India and China in
the ancient world and times as distant from one another as eighth-century B.C. Tuscany and early nine-
teenth-century America, has penetrated non-Greek
cultures more widely than has Greek civilization conveyed in books, and it may be with equal profundity.
The facades of how many of the older homes still
adorning rural prospects from Maine to Georgia and
from Kentucky to Louisiana and the features of how
many statues of the Buddha in present-day India
witness without benefit of language to this widespread
and enduring pervasiveness? Much of this extra-
lingual influence has reached us by way of Rome, but
much of it, and conspicuously in the cases of art and
architecture, has not.

Caveat 3. We who teach a foreign language do not
need to be told that thinking -- religious, philosophical, political, scientific -- requires the agency of
language, but we are not always professionally happy
when we recall how the language in which a given
product of such thinking is first developed shrinks as
a utility after the thought is successfully lodged in
another competent vernacular. Literature, and especially poetry, cannot be so completely transferred,
as a rule; but if our professional energies are chiefly
engaged in what we call translating, who are we to
deny that many of the literary virtues of even a
literary masterpiece can be carried over into alien
tongues? This ironic misfortune of our profession
should give us a modicum of sympathy for the

craftsman who must either build obsolescence into the
product of his talents or be faced with obsolescence
himself and with the legislator and cabinet officer who
must worry about a conflict of interest. This threat
of a diminishing market hovers over all teachers of a
language which first houses an item much desired by
people of another idiom. It is underlined most cruelly
for us when ancient Greek, as in so many things of the
mind, happens to be the language of origin. In this
case the diminishing market rapidly becomes a
vanishing one.

It is not only in unilingual, antilingual, latter-day
America that Greek has had a hard time. All through
the centuries of the Greek impact on the world, including the many centuries which antedate Columbus,
the Greek language has exhibited an over-all tendency
to discharge into another language the riches which it
conveys and thereupon to retire from the scene,
except insofar as it has been sustained artificially by
church or state or scholars or esoteric coteries of
aesthetes and antiquarians or by the somnolent insti-
tutionalism of academic foundations or by the birch rod
of the old-fashioned schoolmaster. The most valuable
gift of Hellenism to other civilizations, most people
would agree, is the complexus of intellectual detach-
ment, critical approach, restless inquiry, sense of
beauty locked up in Greek books and expressed in
Greek architecture and art. These qualities, perhaps
somewhat to our distress, have been completely
caught up into the traditions of non-Greek philosophy
and science and have been reproduced to an impressive
degree in the literary art of non-Greek peoples
through imitation and translation. And how often have
literary devices of Attic Greek in its heyday -- the
figures, the tropes, the cadences, the particles, the
emphasis on the verb, the word-order even been
imported into other languages to ennoble them as
instruments of expression after an initiatory and non-
sensical period of extravagant appropriation and experiment?

Why this benevolent, hit-and-run behaviorism is
so eminently a mark of the Greek language is not a
profound puzzle. The mystery is largely resolved by
the fact that what writers in ancient Greek achieved in
many fields is so superior to indigenous achievements

set down in non-Greek tongues and is of such universal usefulness that the conveying language is only the accidental, passing missionary of much which was conveyed. If these writers in ancient Greek had committed their original achievements to another language, these excellences would still have gotten through the linguistic curtain; and the original language, its mission fulfilled, would have faded away. No one would maintain, for example, that Aristotle has been cherished through the centuries because he wrote in Greek, much less in the kind of Greek in which surviving Aristotle is for the most part written. Another reason for the decline of ancient Greek among non-Greek peoples whom it benefits is the linguistic hurdle which it requires. I refer here not so much to the initial difficulties -- the precision, the analysis, the synthesis, the morphological alertness which it relentlessly demands even of novices -- but to the variety, the compressions, the prolixities, the subtleties, the burgeoning vocabulary whereby highly original authors stretch a highly inflectional and highly conventional medium into expressing things which neither it nor, presumably, any other language had ever expressed before. Homer and Herodotus would not be of this company of innovators nor most of the Attic Orators nor Xenophon, at least not on his own, nor many of the writers of the post-classical period, when the available thesaurus of expression had become enormously enriched by experimental pioneers, when originality had exhausted most of its opportunities, when inflections were breaking down, and grammar and regularity were in the saddle. But Thucydides, the philosophers, most of the lyric poets, the tragic and comic poets, the Hellenistic poets, and Polybius, Plutarch, Lucian -- to each of whom the West owes so much -- are a different story, a different order of magnitude, as many of us could eloquently testify out of our struggles with their texts at one time and another. Now many patient temperaments have doggedly besieged the barriers which the creativeness of these authors has erected and have achieved a large command of their works. But many of the greatest ornaments of the West -- not so patient in the years when foreign tongues come easiest, or living in situations where

opportunities to learn were not available, or distracted by original drives of their own -- derived what
they could from their faulty knowledge of the language
or from translations which werę often faulty, and
made up for their linguistic and background insuf-
ficiencies through the unaccountable inspirations of
genius. St. Augustine, John of Salisbury, Robert
Grossesteste, Roger Bacon, Goethe are examples
which come readily to mind -- witnesses to the
beneficent effects of even a little Greek civilization
and the fugitive character of the language which was
the original carrier of so much of it.

In speaking of the fugitive character of ancient
Greek in the last of the three caveats above, I was
careful to refer to it as an "over-all tendency."
There have been exceptions; and against the sobering
background of these caveats it is pleasant to recall
the names of persons and peoples for whom the
language was something more than an expendable
gangplank to the acquisition of a superior culture. A
long list could be compiled of individuals for whom the
Greek language and literature were an end as well as
a means, and perhaps more end than means in many
cases. Most of the surviving names in the story of
Western Greek studies well down into the nineteenth
century would be included in such a list, although no
one so listed after the second century A.D. would
have known how the ancient language sounded or
would have known much about the literature until the
High Renaissance was under way. Early on such a
list would appear the names of persons in the ancient
world who hated the Greeks from political, military,
or commercial reasons and yet were philhellenists
culturally and gave the language a large place in their
philhellenism -- Mithridates of Pontus, for example,
about whom Cicero worried so much in the last
century B.C., and two centuries before Mithridates
the name of a whole nation would be inserted -- that
of the people of the Sicilian hinterland who fought
against Greek aggression in Sicily before the First
Punic War, while adopting simultaneously and
voluntarily the religion, the art, and the language of
these aggressors.

That a whole people, while beleaguered by live
Hellenes, could be culturally philhellenic, is

probably unique. Less eccentric-seeming to us, because of our cultural history, is the persistent study of Greek for cultural purposes long after the last of the ancient Hellenes had died and long after many of the treasures of the ancient literature had passed more or less successfully into non-Greek vernaculars -- the continuing study of Greek authors as classics, as we call the practice. We expect some provision for such study, at least as a vestigial item, somewhere in the educational programs of all advanced peoples who are Indo-European linguistically. But it also turns up among four European peoples who have resisted successfully the efforts of the Indo-European family to displace their native tongues -- the Basques, the Estonians, the Finns, the Magyars. Among the commonplace items of our everyday information is the enthusiastic study of Greek during the Western Renaissance among the better-known users of an Indo-European language. That these four peoples were equally vigorous in their cultivation of Greek classics at the time may strike a reasonably well-informed person among us as odd, and as all the more eloquent because of its oddity. And when we recall the unsuccessful efforts of Joseph II to impose German on the Magyars and the multiple, prolonged, spectacular resistance of the Basques to outside influences, this hospitality to ancient Greek becomes a nostalgic puzzle to present-day teachers of Greek and Latin. Similar consolations can be found in the stories of ancient Bithynia and Pontus, of the Bactrian and Parthian Empires, and of the Neuhumanismus Movement of eighteenth-century Germany, all the more impressive because of their complete spontaneity, and in the stories of many other nations and groups to whom it became an article of faith that the regions in which they were living would ascend to a higher plane of culture and persist on this higher plane through a first-hand and continuous contact with the survivals of Greek civilization.

We who profess an ancient language today are tempted to fasten on such lists with the eagerness of tobacco companies on the alert against studies about lung cancer, for the story of Hellenism in non-Hellenic regions is chiefly a story in which the language, despite consoling exceptions, departs early. Like the inundations of some beneficent river, it bestows its prodigal sediments in flood-tide and then collapses into a trickle. We are prepared to accept the extra-lingual penetration of Greek art as something which we cannot charm away, since art is the extra-lingual, supra-lingual thing which it is. But an equally intractable fact for us is the view of the ancient Greeks themselves on this issue of language, despite their enormous pride in their own language. In the ancient Greek world you could speak Greek and yet be a barbarian to the eyes -- and ears -- of other Greeks. You could speak Greek and be a Greek ethnically and still be a barbarian to them, though you lived in the Greek motherland itself. This awkward fact, or complexus of facts, is heartlessly underlined for us over many centuries by the peoples of Aetolia, Epirus, Macedonia, and the remoter reaches of Thessaly. These Greeks were for the most part barbarians to their eastern and southern cousins until after the time of Alexander, although some of them (from Epirus and Macedonia) threw off that reproach as early as the fifth century B.C. when they did a thing that was done so often with similar results before and after them by moving out of their fastnesses to conquer Greek city-states militarily and be conquered culturally in turn, adding the Greek way of life to their hereditary proprietorship of the language. This attitude of Greek towards Greek is no more remarkable in its way than our own untutored perception that a tri-lingual Swiss waiter is not thereby an educated human being and that a hopelessly unilingual American may be educated in a highly civilized sense or be scarcely educated at all, but as teachers of a foreign language we do not take readily to this distinction between education and language and are especially disconcerted that the Greeks themselves should have made this distinction even when their native language which we profess was one of the terms of the comparison. The same basic conviction, however, is implied in the action of many ancient peoples who became Hellenized beyond a doubt but who did not include the language as a permanently necessary feature of their Hellenism: the Etruscans of eighth-century B.C. Italy, the equally non-Greek Carians and Lydians of the following century, the Semitic

Syro-Phoenicians of the middle fourth century, the
Latin-speaking barbarians of Central Italy in the
fourth and third centuries, all those who were
Hellenized in the wake of Alexander's armies independently of the need of Greek in official government business; and the many examples of the phenomenon after Alexander's time which could be cited
among Christians and non-Christians alike.

ROMAN HELLENISM

Roman Hellenism, however, is the most striking
witness in the ancient, mediaeval, or modern world
to the singular power of Greek civilization to pene-
trate and conquer another civilization and to maintain
its preeminence long after the Greek language has
faded as a cultural prop. The phrase "Roman
Hellenism" as used here includes phenomena already
operative in Italy before the small town on the Tiber
slipped into its unconscious march towards empire
and phenomena operative throughout that empire long
after the Pax Romana had become a beneficent
social reality. Indeed, one of the factors which
helped the Pax Romana to flourish was a quiescence
which grew into acquiescence as the Greeks discovered
the cultural condominium which the expansion of the
Empire gave them.

When we think of Roman Hellenism today we must
seek its beginnings in a twilight period almost four
centuries before the traditional date for the founding
of the Republic. We have to go back to about 850 B.C.
and the coming of the Etruscans to Italy and their
rapid Hellenization in what became Etruria and their
gradual introduction of the Romans into the superi-
orities of Greek civilization long before the Romans
absorbed still more of it by conquering the Etruscans
in the fifth and fourth centuries. We have to recall
the progress of the Romans down the peninsula
through Campania and Magna Graecia and across the
Straits of Messina and then into the Greek East, with
concomitant augmentations of Hellenism, as they
proceeded, through the contacts of conquest and
commerce. And it is pleasant for language teachers
to remember that in the central administration which
conquest imposed on Rome the imperial chancery was

bi-lingual, Greek enjoying with Latin the prestige of
everyday official use. We should also recall how
Roman emperors from Augustus to Hadrian resumed
Alexander's policy of founding Greek city-states and
how the Romans spread a Latinized Hellenism over the
Appenines and beyond the Alps from the delta of the
Danube to the mouths of the Rhine and across the
Straits of Dover into Britain and southward from
Sicily across the Mediterranean into Africa. Today
we are much given to admiring the late and vigorous
flowering of Hellenism and of the Greek language in
culturally remote Cappadocia of the third and fourth
centuries of our era. One of the remarkable facts of
this phenomenon is that Romans were its evangelists.
This extraordinary and persistent deference to the
Greek language and Greek culture was not completely
divorced from politics and economics but a sincere
conviction about Greek superiority must be accounted
the master-motive.

How deep was this conviction is attested by the
dominance of Greek education in Rome, athletics
excepted, from the third century B.C. and by the
fluency in Greek that was expected of an educated man
or woman even after Latin had absorbed many of the
resources of Greek, and Greek was beginning its long
decline as a spoken and written medium in the West.
It was also attested outside the circles of formal
education by the popularity of plays written in Latin
but based on Greek originals, with the story and
characters unashamedly Greek; by such amazing
announcements, for example, as Plautus' downright
declaration to his Roman audience at the beginning of
the Menaechmi: "writers of comedy ... always
allege that the scene of action is Athens, to make it
seem more Greek to you."[7]

These large and abundantly established facts are
written in capitals across the face of surviving Latin
literature, and in huge capitals in the case of the
Latin literature which most teachers of it profess. If
we use the word "literature" broadly enough, we can
speak of a Latin literature which is innocent of
Hellenism. But I assume that no one here usurps the
province of the graduate seminar and imports into the
classroom what remains of the Song of the Arval
Brothers, the Fabula Atellana and the like; that no one

tries to charm the students of our time with the Latin
equivalent of the nursery jingle, "The Queen was in
her parlor eating bread and honey." I assume that
Latin literature, as we commonly use the word
"literature," does not begin for us until Livius
Andronicus from Greek Tarentum goes up to Rome in
272 B.C. to teach Greek and Latin, to translate the
Greek Odyssey and some Greek tragedies and comedies into Latin Saturnians, and thus to inaugurate,
howsoever unwittingly, that appropriation of Greek
themes and forms and modes of expression which are
an abiding mark of Roman literature long after Latin
had become through Greek nourishment and native
genius a noble instrument of expression and Roman
literature one of the great literatures of the world.

This morning, I take it, I am not expected to
attempt a detailed evaluation of the debt of Rome to
Greece. Several easily available handbooks do about
all that can now be done on this score. The theme of
influences is usually torturous and often treacherous
and in the present instance the inescapable difficulties
are compounded by the fact that so many of the Greek
originals and their Latin imitators are now only rags
and patches. This paper does its full duty here, perhaps, by asking a simple question: what Latin author
can we profess on the high school or college level who
is completely innocent of profound Greek influences,
no matter how impressive his claims to creative
originality? It makes little difference whether our
Latin authors are pagan or Christian; whether
Christian writers are frankly steeped in Hellenism or
profess to be unaffected by it. The mark of Hellenism
is upon them all, and with a little probing becomes
plainly visible beneath the surface of a most unhellen-
ic-seeming facade. It may be useful to recall that
Greek influences -- classical and post-classical --
have worked their way into situations which we tend to
consider most unlikely -- the Latin Old Testament
before St. Jerome, for example; the Latin New
Testament which reflects so faithfully its Greek original; and the liturgy whose Greek origins are
memorialized for us daily by the Kyrie Eleison of the
Mass.

And so, while much is made of the cultural
humility of the Latins when they were confronted by

Greek achievement, their submissiveness was not
unique as we need to remind ourselves from time to
time, in either the ancient world or afterwards.
Roman Hellenism happens to be our most conspicuous
example of a phenomenon often repeated in the cultural
life of the West both before and after the Roman
chapter.

One hundred and fifty years ago all Latin teachers
would have been annoyed, and the more incandescent
among them would have been angry, if the topic of this
paper had been suggested. With much conviction, if
not with much light, they would have pronounced the
subject supererogatory. We know vastly more about
the influence of Greek on Latin than did the contemporaries of Thomas Jefferson, but one of the paradoxes
of our condition is that the more we have gotten to know
about Hellenism among the Romans and among others,
the less attention we have given to Hellenism in our
schools and colleges. Other reasons than human per-
versity can be offered in explanation of this paradox.
But what of the graduate school through whose offices
so much of this added knowledge has been gained?
How many of our graduate schools separate Greek
from Latin in their departmental structures, and how
many departments of Latin allow candidates to follow
a program in Latin, unfortified by a minor in Greek --
unfortified, in other words, by a minor which is a
minor in name only, since the major is so largely
Greek in Latin dress?

These questions -- largely rhetorical, I am
afraid -- are another way of asking how a teacher of
Latin in our day can in good professional conscience
exclude Greek from his professional studies. A
student of Latin whose formal education ceases at the
end of high school or college may ignore Greek and
still sleep soundly at night because of the soothing
claims to his attention made by other subjects which
have grown up since the days when Greek and Latin
were the chief part of the curriculum. But not the
teacher of Latin who is alert. His slumbers are
liable to be disturbed not merely by the pricks of
conscience but by the vastly altered environment in
which he practices his mystery. I refer simply to the
fact that because of the presence and pressures of
other subjects in our day, Latin must be taught

masterfully, if it is not to be pushed aside. And mastery calls for cultivation of the Greek originals from which Latin literature mostly derives.

Because of these pressures from subjects which were once outside the pale, various simplifications have been tried to give a student some sense of tangible achievement in Greek during the short time normally available for a firsthand acquaintance with its riches. Thus, he begins to read the Gospel of Luke and the Book of Acts after an intensive six weeks of summer school induction into the elements of Biblical Greek prose, or he comes swiftly to Homer after an introductory term of Homeric Greek alone. And then there have been all the unfortunate attempts to by-pass the pagan Classics in favor of "the Fathers," to use a large and airy phrase. Of these various quickies towards giving the student the consolation of possessing in a short time something of classical stature which he can call his own, the Homeric short-cut has been the most popular, since Vergil leaned so heavily on Homer, but what about Hesiod, Aratus, Apollonius, and Theocritus on whom Vergil also leaned? For the professional Latin teacher who knows no Greek a "still more excellent way" is one of those modern introductory manuals in which Homer and the minor dialogues of Plato, rather than third-rate Xenophon, are the immediate and early-realized objective and from which one is encouraged to develop a firsthand acquaintance with other authors in realizing Dr. Johnson's aphorism about getting as much Greek -- civilization and language and literature, we would specify -- as we can.

FOOTNOTES

[1]Hermann Diels in an article published in Neue Jahrbuecher ([1905] 692) and Englished in the Jones-McKenzie revision of Liddell and Scott's A Greek-English Lexicon. 1(Oxford 1925) p.v.

[2]G. Birbeck Hill, ed., Boswell's Life of Johnson. 4 (4th ed. Oxford 1887) 23.

[3]The title of Father Musurillo's paper as originally announced was "Latin and Its Place in the

Secondary School and College Curriculum of the
Atomic Age." It was decided later to give the paper
the shorter and better title which it now bears, "The
Place of Latin in Our Modern Curriculum."

[4]John Stuart Mill, Autobiography (New York 1924)
3-4.

[5]G. Thomson, Aeschylus, The Oresteia.
1 (Cambridge [England] 1938) lines 730-758.

[6]Karen Horney, The Neurotic Personality of Our
Times (New York 1937)

[7]Plautus, Menaechmi, lines 7-9.

THE ORIGIN, DEVELOPMENT, AND CHARACTER
OF CHRISTIAN LATIN

by

Martin R. P. McGuire

The systematic investigation of Christian Latin
may be said to have been inaugurated by Roensch's
Itala und Vulgata (1st ed. 1868; 2nd ed. 1875) and
Goelzer's Latinité de Saint Jérôme (1884). Since that
time, constantly increasing attention has been given to
the investigation of the Latinity of Christian authors,
documents, and inscriptions. A number of valuable
studies were published before the end of the First
World War, among them such outstanding works as
Bonnet's monograph on the Latin of Gregory of Tours
and Löfstedt's linguistic commentary on the Peregrinatio Aetheriae.[1] But it is especially from about
1920 that we have advanced beyond the stage of mere
factual recording of linguistic data in Christian Latin
writings, and the general and rather superficial interpretation and evaluation of such data, to a really satisfactory understanding of the origin and precise
character of the Christian element in Late Latin.
Thanks to the pioneer work of the School of Nijmegen,
which approached the problem of Christian Latin from
the viewpoint of General Linguistics as well as from
that of Comparative Indo-European Philology, and in
particular to the many excellent studies published
by its most distinguished representative, Dr. Christine
Mohrmann, Early Christian Latin is now regarded
more and more as a Sondersprache in origin, i.e., as
the specialized language of a definite group closely
united by the bonds of a common interest, revealing in
its origin and development many of the characteristic
features of other specialized languages.[2] It is the
purpose of the present paper to sketch the rise of
Christian Latin largely from this point of view and to
indicate, if very briefly, how the specialized language
of a small and humble group became the distinctive

linguistic element in the great Christian Latin literature of antiquity, and also how it eventually became
the common language of the Christianized Roman
world. For the spoken Late Latin, to use the phrase
of Frédéric Ozanam, became a "baptized Latin," and
thus gave Primitive Romance and the Romance
languages their basic Christian vocabulary.

The Gospel, outside Palestine, was first preached
in Greek throughout the great cities of the Mediterranean world. This Greek was the Hellenistic koinê, a
flexible language of many shades, and the common
language of communication of the Jews of the Diaspora
in Alexandria, Rome, Corinth, Carthage and other
centers, as well as of the great mass of other freemen,
slaves and freedmen of Eastern origin in the great
cities of the East and West, and especially in Rome
itself, the capital of the Empire. It was only natural
that the written Gospel should also be composed in
Greek. The Gospel of St. Matthew, it is true, was
written first in Aramaic, but it was soon translated
into Greek and circulated as a Greek work with the
other books of the Greek New Testament. The Old
Testament employed by the Jews of Alexandria, and of
the Western Diaspora in general, was the Septuagint
Version, and this translation, which was regarded as
inspired, became the authoritative text of the Old
Testament for Gentile Christians. The Septuagint, it
may be added, exercised a considerable influence on
the style of the Greek New Testament. Finally, it
should be observed that the Apostolic Fathers and
Early Apologists wrote in Greek, and that the liturgical
language and the general language of ecclesiastical
communication and administration of the Early Church,
even in the West, was Greek, or almost exclusively
Greek, down to the beginning of the second half of the
second century A.D. At Rome, Greek remained exclusively or in large part the liturgical language until
the second half of the fourth century.

In the light of this background, it is not surprising
to find that the first Christian communities in the West
were Greek and long remained predominantly Greek.
The need and demand for the use of Latin as a vehicle
for the Gospel and as a Christian religious language in
general could only arise when there was a sufficient
number of Latin converts who did not understand

Greek. While our evidence is scanty, it is practically
certain, as Bardy has emphasized in a recent book,
that this condition existed in Africa, Gaul, and
probably at Rome itself, not later than 150 A.D., or
even a little earlier. In one of her studies, Dr.
Mohrmann has attempted to show that, contrary to
prevailing opinion on the matter, the development of
Christian Latin at Rome was not later than that in
Africa nor markedly influenced by it, but is rather to
be regarded as a parallel growth in time and
character.[3] Whatever may be said for this new view,
and it deserves careful examination and further investigation, the earliest extant monuments of Christian
Latin come from Africa, the Acta Martyrum Scilli-
tanorum and the Passio Felicitatis et Perpetuae.
While they date from 180 and 202 A.D. respectively,
they reflect the use of Latin as a well-established
linguistic medium in the Christian communities of
North Africa. Furthermore, the first work mentions
certain libri et epistulae Pauli, viri iusti. There is
every reason for believing that there is question not of
the Epistles of St. Paul in Greek but rather in Latin
translation. Tertullian (died after 220 A.D.) was
already familiar with at least two Latin translations
of the Bible, one of which was a Marcionite text, and
by the time of St. Cyprian (died 258 A.D.) all, or
almost all, the books of the Old and New Testament
were available in Latin. The copious extant remains
of the Old Latin or pre-Hieronymian Bible enable us
to get a fairly adequate knowledge of the language and
style of the early Latin versions.[4]

The problem facing the Latin members of the
Christian communities in the West was the creation of
an adequate terminology in Latin for Christian ideas,
institutions, and practices, and, as a central basic
task, the translation of the Sacred Books of their
religion not only with accuracy but in a form that
would be generally intelligible and acceptable. The
problem was a formidable one, because the Christian
religious terminology in Greek had been long established, and it was in part derived from the terminology
found in the Sacred Books themselves and thus enjoyed
all the greater honor and prestige.

The problem must also be thought of in terms of
the social and intellectual character of the Christian

communities. The great majority of the early
Christians down to the middle of the third century were
drawn from the lower strata of society in urban centers. They had little contact with the small class of
the educated elite or with the artificial literary
language and its productions as expounded in the
schools of the grammarian and the rhetor. There was,
in fact, a tendency to despise cultural pretensions,
bound up as they were with a dominant paganism and a
general hostility to the new religion. The popular
living Latin, and not the literary language, was the
main foundation underlying the development of
Christian Latin in its earlier and freer creative
phase. Hence, it is not surprising to observe a kind
of democratic spirit in the bold freedom with which
the Latin Christians utilized language to meet their
needs. [5]

The authors of the Old Latin versions of the
Bible and the great pioneer Christian Latin writer
Tertullian played such a fundamental role in the
development of Christian Latin and in giving it an in-
delible characteristic stamp that we must examine
their achievement briefly. The Bible occupied a
place of central importance and influence in the early
Christian communities. Copious passages were read
from it in liturgical services, the Biblical psalms and
canticles were sung by all the faithful in religious
assembly or in their homes, and they were known by
heart. The Bible served as the core of early
Christian preaching to such a degree that the greater
portion of our extant early Christian exegesis consists
of collections of homilies on the Books of Scripture.
A large number of scriptural episodes were familiar
to all, as is revealed by early Christian art, and
scriptural language, imagery, and thought permeated
the Christian community. This profound influence of
Scripture gave early Christian Greek and Latin an
Oriental coloring which, because of our long Christian
cultural tradition, we often fail to recognize. [6] At any
rate, we do not appreciate fully how foreign, strange,
and unliterary the Scriptures seemed to the ancients
trained in Greek and Roman schools of rhetoric and
adherents of their literary traditions. In this connection we may recall the famous passage in St.
Augustine's Confessions where he tells how in his

earlier career he had attempted to read the Scriptures
but was repelled by their style. [7]

The Greek-speaking Christians had the special
advantage of possessing the Scriptures in their own
language, and in its more popular and living form, the
Hellenistic koinê. The task of the early Latin translators, then, was to furnish accurate versions of the
Greek which at the same time would be easily intelligible to the ears and minds of Latin Christians, the
majority of whom belonged, as I have said, to the
lower strata of society. These early translators show
little evidence of any acquaintance with the productions
or style of the higher literary Latin. Contrary to an
opinion still widely prevalent, however, they were
certainly not ignorant men, but possessed a fairly
good knowledge of Greek and Latin. Out of reverence
for the sacred text, they frequently do violence to
Latin idiom in their slavish word-for-word rendering
of the Greek, but they seldom betray serious misunderstanding of their original. In choice of vocabulary, they were guided by the needs of the Latin
community for whom they were translating. As will
be shown below, they made use of the religious vocabulary, in part half-Greek rather than Latin, employed
by the first generations of Latin Christians. They
coined words or adopted meanings in keeping with the
spirit of the popular living Latin, and for vocabulary
in general they drew heavily and without inhibitions on
the words familiar to them in their social milieu.
They were, on the whole, so successful that the major
portion of their vocabulary was accepted and became a
permanent part of Christian Latin. [8] St. Jerome could
not ignore the long established phraseology of the Old
Latin versions even in his new and masterly translation of most of the Old Testament from the Hebrew and
Aramaic. Moreover, it is not his translation of the
Psalms from the Hebrew but his second revision of
the Old Latin based on Origen's Hexapla which
constitutes the Psalter in the Latin Vulgate. We still
read portions of Esther and the Books of Wisdom,
Ecclesiasticus, Baruch, and Macchabees in a more or
less revised form of the Old Latin. As regards the
Vulgate New Testament, our Gospel text is Jerome's
thorough revision of an Old Latin version, not a new
translation from the Greek, and the texts of the

remaining books are likewise only revisions of Old
Latin translations.[9]

    Tertullian's role is still represented in the hand-
books of Latin Literature and Patrology, with the
welcome exception of Quasten's, as the father of
Ecclesiastical Latin or even of Christian Latin in
general.[10] In the light of the researches of the
Nijmegen School, this view must be modified. Tertullian, without question, is one of the most original
and powerful writers in the Latin language, but almost
half the coinages ascribed to him were not employed
by later Christian writers. Furthermore, many of the
words which have been assigned to him, especially
those dealing with Christian institutions and practices,
must have been current in the Christian Latin communities for two or more generations before he
wrote. The first Latin translators of the Bible were
the real pioneers in creating Christian Latin terminology. The achievement of Tertullian, and it was a
very significant one, was this. With the freedom of
the great stylist which he was, a freedom which was
emboldened by the intensity of his personality and of
his Christian ardor, he created what may be characterized as the Christian Latin literary language and
style. In his writings the higher profane literary
language of his time, his inherited Christian vocabulary, and his own coinages are freely and even
defiantly blended. St. Cyprian, a generation later,
also represents the higher Christian literary style,
but is much more conservative, reflecting the
stylistic tastes and devices of the contemporary
rhetoric.

    The name of Tertullian recalls also the pressing
and difficult problem facing Christians of East and
West, from the second century, namely, the attitude
which Christians should adopt towards the pagan
literature and learning of the past and present. In
reaction against the contemporary pagan morality and
superstition, and smarting under the scornful attacks
of pagan intellectuals and persecution by the State,
some Christians like Tertullian and Tatian raised the
cry, "What has Athens to do with Jerusalem?" They
advocated a break with pagan culture, although even
Tertullian himself grudgingly modified his own
extreme views in the light of practical needs. But the

majority of the ecclesiastical writers and Fathers in
the Greek East and Latin West accepted the pagan
culture in a number of essential features, justifying
their position on grounds of theory as well as of
practical necessity. The story of the relations between Christianity and pagan literature, learning, and
education has been told in greater or less detail in
recent years, especially by De Labriolle, Marrou,
Courcelle, Ellspermann, and Laistner.[11] A few
points, however, must be discussed here, as they
have such a direct bearing on the rise of Christian
humanism in Antiquity and on its continuance and development in the Middle Ages and Renaissance.

The central question is this: how did Christianity
justify in theory its employment and assimilation of
pagan literature and learning? Origen and Clement of
Alexandria had dealt with this problem, for they were
really the first to make wide and systematic use of
pagan cultural achievements in the service of the new
faith. But it received its classic solution in St.
Jerome, St. Augustine, and St. Basil,[12] and one
which is cited again and again from their own times to
the nineteenth century in the controversies over the
place of the pagan Classics in education. The following passage from St. Augustine's De doctrina
Christiana[13] -- and four centuries later it was incorporated without acknowledgment by Hrabanus
Maurus into his De institutione clericorum[14] -- sums
up the Christian position:

> Furthermore, if those who are called
> philosophers, especially the Platonists, have
> said things by chance that are truthful and
> conformable to our faith, we must not only
> have no fear of them, but even appropriate
> them for our own use from those who are, in
> a sense, their illegal possessors. The
> Egyptians not only had idols and crushing
> burdens which the people of Israel detested
> and from which they fled, but they also had
> vessels and ornaments of gold and silver, and
> clothing, which the Israelites, leaving Egypt
> secretly, claimed for themselves as if for a
> better use. Not on their own authority did
> they make this appropriation, but by the

command of God, while the Egyptians themselves, without realizing it, were supplying
the things which they were not using properly.
In the same way, all the teachings of the
pagans have counterfeit and superstitious
notions and oppressive burdens of useless
labor, which anyone of us, leaving the association of pagans with Christ as our leader,
ought to abominate and shun. However, they
also contain liberal instruction more adapted
to the service of truth, and also very useful
principles about morals; even some truths
about the service of the one God Himself are
discovered among them. These are, in a
sense, their gold and silver. They themselves
did not create them, but excavated them, as it
were, from the mines of divine Providence
which is everywhere present, but they
wickedly and unjustly misuse this treasure for
the service of demons. When the Christian
severs himself in spirit from the wretched
association of these men, he ought to take it
from them for the lawful service of preaching
the Gospel. It is also right for us to receive
and possess their clothing in order to convert
it to a Christian use, i.e., those human institutions suited for intercourse with men and
which we cannot do without in this life.

For, what else have many noble and loyal
members of our faith done? Do we not per-
ceive with what an abundance of gold, silver,
and clothing that very eloquent teacher and
blessed martyr, Cyprian, was loaded when he
left Egypt? With what an abundance Lactantius
was enriched, and Victorinus, Optatus, Hilary,
and innumerable Greeks, not to speak of men
who are still living? That most obedient serv-
ant of God, Moses himself, was the first to do
this, and it was written of him that he 'was
instructed in all the wisdom of the Egyptians.'
The superstitious pagans, especially at that
time when, striking at the yoke of Christ, they
were persecuting the Christians, would never
have bestowed upon all these men sciences
which they themselves considered profitable, if

they had supposed that they were going to convert them to the worship of the one God, in
order that the false worship of idols might be
rooted out. But they gave their gold, silver,
and garments to the people of God who were
leaving Egypt, not knowing how the things
which they were giving would yield to 'the
obedience of Christ.' What happened in the
Exodus is undoubtedly a figure that signified
the present. I assert this without prejudice to
another interpretation, either equal or better.

All that is considered good in pagan education,
literature, philosophy, medicine, and other branches
of learning, then, is to be traced ultimately to divine
Providence. This good is to be separated from the
false and to be appropriated by Christians as rightful
possessors or heirs to the service of Christian
truth. The example of Moses -- and that of Daniel is
frequently added -- gives scriptural support to the
attitude described. The Christian view of pagan
learning as a rightful inheritance was based also on
the widespread belief among the Hellenistic Jews,
and one which later became a commonplace in
Christian apologetic, that the more significant
teachings of Plato and other Greek philosophers on the
virtues, e.g., were borrowed from the Bible itself!
It should be noted, too, that St. Augustine elsewhere
in his works, especially in the De civitate Dei, adopts
a similar attitude toward pagan social and political
institutions.
The most important practical application of the
Christian theory was, of course, in the field of
education. Although the schools of rhetoric were
thoroughly pagan in spirit and in the content of their
curriculum, and remained so pretty much for that
matter to the end of Antiquity, they were attended by
Christians even in the fourth and fifth centuries when
an ever increasing number of students came from
Christian homes. The dangers of such a pagan
environment to Christian youth explain the constant
warnings and criticisms respecting the pagan schools
found throughout ancient Greek and Latin Christian
literature. But the training received in these
schools also did much to acquaint Christian writers

with the intellectual achievements of pagan culture and
to form their literary style in the best traditions of
their age. [15]

But let us turn now to a consideration of the development of Christian Latin, and of the influence of
Greek upon it, in more concrete terms.

The Christian Latin vocabulary proper, the body
of words which Schrijnen has labelled direct Christianisms, was built up in three ways. [16] In the first
place, a considerable number of more or less concrete technical Greek religious terms, and a few
Hebrew words of the same kind found in the Greek
Bible, were merely transliterated into Latin, or were
furnished with Latin suffixes and thus assume a hybrid
form. In this category may be listed words like
angelus, apostolus, baptisma, diaconus, ecclesia,
episcopus, eucharistia, evangelium, martyr,
presbyter, baptizare, blasphemare, prophetare,
scandalizare, apostolatus, episcopatus, baptizator,
gehenna, pascha, satanas. The long established
usage of such basic words in the Christian vocabulary
was the primary factor determining their adoption in
Latin, but the desire to avoid certain familiar Latin
words because of their pagan religious associations
must also be considered. Thus, templum could
hardly be used for "church" in the second century, as
it was later in the fourth and fifth; vates was too
closely connected with paganism to render Greek
prophetes; catechumenus was more suitable than
auditor, and sacramentum than mysterium, for the
same reason. The last word, however, gradually became frequent in Christian Latin usage. The Greek
influence was certainly predominant in the case of
many words which might well have found a good Latin
equivalent. Hence, attempts made by Tertullian and
others to replace baptizare by tingere, clerus by
ordo, diaconus by minister, etc., in the interests of
purism, largely failed.

In the second place, many new words, especially
abstract and compound nouns, verbs, adjectives, and
adverbs were coined under the inspiration of corresponding words in Christian Greek. Among such may
be listed, e.g., abominatio, benedictio, conditio
(= creation), incorruptio, perditio, regeneratio,
deitas, trinitas, humiliare, clarificare, reaedificare,

adgaudere, conregnare, consepelire, convivificare,
corruptibilis, carnalis, coaequalis, coaeternus,
conformis, carnaliter, spiritaliter.

In the third place, a Christian sense, and often a
quite specialized one, was given to common Latin
words in the current vocabulary. Thus Spiritus
was given all the theological meaning of Greek
Pneuma, caro the force of Greek sarx, and dozens of
words like confessio, confessor, ieunium, vigilia,
militia, humilitas, memoria, credere, dimittere,
emundare, regenerare, salutaris, temporalis,
terrenus, infideliter, acquired specific Christian
meanings.

The reason for the choice of certain Latin words
in place of Greek words or of given Latin words in
place of other Latin words has been examined by
Löfstedt, Schrijnen, Mohrmann and other recent
investigators with fruitful results.[17] Thus we have
good studies on oratio, orare, populus, plebs, natio,
gentes, paganus, confessio, etc., and on certain
related groups. The Christian Latin vocabulary
dealing with redemption and salvation is made up
largely of genuine Latin words, and the same is true
of the terminology for Christian charity. The daily
occupations, familiar experiences, and life of the
Christian community suggested the appropriation, with
semantic adjustments, of numerous words from the
specialized vocabularies of agriculture, the trades,
and professions. The Bible, combined with personal
familiarity, was responsible for the development of a
Christian terminology based on military life and
games. Hence the employment with special Christian
meanings of militia, militare, statio, vigilia,
athleta, corona, etc., the rise of the concept of the
devil as adversarius and hostis, and that of the
ecclesia militans and ecclesia triumphans.[18] The
apparent archaisms in Early Christian Latin are not
true archaisms as we find them in Sallust, Tacitus,
and Apuleius, but rather old words that persisted in
the popular, living speech.

The Nijmegen School regards as an essential
part of the Christian Sondersprache a considerable
body of words which are indifferent from the viewpoint
of the Christian religion, but which are found exclusively or almost exclusively in Christian writings

in our extant remains of Latin, and it labels such
words indirect Christianisms. As examples may be
mentioned, cohabitare, cooperari, cooperatio,
cooperator, damnator, imputribilis, insultator,
negator, superseminare, etc. Many are substantives
in -tor and -tio, compound adjectives in -bilis, verbs
in -ficare, and adverbs in -biliter. These indirect
Christianisms were freely created to meet the needs
of the Christian community and show the affective
tendencies of the popular spoken language. In some
cases similar words in Greek suggested the Latin
coinage, e.g., beatificare after Greek makaridzo.

Early Christian Latin reflects the general syntactical usages of Late Latin, especially the usages of
popular speech, but we meet also some constructions
which may be regarded as exclusively or typically
Christian. Thus, a limited number of Semitisms
present in Biblical Greek pass into Christian Latin,
such as genitives of the types homo peccati, odor
suavitatis, vas electionis, canticum canticorum, in
instrumental, the phrase a facie Dei, and the tauto-
logical use of the participle in combinations like
locutus est dicens. Certain Greek constructions
stimulated the use of corresponding constructions already current in popular Latin, e.g., the employment
of quod, quia, and quoniam with a finite verb in place
of the accusative and infinitive after the verba dicendi
et sentiendi, the freer use of the complementary
infinitive, the use of facere as a causative verb with
the accusative and infinitive, the use of ad with verbs
of saying, the transitivization of verbs like benedicere
and maledicere, the use of the indicative in indirect
questions, etc. Some strictly Greek constructions
like the genitive absolute appear in the earlier Latin
versions of the Bible, but these are not really typical
or permanent. [19]

In the realm of style, apart from vocabulary, the
first Latin translations of the Bible reflect the simple
unadorned style and paratactic structure, and often
even the word order, of the Greek original. This
style, however, probably was not very different from
that of contemporary pagan Latin prose of pronounced
vulgar coloring.[20] In marked contrast, the style of
Tertullian is a highly original literary style which can
only be compared with the style of Apuleius or

Tacitus. The Apologeticum of Tertullian is a masterpiece of powerful literary prose. His younger contemporary, St. Cyprian, also wrote literary Latin, but
his style is more conventional, being characterized by
frequent use of parallelism and homoioteleuton, among
other rhetorical devices characteristic of the later
literary Latin in general.[21]

Dr. Mohrmann aptly characterizes the first phase
in the development of Christian Latin, which closes in
the third century, as a linguistic revolution unique in
character:

> This linguistic revolution which in its essential
> features was completed in the course of a few
> generations is a most eloquent witness of the
> spiritual revolution wrought by Christianity in
> the Ancient World. No sect, no other oriental
> religion, produced such a profound linguistic
> differentiation.[22]

The second phase in the evaluation of Christian
Latin begins in the early fourth century, and it differs
from the first phase in important respects. In the
first place, while some additions of a popular nature
continue to be made to Christian vocabulary, the
most significant body of new coinages and semantic
changes are more or less learned in character.[23]
Thus, inspired by Greek models, St. Hilary of
Poitiers (died 367 A.D.), who has been called the
Athanasius of the West, created a technical theological
vocabulary in Latin dealing with the Trinity. The
whole theological vocabulary was then so enriched by
St. Augustine (354-430), that men like Prosper of
Acquitaine (died after 455) and even Pope Leo the
Great (440-461) found the existing theological terminology quite adequate, for there are few if any certain
neologisms in their works. In the second place, this
new creative activity is more conservative than the
earlier one. The new words are almost all strictly
Latin formations and reflect the prefixes and suffixes
still productive in the literary Latin of the fourth and
fifth centuries. This conservatism is explained by the
fact that the great writers of the golden age of
Patristic Latin literature, Lactantius, St. Hilary,
St. Ambrose, St. Jerome, and St. Augustine, had all

been trained in the pagan schools of rhetoric. It is to
be remembered that St. Augustine, the greatest of the
ancient Christian Fathers, was a distinguished
professor of rhetoric at the time of his conversion.
They could not help being influenced by the conservative traditions of these schools, with their employment
of Vergil and Cicero as models of style and with their
exaggerated emphasis on style as such and the elaborate use of various stylistic devices. The investigations of the syntax, vocabulary, rhetorical figures,
word order, and clausulae in the great writers
mentioned, which are published in the Catholic University of America Patristic Studies,[24] indicate
how thoroughly the teachings of the schools were
assimilated.

The great Christian Latin writers were masters of
style, but they did not write literature for its own sake.
They employed their literary talents exclusively in the
service of the Christian faith as need arose in
dogmatic exposition, in defense against pagans and
heretics, and in the moral instruction and exhortation
of Christian congregations. Their style frequently
reveals the characteristic exaggerations of the common
late Latin literary style, but they are primarily pre-
occupied with content and communicating content.
They never subordinate or sacrifice essential content
to stylistic display. They show considerable independence in adapting pagan literary forms -- the
letter, treatise, dialogue, and the epic and lyric
meters to Christian use, and they make the Christian
sermon or homily their constant and most effective
means for instructing and exhorting the Christian
people. The Christian vocabulary of the first
creative period is largely retained as an essential
part of their language, and the Old Latin versions of
the Bible in more or less revised form continue to
serve as their basic text of Scripture. The new
translation of St. Jerome, in spite of its superior
qualities, was adopted very slowly and did not come
into wide use before the second half of the fifth
century.

The great Christian Latin writers, furthermore,
adapted their styles to meet specific religious needs
and conditions. St. Augustine's De civitate Dei is
written in an elaborate literary style to attract pagan

intellectuals in an age when literary style was an obsession and the chief proof of intellectual prestige.[25] In marked contrast, his popular sermons reveal a choice of language, rhetorical devices -- especially parallelism combined with figures of sound -- a syntax, and word-order, which make them master-pieces of popular preaching in form as well as in content.

Christian Latin in its second phase, then, became the vehicle of a great literature. It is more conserva-tive, showing a conscious attention to style and to the Latin literary tradition in general. But it did not lose its freedom or suppleness. Dr. Mohrmann has well said:

> In the classical period of Christian Latin literature, all the resources of the Christian idiom were utilized: the freedom which, as in the second century, allowed the creation of neologisms, the ease with which this idiom lent itself to the interpretation of abstract thought, and the wealth of stylistic elements drawn from Roman rhetorical tradition, from the Bible, and from the spontaneous resources of the popular living language.[26]

Christian Latin, in the course of the fifth and sixth centuries, became the common literary Latin and spoken Latin of the West. Triumphant first in the urban centers, it penetrated slowly but successfully into rural areas also, as is indicated by that most interesting and precious religious and historical document, the De correctione rusticorum of St. Martin of Bracara (c. 515-580). Men like Cassio-dorus (c. 490-c. 583) employed a Latin in which Christian and other elements were completely and unconsciously merged, and, as I said at the beginning, it was a "baptized" popular Latin which became Primitive Romance.

In this short paper I have not attempted anything more than a sketch of the origin and character of Christian Latin. Thus, I have not dealt in any detail with the question of the linguistic differentiations within Christian Latin itself, i.e., Liturgical Latin, the Latin of ecclesiastical administration and communication, and the broader common Christian Latin of the whole Christian community. [27] I have merely touched upon the relations between Christian Latin and Vulgar Latin in general, and I have not discussed the problem of possible regional differences in Christian Latin, although it may be said in passing that they are neither significant nor numerous. I have confined my treatment of the second phase in the development of Christian Latin to a few general observations. I have not dealt with the important subject of Christian Latin poetry, nor, in particular, with the Ambrosian hymn. [28] My primary purpose has been achieved if I have succeeded in indicating, however sketchily, the present state of our knowledge of Christian Latin, its development, and its essential character. The bibliographical references should be useful to those who wish to pursue this interesting and important subject more deeply.

FOOTNOTES

[1] M. Bonnet, Le Latin de Grégoire de Tours (Paris 1890). E. Löfstedt, Philologischer Kommentar zur Peregrinatio Aetheriae (Uppsala-Leipzig 1911; reprinted 1936).

[2] See J. Schrijnen, Charakteristik des altchristlichen Latein (Nijmegen 1932), but especially the following studies by C. Mohrmann: "Altchristliches Latein: Entstehung und Entwicklung der Theorie der altchristlichen Sondersprache," Aevum 13 (1939) 339-354 (reprinted in her Études [see below] 3-19); "Quelques traits caractéristiques du latin des chrétiens," Miscellanea Mercati I (Rome 1946) 437-466 (reprinted in her Études); "Le latin commun et la latin des chrétiens," Vigiliae Christianae 1 (1947) 280-297; "Le latin langue de la chrétienté occidentale," Aevum 24 (1950) 133-161 (reprinted in her Études 51-81); "How Latin Came to Be the Language of Early Christendom," Studies 40 (1951) 277-288; Latin vulgaire. Latin des chrétiens. Latin medieval (Paris 1955); Études sur le latin des chrétiens (Rome 1958; a collection of 26 studies published in widely scattered journals, etc., during the past twenty-five years). See also: E. Löfstedt, "Zur Entstehung der christlichen Latinität," in his Syntactica. II (Lund

1933) 458-473. J. De Ghellinck, S.J., "Latin chrétien ou langue latine des chrétiens," Les Études Classiques 8 (1939) 449-478.

[3]On the use of Greek in the Early Church, and on the shift from a Greek to a Latin Liturgy in the West, see: C. Mohrmann, "Les origines de la latinité chrétienne à Rome," Vigiliae Christianae 3 (1949) 67-106, 163-183; "Les emprunts grecs dans la latinité chrétienne," ibid. 4 (1950) 193-211; Liturgical Latin: Its Origins and Character (Washington 1957). G. Bardy, La question des langues dans l'Eglise ancienne. I (Paris 1948), especially I-121. J. Quasten, Patrology. I (Utrecht-Brussels 1950) 20-22.

[4]In addition to the references given above in notes 1-3, see Robert-Tricot, Guide to the Bible. I (2nd ed. Tournai and New York 1960) 609-610, 675-676.

[5]On the democratic character of Early Christian Latin, see especially C. Mohrmann, "Latin langue de la chrétienté occidentale," Etudes 57-58.

[6]L. Traube employed the phrase, griechisch-orientalischer Schimmer, to characterize this influence. See his Einleitung in die lateinische Philologie des Mittelalters. Herausgegeben von P. Lehmann (Munich 1911) 45.

[7]Cf. Augustine, Conf. 3.5.9.

[8]On the role of Scripture in the Early Christian communities and on the character of the Old Latin versions, see Mohrmann, "Latin langue de la chrétienté," Etudes 56-58, and also her art., "Les éléments vulgaires du latin des chrétiens," Vigiliae Christianae 2 (1948) 89-101, and 163-184.

[9]On St. Jerome and the Vulgate, see Robert-Tricot, op. cit. 645-652.

[10]See J. Quasten, Patrology. II (Utrecht-Brussels 1953) 249-251, and the bibliograpny listed.

[11]See P. De Labriolle, Histoire de la littérature latine chrétienne. Revised by G. Bardy I. (Paris 1946) 1-43. H. I. Marrou, Saint Augustin et la culture antique, with Retractatio (Paris 1938-1949); id., History of Education in Antiquity (New York 1956) 314-329. P. Courcelle, Les lettres grecques en Occident de Macrobe à Cassiodore (new ed. revised

Paris 1948). G. L. Ellspermann, O.S.B., The
Attitude of the Early Christian Latin Writers toward
Pagan Literature and Learning (Washington 1949;
Catholic University of America Patristic Studies 82).
M. L. W. Laistner, Christianity and Pagan Culture in
the Later Roman Empire (Ithaca 1951).

[12]On St. Jerome and pagan literature, see: E. A.
Quain, S.J., "St. Jerome as a Humanist," in a
Monument to St. Jerome. Edited by F. X. Murphy,
C.SS.R. (New York 1952) 203-232. H. Hagendahl,
The Latin Fathers and the Classics (Göteborg 1958).
On St. Augustine's attitude, see Marrou, op. cit.,
above, and the quotation from his De doctrina
christiana given below). For St. Basil, see: R. J.
Deferrari and M. R. P. McGuire, "Basil the Great's
'To Young Men, on How They Might Derive Profit
from Pagan Literature'," in R. J. Deferrari, ed.,
St. Basil, The Letters. IV (Loeb Classical Library,
London and Cambridge [Mass.] 1934) 365-435.

[13]Augustine, De doctrina christiana 2.40.60 ff.
The translation, with minor changes, is that of J. J.
Gavigan, O.S.A., in Writings of St. Augustine.
Vol. 4 (Fathers of the Church. A New Translation,
New York 1947) 112-114.

[14]See his De institutione clericorum 3.26
(Migne, PL 107, cols. 404A-405A).

[15]On Christian attendance at pagan schools and on
the pagan character of the curriculum to the end of
Antiquity, see Marrou, History of Education in
Antiquity 321-326.

[16]See Mohrmann, Latin vulgaire. Latin
chrétien. Latin médiéval 20-27.

[17]See Mohrmann op. cit., and the "Index des
mots grecs et latins," in her Études sur le latin des
chrétiens 457-461. See also H. Pétré, Caritas:
Études sur le vocabulaire latin de la charité
chrétienne (Louvain 1948; Spicilegium Sacrum
Lovaniense 22).

[18]For the Christian adaptation of the vocabulary
of military life and the games, see, in addition to the
references given to Mohrmann above, W. J. Teuuwen,
Sprachlicher Bedeutungswandel bei Tertullian
(Paderborn 1926; Studien zur Geschichte und Kultur des
Altertums 14.1).

[19]On typical Christian syntactical usages, see, e.g., Mohrmann, "Traits caractéristiques du latin chrétien," Études 45-49. See also ibid. 38-40.

[20]See Mohrmann, Latin vulgaire. Latin des chrétiens. Latin médiéval 28-30.

[21]On the style of Tertullian, see Quasten, Patrology. II 249-251, and the bibliography listed. On the style of St. Cyprian, see: E. W. Watson, "The Style and Language of St. Cyprian," Studia Biblica et Ecclesiastica 4 (1896) 189-324. L. Bayard, Le latin de saint Cyprien (Paris 1902). Sister George Edward Conway, Thasci Caecili Cypriani De bono patientiae. A Translation with an Introduction and a Commentary (Washington 1957; Catholic University of America Patristic Studies 92).

[22]Mohrmann, "Latin langue de la chrétienté occidentale," Études 65.

[23]Mohrmann, ibid. 66 ff.

[24]This series, edited by R. J. Deferrari, J. M. Campbell, M. R. P. McGuire, and B. M. Peebles, comprises 93 volumes to date (1959), covering the great Christian writers from St. Cyprian to St. Gregory the Great. The majority of the studies are concerned with language and style. Each volume contains a good select bibliography and good indices. See also the excellent studies published in the Nijmegen series, Latinitas Christianorum Primaeva, edited by C. Mohrmann and H. H. Janssen (12 vols. to date).

[25]On Christian humanism in the fourth and fifth centuries, see, in addition to the reference to Mohrmann's article in note 23, the references listed in notes 11-12 above. See also G. Bardy, "Aux beaux temps de l'humanisme chrétien (380-430," La France franciscaine 22 (1939) 101-130.

[26]Mohrmann, "Latin langue de la chrétienté occidentale," Études 68.

[27]See the references given in note 2 above.

[28]See Mohrmann, "La langue et le style de la poésie latine chrétienne," Revue des Études latines 25 (1947) 280-297 (reprinted in Études 151-168). See also F. J. E. Raby, A History of Christian Latin Poetry (2nd ed. Oxford 1953) 11-71.

CHRISTIAN LATIN IN THE HIGH SCHOOL AND COLLEGE

by

Herbert Musurillo, S.J.

In our discussion of the place of Christian Latin in our modern curriculum, we must be guided -- as in all problems -- by a sense of reality, and attempt to see things as they are without subjective bias or partiality. It is hard to be unbiassed about the past, especially about a past that is so intimately present, so closely linked with our Christian growth and vision. The literature of the Patristic and early Middle Ages cannot be filed into neat categories: it ranges from the austere theological or scientific treatise to the gay love poem, from the obscurities of Augustine to the obscenities of the Goliards and the Carmina Burana. It has been said that as an aesthetic phenomenon Christian literature, in the strict sense, does not exist -- that is to say, there is nothing to distinguish it as literature save for the fact that it happens to be written by Christians.

But I think there is a deeper meaning, a more profound function fulfilled by a truly Christian art and literature. All Christian art is fundamentally an exploration of the problem of the Christian imagination. Christian dogma proceeds in time and space by the historical unfolding of the implications of the primitive kerygma, the "announcement" of the Good News; and this announcement has proceeded outward from the community of the baptized, the "enlightened," who wait for the Parousia while celebrating the mysteries of their Lord. But the baptized are still citizens of this visible world and members of the human family. Christian art and letters, therefore, as an imaginative product, is the aesthetic expression of the tension felt by Christians between time and eternity, between the sensual world and the secret doctrines that have been revealed to them. Sometimes

56

they feel an opposition: when the brilliance of this
world's light only heightens the shadow of faith. At
other times there is a correspondence: when the
world is seen as a forest of symbols[1] that can only be
deciphered by the eye of faith.

It must be borne in mind that the greater proportion of what we call, for want of a better term, the
literature of the Patristic and Middle Ages, is not
literature in the strict sense, the product of the
creative imagination. Rather, it is the written record
of centuries of instruction, evolving from the methods
of the primitive catechesis which began with the
Gospels. The apocalypses, sermons, letters,
treatises and commentaries, Platonic dialogues,
didactic hymns and poems -- it is a vast network of
doctrinal dissemination.[2]   Even the art of fiction
was pressed into service; and we see the rise of
edifying tales, like the Acts of Paul and Thecla,
Jerome's Life of Paul the First Hermit, the Acts of
St. Cecilia, and many more. In all of this the
imagination is indeed at work, not so much in a
creative as in an ancillary role, in quest of the means
to illustrate the traditional catechesis. For what need
is there of creation when all the soul needs for salvation has already been given? I will not say that this
tendency, stated in so crude a form, was universal;
it does, however, emerge from time to time with
peculiar persuasiveness in the history of Christian
literature. In its extreme form, the tendency to
didacticism has perhaps kept some of the patristic
writers from a clear understanding of the role of
poetry in general, and even of the poetic, imaginative
books of the Old Testament, as for example the Book
of Job and the Song of Songs.

In our approach to the Latin literature of the
Christian period, we ourselves must not be led astray
by the fallacy of didacticism -- I mean that attitude
which judges all writing not by its intrinsic excellence
or literary craftsmanship but by the sole fact that it
teaches an acceptable lesson or serves some other
moral purpose in our educational syllabus. In the
course of a controversy long since past, I pointed out
some of the merits and defects of a system which would
restrict itself to Christian literature.[3] In doing so, I
perhaps did an injustice to Christopher Dawson, whose

plan for a revision of the Catholic liberal arts curriculum had not envisioned such a restriction. In any
case, I should not here repeat the obvious objections
which I then put forward. Apart from what I considered an unfortunate narrowing of the liberal arts
program, I pointed out that a good number of the most
important patristic texts were highly technical and far
too difficult for an undergraduate who had no special
training in the history of dogma or in scriptural
exegesis. For the same reason, many of the texts
lacked good commentaries -- at least of the sort that
could be used either by the college student or even the
teacher -- and thus we would be in constant danger of
thrusting our best as well as our poorest pupils into
difficulties with which neither we nor they would be
fully prepared to cope. Thus I do not see how we can
inaugurate a successful program which is restricted
to Christian Latin.

At the same time, I feel we can supplement our
high school and college curriculum with a judicious
selection of Christian texts, provided we choose those
that have definite literary and cultural value, carefully
excluding complicated theological ones. In such a
program, which would be secondary to our main
effort, I would suggest as our goal the exploration of
the Christian poetic imagination and its development
in close dependence upon its historical environment,
the Greco-Roman world. This is an area which still
requires scholarly thought and discussion; and it is
one which our young students will find rewarding.
Like so many other fields, it would profit by fresh in-
sights and enthusiasm.

The problem of Christian literature centers about
two polarities: the one, which we have touched on,
concerned the acceptance or rejection of the creative
imagination; the other, the acceptance or rejection of
the captive maiden, Greco-Roman culture and education.

But the dilemma between acquiescence and
avoidance was not nearly so much a matter of free
choice as St. Jerome in his famous anxiety-dream
seems to have believed.[4] Ciceronianus es, non
Christianus, says the grim figure on the judgement-
seat. But the truth was that Jerome could not help
but be both. And we today would do a serious

disservice to patristic studies if we attempted to cut
them off completely from their classical background.
For the evolution of Christian literature cannot be
understood apart from its classical heritage; to think
otherwise would be to manifest a deep incomprehension
of the forces of history. We would also be forgetting
that the Fathers who, as individuals, exercised perhaps the greatest influence on the growth of doctrine
were precisely those whose immersion in secular
learning was the most profound: witness Origen,
Augustine, the Cappadocians, Ambrose, and Jerome;
and the same was true of the later theologians like
Denis the Areopagite, John of Damascus, and Thomas
Aquinas. But the influence of pagan Latin literature
on the Latin-speaking Fathers was totally different
from the influence of Greek literature upon the Greek
patristic writers. For one thing, it would seem that
the Roman authors -- for example, Cicero, Sallust,
Vergil, Horace -- were far more acceptable to the
Latin Fathers than the corresponding Greek authors --
Demosthenes, Homer, the lyric and tragic poets --
were to Greek-speaking Christians. Part of the reason
was that the most popular Latin authors were post-
philosophical; they had profited by the development of
Platonism and Stoicism. And in the case of Cicero at
least there is a quiet rejection of the old pantheon of
gods and mythical heroes so beloved of the Greek
poets. Latin Fathers like Augustine, Ambrose, and
Jerome, were too well read in their Latin literature
not to realize its importance in the educational
process of the Christian, and in their preparation for
a deeper understanding of the Scriptures. This is
especially emphasized by Augustine in his De doctrina
christiana. And consider the important role played by
Cicero's Hortensius in Augustine's conversion. On
the Greek side, only Plato, and later Plotinus, exercised a comparable influence; the Peripatetics only to
a limited extent. For the Greek Fathers, Greek
literature remained a problem. And even Basil's
Magna Carta, his Letter to the Youth on the intrinsic
values of Greek literature, did not completely rid the
Greek Church of its long and deep-seated suspicion.
It was a suspicion which, allied with ignorance, persisted down to the Renascence.
     A similar conflict manifested itself in the growth

of what I have called the Christian imagination -- and
this is a problem which should concern us in our
teaching today. Poetic creative talent in the early
Christian period found itself in an embarrassing
dilemma: on the one hand there was, especially in the
Greek world, an understandable aversion for the
myths and symbols of traditional poetry; on the other,
there was no established method for transforming the
Judaic symbols of the Christian kerygma into acceptable poetic dress. Again, should the poet write in the
manner of Vergil, Horace, Catullus? How could he
use their techniques to speak (as he felt he should) of
the Bible or of the Church? Indeed, why should he
write poetry at all when the means of salvation lay
close at hand, in the catachesis and in the Liturgy?
With some differences the same dilemma is still with
us today, and the same gnawing questions continue to
dishearten Catholic creative writing and scholarship.
And yet, man's original and creative drives cannot
long be repressed; nor was Christianity intended to
repress them. Man's constant urge to rethink and re-
shape the world remains the same; and he cannot
create on command, but only in accord with his own
experiential vision. And this drive, and this vision,
should not be frustrated because he has been baptized;
rather they should thereby be sharpened and more
keenly focussed.

With Hilary and Ambrose we see the first successful efforts to create a community poetry for use during
liturgical services, by way of varying the regular
psalmody and antiphonal chant. Non-liturgical verse
had a more difficult existence. Paulinus, the lovable
bishop of Nola and the scrupulous custodian of the
venerable shrine of St. Felix, was the first to carve
out a specifically Christian theory of poetry. In
Carmen 10, a poetic epistle to his master Ausonius,
he expresses the dilemma of the Christian poet as
clearly, I think, as it has ever been put:[5]

    quid abdicatas in meam curam, pater,
      redire Musas praecipis?
    negant Camenis nec patent Apollini
      dicata Christo pectora.

Why urge me, Father, to take up again

With the Muses I've long abandoned?
Hearts pledged to Christ are closed to Apollo,
And must deny entrance to the goddesses of song.

And he continues: "Now another force, a greater God
(alia...vis, maior deus) drives me on, demanding a
new life, claiming of every man a sacred duty." Then
he goes on with a charming change of metre:[6]

Namque caduca patent nostris, aeterna negantur
visibus, et nunc spe sequimur quod mente
                    videmus.

Indeed, what the eye sees is but passing;
Invisible are the things that are eternal,
Seen only in spirit and embraced by hope.

Thus the denial of pagan tradition and symbol, though
based on belief, is more suggestive of the interior
change that conversion has achieved, but the poet's
heart, though now pledged to Christ, still feels the
shock of the conflicting vision of time and eternity.
And this statement of Paulinus is all the more impressive inasmuch as it comes from a bishop who was
as immersed in the Bible and in the liturgy of his
shrine as he had once been in the pagan poets at the
feet of Ausonius.
    But if Paulinus' statement was an Ars poetica
christiana, surely the mysterious Prudentius of
Tarragona, [7] who first published his poetry at fifty-
seven, wrote by no set plan. Like Melchisedech, we
do not know his generation; and yet his Cathemerinon
contains perhaps the most poetically perceptive of all
the verse of the early Church. Catholic University has
indeed done much to advance the study of Prudentius;
and Bernard Peebles has acutely set forth the poet's
artistic achievement. [8] It was unfortunate that
Richard Bentley spoke of Prudentius as the "Vergil
and Horace of the Christians": as Peebles, among
others, has shown, [9] he has no title to such high rank.
But he is a truly great Christian poet, who allows us
to share his own insight into the new role of the
creative imagination, fired by the grace of Christ's
Atonement. In our classroom dialogue on the growth
of the Christian poetic achievement, both Prudentius

and Paulinus of Nola must be allowed an impressive
contribution.

But I am forced to pass over the vast bulk of
Latin verse that followed; some of it is good, some
(like Commodian, and the Vergilian Laudes Domini
and Proba) shockingly bad. Unfortunately, sound
theology need not make good poetry. The Carolingian
Renascence improved both the Latin and the literary
quality; and the rise of Benedictine monasticism gave
us charming liturgical sequences and hymns in great
quantity. Perhaps one of the greatest hymns of the
early Middle Ages, the Victimae Paschali, was composed by an obscure Burgundian (or Swabian) priest
named Wipo, who was chaplain to Conrad II and died
about the year 1050.[10] It is clear that Wipo had some
knowledge of Sallust, Horace, Vergil, Lucan, Statius,
and many other writers of the now distant classical
period. He liked the rhyming, Leonine hexameters,
but the Victimae is composed in rhythmic prose with
occasional isosyllabic correspondence and homoioteleuton   -- almost as though it were a rhetorical
composition. The poem begins as a vivid vision of
Easter morn, put into the mouth of the Christian
community as they celebrate the Paschal Liturgy.
They are swept back in time as they meditate on the
meaning of the Atonement, summed up in the image of
wrestling or single combat -- the fierce duellum
between Life and Death. But now we are suddenly
back in Jerusalem, speaking to Mary, the apostola
apostolorum, who delivers breathlessly the exciting
message of Christ's triumph. In our printed Missals
the Church has chosen to omit Wipo's sixth strophe,
"Let us believe Mary rather than the mob of faithless
Jews." But the final stanza, Scimus Christum sur-
rexisse, recalls us back to the liturgical present with
a communal act of faith in the Paschal Victim now
reigning gloriously.[11]

We should allow a place in our program to some
of the plays of that extremely talented nun of
Gandersheim, Hroswitha -- especially the Dulcitius
and perhaps some scenes from the Abraham and the
Paphnutius, plays which were originally enacted --
I have no doubt -- by the young girls or even by the
nuns of the monastery. They possess a charm which
brings to life most vividly the life and faith of the

early Middle Ages. We must not forget, too, all the
fine Eucharistic poetry of the thirteenth century that
clustered about the institution of the feast of Corpus
Christi; a good deal of it, as we know, comes from
the hand of Thomas Aquinas. Our more mature students will perhaps enjoy the shocking self-revelation
attributed to Abelard called the Historia calamita-
tum;[12] both this narrative and the collection of Latin
letters attached to the names of Abelard and Heloise
are, in my humble view, charming mediaeval
forgeries. But they have an authentic flavor of their
own, and are worth reading as a revelation of one side
at least of twelfth and thirteenth century Christianity.

A great artistic revival was inaugurated by the
Franciscan Order at this time, and it has survived in
some deeply moving poetry, St. Francis' Hymn to the
Sun, and the hymns now incorporated into the Roman
Missal, the Stabat Mater and Dies irae. The author-
ship of the last two is uncertain. In the Stabat Mater
the pious poet, before a representation of the death of
Jesus, asks to feel the sufferings of His Mother, and
in this way to achieve penitence and the grace of final
perseverance.[13] Though a great religious document,
the poem lacks focus and unity, and seems excessive
in its vast orgy of emotion. The Dies irae,[14] on the
other hand, is a model of mediaeval poetic creation.
Based on the ominous words of the prophet Zephaniah
(Sophonias) predicting the Day of Yahweh, which the
Liturgy adapted for the Absolutio super tumulum, the
poem is a meditation on the Last Judgement, somewhat as the scene was depicted over the gates of
mediaeval cathedrals. As the Judge takes his seat
(in the manner of the imperial magistrates at a
cognitio extraordinaria), the poet finds himself bereft
of a patronus to plead his case, and appeals to the
Judge for mercy instead of rigorous justice. And the
ultimate result of this spiritual confrontation is a
sense of humility and contrition -- cor contritum
quasi cinis -- which the poet hopes will persevere until his own death. The last six lines have been added
by the Church in order to adapt the poem (which was
personal, and perhaps not originally connected with
the Liturgy of the Dead) to the immediate context of
the funeral Mass. Apart from the vast influence the
poem and its plainchant melody have exercised on the

imagination of so many Christian poets, artists, and
musical composers, it stands as a monumental
example of the ideal Christian poem according to the
doctrine of Paulinus of Nola. Hebrew, Christian, and
pagan symbols are fused in the poetic structure to
express the poet's ultimate anxiety and the firm decision to which he has come on the problem of his sin-
ful, guilt-ridden condition. No Christian Latin poem
has better expressed man's inner torment against the
setting of an eschatological view of history: that the
growth of the Church is the trajectory, as it were,
between two divine theophanies, Christ's death and
His Final Coming.

But we should be giving a false portrait if we
restricted our discussion to the purely religious
poems. We must make our students familiar with
some of the delightfully irresponsible student songs
(often called, by a misnomer, Goliardic poetry) and
the Carmina Burana. The lovely winter love-song, De
ramis cadunt folia, from a thirteenth-century French
manuscript, [15] should be included in every syllabus, as
well as the bilingual Stetit puella rufa tunica. [16] There
is a peculiarly surrealist poem in the Carmina
Burana, Olim latus colueram, [17] which is like the
whimsical paintings of Hieronymus Bosch, and must
surely be a product of Germany or the Lowlands. The
song is put into the mouth of a swan that dreams of the
free life it used to have, now that it is being roasted,
basted, and prepared for a fine banquet. Miser,
miser, is the repeated refrain, "Alas, alas, burnt
black I am, and roasted thoroughly. Turned and
turned by the fork, tasted and burnt..." Miser,
miser. The final stanza shows the poor swan as it
lies in the platter, gazing at the banqueters' flashing,
hungry teeth. It is a brilliant piece of virtuosity,
quite advanced for its day; and I cannot but think that
a bit of mediaeval allegory is lurking somewhere in
the background. The constant refrain, Miser, miser,
and the prodding of the fork suggest a macabre, mock-
serious vision of Hell, with the white swan that
"once cultivated the body" (latus) as a symbol of the
soul. In any case, the poem is an intriguing one and
would repay further examination.

There are many other pieces we could consider,
but these will suffice to indicate the general direction.

We must not, of course, forget the fine Marian
hymns of monastic tradition, the Ave Maris Stella and
the Alma Redemptoris which Chaucer loved. 18 For
prose-passages, there is the quaint Gesta Romanorum,
some of the early authentic martyr acts, the less
philosophical passages of Augustine's Confessions,
and perhaps something from Ambrose and Jerome.

But we must above all beware of falling into the
fallacy of the Abbé Gaume by attempting to reject non-
Christian literature entirely. It was a cause célèbre
of the nineteenth century; but the forces which
brought it about are still, I fear, with us today. The
Abbé Jean-Joseph Gaume (1802-79) taught theology at
the seminary of Nevers until his resignation in 1852:19
this was occasioned by the publication, in the previous
year, of the fiery denunciation entitled Ver rongeur
-- "The Gnawing Worm: Paganism in Our Education"
(1851). Here he attacked the reading of the Classical
authors in the French schools, and suggested that in
Catholic secondary schools at least the students
should substitute the Fathers of the Church. There
subsequently appeared some thirty volumes of texts
incorporating selections for the use of schools.

But the monstrous fallacy here -- and it is a
complex one -- shows a complete incomprehension of
the meaning of literature -- as opposed to doctrinal
teaching, catechetical instruction -- and of the goal
and potentialities of secondary and even college
education. The Latin and Greek authors taught in our
classical syllabus were originally chosen because of
their importance in the development of world history
and literature. If patristic and mediaeval texts are
also chosen with this view in mind, as I have attempted to show, all will be well. But if they are
chosen as a doctrinally acceptable substitute, we
shall be making a serious paedagogical mistake. My
own experience has suggested that American boys and
girls, even on the college level, are not prepared to
grapple with the many problems involved in reading
the Fathers as a regular course; and for this reason
they may sometimes find them a bore. And the
reasons for this are not far to seek: we cannot expect the fine points of the development of dogma or
Scriptural exegesis to interest the ordinary boy or
girl. Again, even in non-doctrinal texts, the fact that

a piece of poetry or prose has been written by a
patristic writer does not guarantee that it may not,
from a literary point of view, be trite and banal. We
must recall that the main fibre of much of this early
literature was directly or indirectly instructional.

But as I have already suggested, the question of
Christian Latin and the Gaume controversy are
intimately connected with the more general problem,
the growth of the Christian imagination. It was this
problem that I especially commended for consideration
as a source of unity in making the transition from the
strict classical syllabus to Christian Latin. For the
dilemma of acceptance or rejection of the world of the
imagination was at the heart of the Fathers' attitude
towards the pagan Classics; and the dilemma is still
urgently with us today. We must be wary of being
misled into an easy solution. Perhaps the ultimate
solution is beyond us. But I think that a study of
Christian literature should direct our thinking along
the following lines. First, the poetic-artistic
creativity of a people cannot be long checked or sup-
pressed; it is a human drive that must somehow
emerge and have its way. Second, the Christian
imagination is unique, in that it has been super-
naturally elevated by Baptism in the Mystical Body and
is under the influence of the truths and symbols of
divine revelation. Third, it need not always view the
world in the uniquely Christian way, and thus sometimes its creations are not distinguishable from those
of the non-Christian; as we have seen, the Christian
poet to be honest and faithful to his vision, need not
always produce a "Christian poem." Lastly, the
Christian imagination, working in its specific function,
is concerned precisely with the polarity which arises
between Christian revelation and the world of the
visible and the sensuous, between the actualities of
time and the substance of things hoped for. Thus our
ideal Christian poet will have a difficult task. And
only very rarely in the literature of Christianity was
success achieved. For if in some areas there is a
correspondence between faith and the world, in others
there is ambiguity, contradiction, and obscurity.

The problem still remains, and the mystery is
still hidden in the story of Christian literature. It
should always be borne in mind in our program of

Christian Latin and commended to our maturer students. For the art of teaching is not merely paideia, the transmission of a cultural heritage; it is also a common dialogue and discourse in which all voices are raised in a dedicated quest for truth.

FOOTNOTES

[1] The phrase is Baudelaire's; see his poem, Correspondances, first published in 1857.

[2] See my article, "History and Symbol: A Study of Form in Early Christian Literature," Theological Studies 18 (1957) 357-386.

[3] See "Dawson's Program: A Criticism," Thought 30 (1955) 174-187.

[4] The story of the dream, or rather vision, is related in Epistle 22.30, a letter written to Eustochium. The incident, if it can be believed, seems to have occurred during Jerome's first journey to the East about the year 374. Suffering from fever and near to death, Jerome claimed to have had a vision in which he found himself before the judgement seat of Christ, and was condemned and scourged until he promised to give up the reading of pagan authors. Actually when he is restored to consciousness he does not assert that he gave up these favorite authors but that he now read the Scriptures with as much care (tanto studio) as he had given to the pagan writings. The significance of the vision is perhaps exaggerated by some authors. If it was not merely Jerome's pious embellishment of a resolution he had taken -- put into the form of a dream or vision for the edification of Eustochium -- it perhaps merely reflects Jerome's feelings of guilt for his neglect of the Scriptures. Augustine surely felt no such guilt for his devotion to Cicero; and Ambrose is deeply indebted to him, especially for many of the concepts of the De officiis ministrorum.

[5] Carm. 10.19-22. On Paulinus, see F. J. E. Raby, A History of Christian-Latin Poetry from the Beginnings to the Close of the Middle Ages (2nd ed. Oxford 1953) 101-107, and The Oxford Dictionary of the Christian Church. Ed. by F. L. Cross (London 1957) 1035-6, with the bibliography cited.

[6]Carm. 10.174-5.

[7]See Raby, op. cit. 44-71; Cross, op. cit. 1119.

[8]Bernard M. Peebles, The Poet Prudentius (New York 1951; Boston College Candlemas Lectures on Christian Literature 2) with the bibliography 105-111.

[9]Op. cit. 101 f.

[10]See Cross, op. cit. 1470 and 1418.

[11]For the text, see Raby, op. cit. 217 ff.

[12]For a good translation and commentary, see J. T. Muckle, The Story of Abelard's Adversities, with an Introduction by E. Gilson (Toronto 1954; Pontifical Institute of Mediaeval Studies). On the authenticity of the document Gilson remains non-committal. The Historia is, however, accepted in Cross, Oxford Dict. of the Christ. Church, s. v. "Abelard," 3-4.

[13]On the poem, see Raby, A History of Christian Latin Poetry 437-440, and Cross, op. cit. 1385.

[14]Cf. Raby, op. cit. 443-450; Cross, op. cit. 398.

[15]See Helen Waddell, Mediaeval Latin Lyrics (New York 1930) 274, with her remarks on 346. See, also, F. J. E. Raby, ed., The Oxford Book of Mediaeval Latin Verse (new ed. Oxford 1959) no. 234.

[16]Carmina Burana. Edd. A. Hilka and O. Schumann. I.2 (Heidelberg 1941) no. 177. It is also to be found in Raby, op. cit. no. 219.

[17]Carmina Burana. Hilka-Schumann, no. 130. For a discussion of the collection, see Raby, A History of Secular Latin Poetry in the Middle Ages. 2 (2nd ed. Oxford 1957) 256-279.

[18]For a discussion of the symbolism of these Marian hymns, see my article, "The Mediaeval Hymn, Alma Redemptoris: A Linguistic Analysis," Class. Journ. 52 (1957) 171-174.

[19]On the controversies connected with Gaume, see G. E. Mangenot, Dict. de la théol. cath. 6 (Paris 1920) 1168-71; and Cross, op. cit. 542.

THE PRONUNCIATION OF LATIN: ITS HISTORY AND PRACTICAL PROBLEMS

by

Martin R. P. McGuire

The science of Comparative Grammar, which had its beginnings in the early nineteenth century, and the relatively new science of General Linguistics have enabled us to trace, catalog, and, in part, explain the changes that have taken place in the Greek and Latin languages throughout their long history. All languages are subject to a process of change, and to such a degree, that the later stage of a given language can be so different from an earlier one that we are justified in calling the later stage a new or different language, as in the case of Modern English as distinct from Anglo-Saxon and the Romance Languages as distinct from Latin. The process of linguistic change, as is so clearly indicated by the title of Du Cange's great Glossarium mediae et infimae Latinitatis, was once regarded as a form of decay, but such a notion is completely antiquated.

The science of General Linguistics, through its investigation of modern living languages, has helped us very much not only by supplementing the data furnished by the written remains of Greek, Latin, and other ancient languages, but also in the evaluation of these data themselves. Thus, we now have a clear idea of phonemes and realize that the Greek and Latin alphabets do not give us fully satisfactory control of the Greek and Latin phonemes, i.e., the precise control of all the consonantal and vowel sounds as they can be described by the modern international phonetic alphabet. The questions of accent and sentence phonetics have turned out to be more complicated than we once thought. What we call standard speech admits and comprises a wide range of minor variations. There can be marked differences between written language and spoken language, and these differences

were much greater in the past than at the present
time when, through the mass media of oral and
written communication, a levelling has taken place
which under past conditions was quite impossible.
Finally, we have learned that the psychological factor
plays a major role in linguistic usage and in
linguistic change.

The sources for our knowledge of the pronunciation
of Latin in Antiquity are the following:

(1) the direct statements of the ancient
    grammarians and metricians;

(2) the evidence of the meters of poetry, which
    show the quantities of vowels in open initial
    and medial syllables, and in final syllables;

(3) ancient puns, old etymologies, representa-
    tions of animal cries, etc.;

(4) the spellings in inscriptions, including the
    use of the apex -- this evidence is especial-
    ly important;

(5) the spellings in our earliest and most ac-
    curately written manuscripts;

(6) the spellings used in Latin for words bor-
    rowed and transliterated from other
    languages, and those used in other lan-
    guages for words borrowed and transliter-
    ated from Latin;

(7) the pronunciation in Vulgar Latin as re-
    vealed especially by inscriptions and
    reflected in the Romance dialects; and

(8) the value of sounds as shown by compara-
    tive grammar.[1]

Ancient Latin writing was phonetic, i.e., a close
relationship was maintained between pronunciation
and orthography. This does not mean that conventional spelling does not play any role in Latin
writing, but rather that, for a considerable time,
there was no wide divergence between spelling and
current pronunciation. In the age of Cicero and
Augustus, the relationship between orthography and
pronunciation was particularly close. However, we
moderns should not look for an absolutely standardized orthography in our sense. The most carefully
written inscriptions of the Late Republic and Early

Empire reveal variant spellings for the same word in
the same document, as in the Res gestae divi
Augusti. The strictly standardized orthography of our
modern languages is fairly recent. As regards English, e.g., Noah Webster (1758-1843) was a pioneer
in advocating and disseminating a standardized English orthography.

Since the middle of the last century, scholars
have gradually succeeded in establishing with reasonable exactness the pronunciation of Latin throughout
its long history. The pronunciation of Latin was never
static. Marked changes can be noted between the
pronunciation of Plautus and that of Cicero, and much
more striking changes in the period between Tacitus
and Suetonius and the beginning of the Middle Ages.
By the sixth century, the spoken Latin of the masses
was approaching in its pronunciation, morphology,
and syntax, the linguistic stage that we call Primitive
Romance. Writers, however strictly trained in
literary Latin and however tenacious in adhering to
Classical norms as inculcated in a conservative
school tradition, could not escape popular influences,
especially in pronunciation. The Latin grammarians
of Late Antiquity, with their increasing preoccupation
with orthography, reveal the difficulties that faced
them in their attempt to maintain a traditional
literary usage that was becoming more and more
artificial, as the spoken living language was exhibiting
greater vigor and a faster tempo in its evolution.
Classical orthography was restored -- but not always
with exactness -- in the great editions of Vergil and
other Latin Classical writers prepared in the fourth
and fifth centuries and was maintained in the more
carefully written Patristic works of the same
period.[2] Together with the treatises of the grammarians, these carefully edited editions of profane
and Christian writings served as models for the
reform of Latin studies inaugurated by Charlemagne
and carried out by Alcuin and his colleagues and
their successors. But the restoration of the study of
Latin grammar and the careful copying of good manuscripts of Classical authors did not include any change
in the current pronunciation of Latin.

From the close of Antiquity, or at the very
latest, from the beginning of the Carolingian Age,

Latin in the strict sense was a language of the school.
However thoroughly mastered and widely used in
writing and speaking by an educated elite -- very
small in number in relation to the total population, it
was not a mother tongue acquired in the circle of the
home from earliest childhood. It was never a living
language in the sense that English, French, German,
Spanish, and other modern languages can be called
living, i.e., languages that have had a truly organic
life and which have even undergone radical changes in
phonology, morphology, and syntax. But enough on
this point, as it will be discussed fully in my lecture
on Mediaeval Latin. Let us now take up rather the
history of the actual pronunciation of Latin from the
close of Antiquity to the middle of the nineteenth
century.

The writers of Latin in the Merovingian period,
including Gregory of Tours, pronounced Latin as the
emerging Romance vernacular was being pronounced,
and the newly Christianized Celts, Germans, and
other non-Latin peoples of Europe, in committing
their respective vernaculars to writing, employed the
Latin letters with the sound values which the Latin
letters had at the time in each case. Latin itself was
pronounced as the vernacular was pronounced. Then,
as each vernacular language changed its sounds,
corresponding changes were made simultaneously in
the pronunciation of Latin. In spite of the influence of
a school tradition and the striving to maintain an accurate transmission of Classical and Patristic texts,
Mediaeval Latin orthography was affected very much
by the vernacular pronunciations of Latin, especially
because so much school instruction had to be given
orally and men by habit visualized words more as they
had heard them and as they pronounced them themselves than as they were actually found in written
form before their eyes. Hence, a mediaeval scribe,
in copying, often employed a spelling, particularly of
familiar words, which did not correspond to the
spelling in the text being copied.[3] Under the circumstances, there can be no question of a standardized
Latin orthography in the Middle Ages. The grammarians know the Classical treatises on orthography,
but they do not follow them in practice. On the whole,
there is fairly careful and uniform observance of the

inflectional endings of nouns, pronouns, and verbs,
but otherwise there is marked variety in orthography
in the same period and in succeeding periods. Thus,
we can speak of Irish Latin, German Latin, Italian
Latin, in the sense that the Latin writers of Irish
origin or training, etc., show identifiable peculiarities
in their orthography. But given the general similarity
of the vowel sounds and of many consonantal sounds in
the languages of Western Europe, there are also a
number of spellings that may be regarded as universal
in Mediaeval Latin. The following spellings may be
considered as typical in this respect: e = ae and oe,
ci and ti interchange, que (quae), aeclesia, diptongus,
sydera, limpha, agurium, yconomus, precium,
michi, nichil, pasca, cifus (scyphus), accio, fatio
(factio), Gretia (Graecia), anticus (antiquus), hortus
(ortus), ortus (hortus), salmus, sollempnis, rethor,
rethorica, locuplex, thaurus, spera (sphaera),
magestas, zabulus (diabolus), selum (caelum),
conserno (concerno), signus (cygnus), zeta (diaeta),
scalores (squalores), mistus (mixtus), eptaticus
(Heptateuchus), Feton (Phaeton), tunica = tonica and
vice versa, monimentum = munimentum and vice
versa. And the following accentuations are typical
also: theología, philosophía, filología, etc.[4]
In the Renaissance and post-Renaissance period,
with the new interest in the Classics and the renewed
study of excellent manuscripts preserved from late
Antiquity and the Carolingian Age, we note a marked
improvement in orthography, although Renaissance
and post-Renaissance Latin spelling is by no means as
consistent and Classical as is usually assumed.
Erasmus criticized all contemporary pronunciations
in his De recta Latini Graecique sermonis pronunti-
atione (1528) and advocated a pronunciation corresponding to the Classical. Yet with the possible
exception of the great Dutch scholar Justus Lipsius
(1547-1606), who in a work on Latin pronunciation
dedicated to Sir Philip Sydney (1586) maintained that
C should be pronounced as K and V as W, there was no
further systematic investigation of Latin pronunciation
nor was any further attempt made to change the
traditional practice. Latin continued to be pronounced
as the respective vernaculars. Erasmus admired the
Italian pronunciation of the Latin vowels, and it was

the regular one of the University of Cambridge as late
as 1542. Under the influence of the Reformation, however, the Italian pronunciation was then abandoned,
and by 1600 the English pronunciation of Latin had
triumphed -- much to the disgust of Scaliger (1608) and
later of Milton (1644).[5]

No marked changes took place in the method of
pronouncing Latin before the middle of the nineteenth
century. National pronunciations were in vogue, but
with the exception of the English, all these had much
in common. In the case of the vowels, they showed
almost complete uniformity. But our modern English
vowels represent a number of sounds which have no
counterparts in the languages of the European
continent, and the sounds in question when applied to
Latin vowels make English Latin practically unintelli-
gible to continental scholars.

The rise of the science of Comparative Philology
in the early nineteenth century and the historical investigation of the development of the Latin language by
Ritschl, Corssen, Seelmann, Bücheler, and Lindsay,
among others, revolutionized our knowledge of Latin
pronunciation.[6] On the basis of a utilization of all the
sources mentioned earlier in this paper, the pronunciation of Latin throughout Antiquity, but especially in
the days of Cicero and Vergil, was determined with
reasonable accuracy. The study of inscriptions enabled scholars to establish the general standard of
orthography in the Classical period, and also to
correct the Latin grammarians in their teaching on the
division of syllables.[7] The sound values of vowels and
consonants were determined with practical certainty,
and even the nature of hidden quantities was ascer-
tained in most cases.

But the known values of the vowel and consonant
sounds does not solve the problem of Latin pronunciation completely, for we must still consider the question
of the Latin accent, so vital for Latin sentence phonetics. Granted that we know the individual sounds of
Latin, how were they pronounced in the succession of
syllables and words that constitute a unit of connected
discourse? Most scholars are agreed that Latin had a
strong stress on the initial syllable of disyllabic and
polysyllabic words in the very early period and that
this kind of stress continued for some time after the

introduction of the Penultimate Law of Latin accentuation. Most scholars are likewise agreed that Latin had a stress accent on the penult or antepenult syllable in the later Silver Age, and that this stress by the fourth century A.D. had become fairly heavy. Following the Latin grammarians and relying on the undisputed fact that Classical Latin poetry is purely quantitative like the Greek, French scholars and a few others hold that in the Classical period the Latin accent was a pitch accent. German, English, American, and Italian scholars for the most part, on the other hand, maintain that Latin in the Classical Period had a very mild stress accent, so mild that it was possible to adapt the Greek system of quantitive metrics to Latin use. The present writer adheres to this view, and cannot accept the explanation offered by the late Professor R. G. Kent:

> Greek teachers of the Roman youth set the fashion of speaking Latin with a pitch accent, for as Greeks they kept this peculiarity of their mother tongue when they learned Latin. From that time (c. 150 B.C.) on, Latin was spoken with a pitch accent by the highly educated class, while the general populace retained the stress accent.[8]

Such an explanation, in my opinion, is as artificial as it is unconvincing. That Greek rhetoricians could not learn to speak Latin without a marked foreign pronunciation is understandable, but that Romans could be taught to exchange the natural accent of their language for a foreign one of different character, and that they then proceeded to write great literature in a language to the intonation and rhythm of which they had done much violence, is simply out of the question. The late Professor G. D. Buck gave a much more satisfactory explanation:

> The familiarity of educated Romans with Greek accent and technique, while it certainly could not have caused them to adopt an element of accent wholly foreign to their natural speech, might well have made them more conscious of an existing element of pitch [in Latin] and even

led them to a studied enhancement of it in
actual practice, for example in oratory.[9]

The Classical or "restored" pronunciation of
Latin spread rapidly through the German and Scandi-
navian universities, but more slowly in secondary
schools. In England, Roby supported it in his Latin
Grammar (1871) and it was soon employed in Scotland,
but it made little real headway in Britain before the
beginning of the present century. It was recommended
by the English Classical Association's Committee on
the Pronunciation of Latin in 1906, and from that date
it has become general in England, and in English
Canada, and Australia.[10] In France, Italy, Belgium,
and Holland, the "restored" pronunciation is still
confined pretty much to university circles or even to
individual professors and their seminars.[11] Its
dissemination in our own country has been wider than
in Germany itself. The numerous graduates of
American colleges who received their doctorates in
Classical Philology at German universities in the
second half of the last century returned to this country
to become enthusiastic advocates of the new pronunciation in the leading American colleges and universities
of their time. It spread very rapidly, and since the
beginning of the present century it has been employed
almost universally in secular and non-Catholic high
schools, academies, colleges, universities, and in
Protestant seminaries. It is also used to some extent
in similar Catholic institutions, with the exception of
seminaries.

In Catholic circles, the "restored" pronunciation
was not, in general, viewed with enthusiasm, and
Catholics tended to adhere to traditional pronunciations. In our own country down to the early 1900's,
priests trained abroad, or trained by teachers who
were continuing the continental tradition in their Latin
pronunciation, used the French ("Continental"), or
German, or Italian pronunciation of Latin. The
writer recalls that in his boyhood almost all the
priests in what is now the Diocese of Worcester had
been trained in Montreal or Paris and pronounced
Latin in the "Continental" manner. The reign of Pope
St. Pius X (1903-1914) marks the beginning of a new
epoch in the history of Latin pronunciation among

Catholics. In his Motu proprio on sacred music
issued in November, 1903, and again in his Letter of
July 10, 1912 to Louis E. Dubois, Archbishop of
Bourges, he strongly recommended the use of the
Italian pronunciation of Latin as an aid in the revival
of Gregorian Chant, and he expressed the hope that the
adoption of the Italian pronunciation in France would
do much to promote liturgical unity. Since the publication of these documents, the Italian pronunciation
has made steady progress and has become the official,
or at least the quasi-official, Latin pronunciation of
the Roman Catholic Church. While it met some opposition on the Continent of Europe, it was quickly
adopted throughout the Catholic English-speaking
world. The Italian pronunciation -- often called the
"Roman" pronunciation -- is simply the traditional
Italian pronunciation of Latin, reflecting in the course
of its history the changes that have taken place in the
pronunciation of the Italian vernacular. 12

Before passing to the question of the Classical
and Italian pronunciation in the schools it may be
helpful from the theoretical as well as the practical
points of view to make the following observations. It
is hardly necessary to describe the sound values of
the vowels and consonants in the Classical pronunciation, for this information is presented clearly enough
in the textbooks of Elementary Latin, and it is easily
available in scholarly detail in Bennett's Latin
Language and Sturtevant's Pronunciation of Greek and
Latin. 13 Nor will it be necessary either -- nor would
it be possible within the time limits of this lecture --
to give a full description of the Italian pronunciation of
Latin. 14

The Classical or "restored" pronunciation of
Latin reproduces with reasonable exactness the sounds
of Latin as Latin was pronounced by the educated in
the day of Cicero and Vergil. In its broadest range,
and with some minor adjustments, it covers the
pronunciation of Latin in the period from about
150 B.C. to about 200 A.D. The pronunciation in the
age of Plautus was somewhat different, and by the end
of the second century A.D. pronunciation was beginning to show marked divergences from the
Classical norm. The Classical pronunciation can be
used for the literary works of the Latin Fathers, just

as we use our current English pronunciation when we
read Shakespeare, but it is not suitable for Mediaeval
Latin. Mediaeval Latin reflects a pronunciation quite
different from the Classical, and the Classical pronunciation of Latin impairs or destroys the rhythm and
the rime schemes of Mediaeval Latin verse.

The problem of the Classical accent has already
been mentioned, but it need not cause trouble in
practice, provided one tries to pronounce accented
syllables with a light stress. Many imagine that they
are employing the Classical pronunciation accurately
when they pronounce their c's, t's, g's, and v's in the
Classical manner, but matters are not so simple.
Long syllables, even when unaccented, should be kept
long, and short syllables, even when accented, should
be kept short. Vowels should be kept "pure", but this
is difficult in English, as we frequently pronounce
simple vowels as diphthongs. Full attention should be
given to hidden quantity. Short vowels in long syllables
should be pronounced short, and long vowels should be
pronounced long -- apart from the rare cases of semi-
shortening in verse. Double consonants should actually be pronounced as double consonants. The accurate use of the Classical pronunciation is not easy,
but, with much practice it can be attained. The
Classical pronunciation is often an object of ridicule
in Catholic circles, but such an attitude is not justified. The Classical values of the Latin vowels and
consonants have been established on a scientific
basis. Cicero called himself Kikero, Caesar called
himself Kaisar, and his veni, vidi, vici was pronounced wainee, weedee, weekee, whether we like
these sounds or not. Cicero would probably regard
our "restored" pronunciation of his Latin sounds
definitely foreign, and he would surely think our
sentence phonetics rather bad, but I think -- perhaps
not with the same confidence as the late Professor
Kent -- that he would understand us.[15] All teachers
should have a knowledge of the Classical pronunciation
and its evolution, whether or not they use it in the
classroom. Such a knowledge is indispensable for
persons taking graduate degrees in Latin, and also for
graduate students in the Romance languages.

St. Pius X and later, Pius XI, were eminently
practical in advocating the use of the Italian

pronunciation of Latin in the Liturgy and in encour-
aging the spread of this pronunciation throughout the
Church. [16] The use of Latin as the liturgical and
official language of the Church symbolizes the unity of
the Church and is a tangible proof of that unity. A
uniform pronunciation of Latin in the Church likewise
not only symbolizes and emphasizes unity, but also
greatly facilitates seminary instruction and ecclesiastical communication in general. Given the fact that
Rome has been the capital of the Church and the
residence of the Pope since the days of St. Peter, it
is only natural that the Italian pronunciation of Latin
has been employed in Rome since the rise of the
Italian language and that this pronunciation should be
used in the numerous ecclesiastical establishments of
the Holy City. Foreign ecclesiastics taking up
residence in Rome as students, scholars, heads of
orders, etc., adopt the Italian pronunciation of Latin
as a matter of course and normally continue to use it
when they return to their respective countries. The
recommendations of St. Pius X gave formal support
to a movement that was long under way before his
pontificate.

But uniformity of pronunciation is so obviously
desirable that the question may be asked: Why
would it not be a good thing to recommend the employment of the "restored" pronunciation of Latin instead
of the Italian, now that its principles have been solidly
established, that it is widely taught, and that it is
free from any charge of being nationalistic? An effective answer in the negative can be readily made.
The Liturgy of the Church contains elements that
range from the second century of our era to the
present time, and many of these elements entered the
Liturgy when Latin was being pronounced in a manner
quite different from the Classical. I have in mind, of
course, the considerable body of liturgical texts
composed in Late Antiquity and in the Middle Ages.
In actual fact, Latin pronunciation was no longer
Classical in any strict sense when the earliest Latin
liturgical texts were being composed. The Church has
really never had a uniform, unchanging pronunciation
of Latin throughout its long history, nor could this
have been possible. Hence, any pronunciation that it
adopts for the sake of uniformity must be arbitrary,

because it must be applied to texts composed at dates
as much as eighteen hundred years apart. Under the
circumstances, the Classical pronunciation would be
quite unsuitable as a Church pronunciation of Latin.[17]
A vernacular pronunciation of Latin based on the
pronunciation of one of the Romance languages is
clearly the best solution, and Italian has most in its
favor. It not only has superior claims because of its
usage in Rome, but, as compared with French or
Spanish, it preserves the vowel and consonant sounds
of the ancient Latin more faithfully. Furthermore, it
is much easier for foreigners to learn and use the
Italian sounds than those of French or Spanish.

Finally, in the light of the background which I
have given, let us consider the pronunciation of Latin
in school. In secular or non-Catholic schools, I see
no reason why the Classical pronunciation of Latin
should not continue to be used, provided that the
necessary modifications be made if mediaeval texts
are being read.[18] As regards our Catholic schools,
on the other hand, I strongly recommend that the
Italian pronunciation of Latin be adopted from the
first day of Latin instruction and that it be used
exclusively. Students will thus become accustomed to
one pronunciation. They will use it habitually, and
there will be complete integration between the
pronunciation employed in the school and that in the
Liturgy. It is hard enough to master one pronunciation without trying to master two. I have found by
experience that even teachers who use the two pronunciations often confuse them, without being
conscious that they are doing so. Cicero and Vergil
have been read with various pronunciations through
the centuries and will not suffer too much if their
Latin is pronounced in the softer and more liquid
sounds of the Italian tongue.[19] If the Italian pronunciation is adopted as the exclusive pronunciation,
it will be possible for both teachers as well as pupils
to develop greater accuracy in its use. The Italian
pronunciation of too many teachers is bad, and
should certainly be corrected. Familiarity with the
Italian language itself is the best foundation for a good
Italian pronunciation of Latin. But, even without
knowing Italian, it is possible, through the careful
study of the Italian sounds and the use of recordings,

to acquire a satisfactory Italian pronunciation of Latin.

FOOTNOTES

[1]See E. H. Sturtevant, The Pronunciation of Greek and Latin (2nd ed. Philadelphia 1940) 21-29; R. G. Kent, The Sounds of Latin. A Descriptive and Historical Phonology (2nd ed., revised, Baltimore 1940) 43-45.

[2]On the changes in Latin pronunciation in the last centuries of Antiquity, and on the preoccupation of the Latin grammarians with problems of orthography, see L. R. Palmer, The Latin Language (London 1954) 148-166; W. M. Lindsay, The Latin Language (Oxford 1844); the pertinent treatises of the grammarians printed in H. Keil, Grammatici Latini (7 vols. Leipzig 1857-1880).

[3]See H. J. Chaytor, From Script to Print. An Introduction to Mediaeval Vernacular Literature (2nd printing Cambridge [England] 1950) 13-14.

[4]On the pronunciation and orthography of Latin in the Middle Ages see: K. Strecker, Introduction to Mediaeval Latin. English Translation and Revision by R. B. Palmer (Berlin 1957) 58-60; D. Norberg, Introduction à l'étude de la versification latine médiévale (Stockholm 1938) 7-28; F. Brittain, Latin in Church. The History of Its Pronunciation (new ed. revised and enlarged London 1955) 13-25.

[5]On the views of Erasmus, Lipsius, and Milton on the pronunciation of Latin in their time, see J. E. Sandys, A History of Classical Scholarship. II (Cambridge [England] 1908; reprinted New York 1958) 232-234; Brittain, op. cit. 27-31, and 49. On the English pronunciation of Latin Milton observed: "To smatter Latin with an English mouth is as ill a hearing as Low-French," and he recommended that the pronunciation of boys should "be fashioned to a distinct and clear pronunciation as near as may be to the Italian, especially in the vowels." (Quoted in Sandys 234).

[6]See, especially: W. Corssen, Ueber Aussprache, Vokalismus und Betonung der lateinischen Sprache (2 vols. Leipzig 1858-1859; 2nd ed., revised, 1868-1870); E. Seelmann, Die Aussprache des Latein nach physiologisch-historischen Grundsätzen (Heilbronn

1885).

7On the division of syllables, see C. H.
Bennett, The Latin Language (Boston 1907) 31-35,
and, especially, Kent, op. cit. 62-64.

8Kent, op. cit. 66.

9C. D. Buck, Comparative Grammar of Greek
and Latin (3rd impression Chicago 1942) 167.

10See The Teaching of Classics. Issued by the In-
corporated Association of Assistant Masters in
Secondary Schools (Cambridge 1954), "Appendix I.
The Pronunciation of Latin," 211-219.

11For the "restored" pronunciation in France, see
J. Marouzeau, La prononciation du latin (histoire,
théorie, pratique) (Paris 1931); for Italy, G. B.
Pighi, "La pronunzia del latino," Aevum 8 (1934)
215-233.

12On the Italian pronunciation of Latin, see Pighi,
art. cit., and Brittain, op. cit. 61-87.

13See the works by Kent, Sturtevant, and Bennett
cited in notes 1 and 7 above.

14For a convenient summary of the rules for the
Italian pronunciation of Latin see the last part of the
section "Rules for Interpretation [of the Chant]" in
the English language edition of the Liber Usualis published by Desclée and Co. (Tournai, Paris, Rome,
and New York; in the edition of 1938, e.g., pp. XXXVI-
XXXIX). The rules given, however, are primarily
concerned with pronunciation in singing. It is to be
hoped that Dr. George J. Siefert will prepare and
publish a description of the Italian pronunciation
which will give adequate guidance for its use in reading Latin prose and verse.

15Kent, op. cit. 44.

16See the Letter of July 10, 1912, sent by Pope
Pius X to Louis E. Dubois, Archbishop of Bruges
(AAS 4 [1912] 577-578), and the Letter of Aug. 25,
1929, sent by Pope Pius XI to the same as Cardinal
Archbishop of Paris (AAS 21 [1929] 619).

17For general surveys of the pronunciation of
Latin in the Church from Antiquity to the present
time, see, especially, Brittain and Pighi.

18On this point, there are some excellent observations in R. A. Browne, British Latin Selections

A. D. 500-1400 (Oxford 1954) LIX-LXI.

[19]But they do suffer, at least in this writer's opinion! Something of the characteristically Roman strength and majesty of Cicero and Vergil is lost when they are read aloud in the Italian pronunciation.

THE READING OF LATIN VERSE

by

George J. Siefert, Jr.

It would in a very real sense be easier to cover adequately in so short a time a more theoretical subject, of which the lines could be more largely drawn. The reading of Latin verse is a technique, not to say, in plainer English, an art; it is in the nature of a technique that it must be acquired by practice; and practice takes time. Moreover, one does not put off the beginning of practice until one has mastered the theory; rather, the two proceed pari passu, with mutual corroborations all along the line. The case is somewhat as with the newly invented lyre that Hermes presents to Apollo in the Homeric Hymn (to Hermes 482-8): "Whoso with wit and wisdom enquires of it cunningly, him it teaches through its sound all manner of things that delight the mind, being easily played with gentle familiarities, for it abhors toilsome drudgery; but whoso in ignorance enquires of it violently, to him it chatters mere vanity and foolishness."

"But," as the Hymn goes on to say in the very next line, "you are able to learn whatever you please;" and it is in the assurance that you do please to learn to read Latin verse, and can in fact do so, that I shall try in the short time at our disposal to give you as much theory as I regard as necessary for an intelligent beginning of practice, and then, if it is at all possible, a few pointers with regard to the practice itself. Almost every theoretical statement that I shall make could be refined upon; and there will not be time enough to touch upon many a specific difficulty that will arise in practice. For help with the latter I would recommend in the strongest terms a little book called An Introduction to the Latin Hexameter, by Charles Gordon Cooper, of the University of Queensland in Australia, published in

84

Melbourne (1952) by Macmillan and Company, and
procurable at a very low price.

First of all, then, to the theory. To set our
problem in its proper frame, we should keep in mind
the commonplace that language is used for three purposes, or, to put it in another way, at three levels:
first, to communicate ideas; second, to stir the
feelings and to move to action; third, to serve in
itself as an object of contemplation. These three
levels are not of course in practice kept distinct. As
soon, for instance, as one brings to a simple statement, at the first level, such rhetorical art as is
designed to convince one's audience of its truth, one
has already reached the second level; and as soon as
one consciously begins to form one's utterance with a
view to what we call style, one approaches the third,
which is that of the poem, that is, as the etymology of
the word itself clearly indicates, something not so
much said as made.

Artistic prose is from this standpoint "poetic";
but traditionally poetry has been marked throughout by
a formality and regularity that go beyond anything
admissible in prose, where such evident art, as
Aristotle says (Rhetoric 3.8.1), would reduce persuasiveness (at the second level) and so defeat the
rhetorical end. On the other hand, it is worth pointing
out that ancient poetry, and indeed poetry in general
until quite recent times -- although what makes it
poetry is always the formal structuring, as an object
of contemplation, of a rich complex of elements which
we have not the time to specify more exactly -- never
failed to subsume within itself the two lower levels to
which we have referred: in other words, it always
said something, at the first level, and at the second
more often than not made a direct appeal to the heart
and to the feelings of mankind.

Of this rich complex of elements that are formally
structured in poetry, we are here specifically concerned with the rhythmic. Coming from a Greek word
generally interpreted as meaning "measured motion"
(itself derived from the verb "to flow"), rhythm may
for our purposes be defined as a patterned alternation, measurable in time, of some quantitative difference in duration, pitch, or stress, in contra-
distinction to such phonetic and semantic differences

as may be regarded as qualitative in character. In terms of the art of painting, the word rhythm might be applied analogously to patterns constituted by those elements, such as mass, line, and intensity of color (or light and shade), that can be measured quantitatively, leaving the colors themselves and the larger significances of the subject matter, which must be spoken of in qualitative terms, as analogues to certain phonetic and semantic aspects of poetry.

We have defined rhythm as a patterned alternation, measurable in time, of some quantitative difference in stress, duration, or pitch. Classical Greek (without some conception of which we cannot begin to understand the Latin) differed radically from English in that it kept these three elements almost purely distinct; in other words, a syllable could be long without receiving any accretion of stress or heightening of pitch; or it could be stressed and yet not raised in pitch or lengthened; or it could be higher in pitch without being lengthened or stressed -- quite as in music a quarter-note may receive the down-beat when a subsequent half-note does not; while an eighth-note may be higher in pitch than every other note in the measure. In their prosody the Greeks paid attention solely to the temporal duration of syllables; the pattern as thus determined was then marked by a degree of stress, perhaps very slight, that constituted what we should call the beat (or the ictus), while the accents of the words, which were purely tonic in character, floated as freely over the rhythmic pattern as the melodic line does in our music. In English, on the other hand, in patterning our rhythm we think primarily in terms of stress; and the stressed syllable receives, from the fact of being stressed, something of an accretion in both pitch and duration. For example, the initial i in the words Italy and Italian is about the same in quality; but the i in the word Italy takes somewhat longer to pronounce, and is pronounced on a somewhat higher note, than the first i of the word Italian. The keeping of these three elements distinct in Greek, and their amalgamation in what may be called a centroidal syllable in English, constitute the chief difference between the languages in this regard.

Latin originally had a stress-accent more like

that of English; and this perdured to an extent that
made it difficult if not impossible ever to ignore it.
But as time went on, with a more self-conscious
practice of the arts of speech, and to no small extent
under the influence of Greek teachers, the stress-
accent was, in the mouths of the most highly cultivated
speakers, moderated to the extent that it no longer
caused an obscuration of the quality and an abridge-
ment of the quantity of unaccented syllables in its
neighborhood. In other words, that accent became one
in which the element of tone had become somewhat
more prominent, and the element of stress somewhat
less prominent -- which is to say that it had become
more musical, much as in the best Italian of the
present day. (In this connection it is interesting to
note that the very word accentus, which is itself a
translation of the Greek prosodia, means a "singing
to" and not a "stressing of" a syllable.) But, however
softened, the element of stress still remained in the
Latin word-accent, and, as we shall see, frequently
brought this accent into conflict with the metrical
stress, or ictus, which was determined primarily by
the durational pattern of long and short syllables.
How the Latin poets of the great age partly resolved
and partly made use of this conflict we shall discuss
when we have disposed of more elementary matters.

Now, as to the practice. We have said that in
their prosody the Greeks paid attention solely to the
temporal duration of syllables. The word syllable,
itself from the Greek syllabein, "to take together,"
may perhaps best be defined as follows: a syllable is
as much of articulate utterance as can be comprised
in what is felt to be one effort of the vocal apparatus.
The utterance must be articulate, i.e., "jointed"; we
do not speak of syllables in connection with the
barking and growling of animals. The psychological
element involved in the word "felt" is also important.
A close analysis can determine several discrete
efforts within the one impulse with which we utter a
heavy syllable like the English bridged; but we feel
that we produce the word with one compound effort,
however difficult, of the organs of speech. In Greek,
as in Latin, a syllable must in effect contain one
vowel or one diphthong, no more; and it may contain
as many consonants ("with-sounding" elements) as the

habits of the language permit. As for the matter of
temporal duration, a syllable is long (1) if it contains
a long vowel or a diphthong, (2) if it ends in a consonant (in which case it is referred to as "closed").

The last consideration alone should make it clear
how important it is to divide a line of verse (or for
that matter of prose) correctly into its component
syllables. For details I will refer you to Cooper's
book, which I have already recommended. Here we
have time only to summarize as follows: every vowel
or diphthong will form the nucleus of one syllable. A
single consonant between two vowels (or diphthongs)
will go with the following; two or more will ordinarily
be so distributed that as many as can comfortably be
pronounced with the following vowel will go with it.
In this connection we may ask ourselves the question:
could the combination of consonants we have arrived
at in our syllabication stand at the beginning of a
Latin word? The great exception to this rule is in
connection with the letter s followed by a consonant.
Such a combination may stand at the beginning of a
Latin word; but standing alone between two vowels in
the middle of a word it will be divided between them.
As x and z are double consonants, standing for cs and
ds respectively, they should be so represented in
scansion, and divided between the antecedent and subsequent vowels. H (which represented an increasingly
weak aspiration) does not count in any position, nor
does m (which was probably little more than the
representation of a nasal quality of the preceding
vowel) before an initial vowel in the following word;
they should therefore be set off with parentheses.

A most important thing to remember is that the
pronunciation of both Greek and Latin (like the writing
itself, originally) was characterized by an extreme
degree of liaison, i.e., the utterance was produced as
a continuum, with no breaks between words except
where the sense demanded it -- and even here, for the
purposes of versification, there is generally a carry-
over of a single final consonant to an initial vowel in
the following word, quite as there would be within a
clause. Furthermore, a final vowel is regularly
elided into an initial vowel following, as in Italian
verse (it being remembered always that initial h, and
final m preceding an initial vowel, do not count). The

exact nature of this elision is in dispute; in practice it
is perhaps best to make no attempt to pronounce the
prior vowel. (Aphaeresis of the e in est, or es,
which allows the preceding word to remain intact, is
a different figure, countenanced in positions where
elision proper is avoided.) Failure to elide produces
a hiatus, which is relatively rare in Latin verse.
When it does occur, it is generally at a clear break in
the sense (as in Georgics 1.3-4: qui cultus habendo
Sit pecori, // apibus quanta experientia parcis), or in
imitation of a Greek rhythm (so twice in Aeneid 3.74:
Nereidum matri // et Neptuno // Aegeo), or for some
special effect (as in Aeneid 4.667 and 9.477: femineo
// ululatu).

The first thing to do therefore is to write the line
as one continuum and to mark off the syllables:

Ar/ma/vi/rum/que/ca/no/Troi*/iae/qui/pri/
    mu/sa/bo/ris
I/ta/li/am/fa/to/pro/fu/gus/La/vin/ia*/que/
    ve/nit
li/to/ra/mul/t(um)il/l(e)et/ter/ris/iac/ta/tu/
    se/tal/to . . .

Or, if this seems too confusing to the eye, we may
leave the printed space between the words, and indicate elision by a slur; so, for line 3:

li/to/ra/ mul/t(um)‿il/l(e)‿et/ ter/ris/
    iac/ta/tu/s e/t al/to.

Next, these syllables should be marked as long or
short (with macrons and breves placed well above the
line), according to the twofold rule already given:

   — ◡ ◡   —   —   — —
li/to/ra/ mul/t(um) il/l(e) et/ ter/ris/

   —   — ◡ ◡   —
iac/ta/tu/s e/t al/to.

---

* The ad hoc spelling of the word Troiae, and the
syllabication of the word Laviniaque, will be explained
orally, with references to Kent, The Sounds of Latin
§§25 and 60, for the first, and to Gildersleeve and
Lodge, §723, for the second.

An intermediate step, to be recommended for be-
ginners, would be the marking of every long vowel
with a macron placed immediately above it. So,
again for line 3:

lī/to/ra/ mul/t(um)_il/l(e)_et/ ter/rīs/
iac/tā/tu/s e/t al/tō.

The length of a diphthong is obvious to the eye, as is
also the length of a closed syllable, if the division has
been made properly. The difficulty arises in recog-
nizing, in an unmarked text, the quantity of the
vowels; and it is here that the peculiar interchange
that characterizes all practice of an art is most
marked: we bring what knowledge we have to it, and
come away with more that we have gained from it.
There is no better way to learn the quantity of Latin
vowels than by practicing scansion; indeed, although
there may in specific instances be other sources for
the knowledge, the commonest authority for the
length of a vowel as given in our lexicons is that of
some classic poet who so used it. We may leave out
of consideration, as having no bearing on the scansion,
the whole question of "hidden" quantities, i.e., of
vowel-quantities, like that of the a in actus, obscured
by the fact that they occur in permanently closed
syllables.

As for the knowledge of vowel-quantities that we
can bring to the problem of scansion, it might help to
keep in mind the following facts. Words, like most
other things, have beginnings, middles, and ends. To
start with the last, Latin is a highly inflected language,
and the ending of a large proportion of words will be
some common inflection, the quantity of which should
long since have been learned, along with the form
itself. No one really knows the inflection of the
neuter plural arma, for instance, who does not know
that the final a is short. Of forty-eight words,
counting them as they are printed, and ignoring
enclitics, in the first seven lines of the Aeneid,
thirty-nine are inflected. The other nine are either
conjunctions: et (three times), atque and dum; or
prepositions: ab and ob; or adverbs: quoque and unde
-- all of them so common that their quantities should
soon be learned, even if they are not already evident

to the eye.

As for the penultimate syllable, the correct accentuation will remind us of its quantity, for it was of course this quantity that determined the accentuation in the first place. We say Itáliam, prófugus, mémorem, and cónderet because the penultimate vowels are short, and open; on the other hand, we say Latínum and Albáni because the penultimate vowels are long. The fact that we do so pronounce them, if we are careful, should remind us of their correct quantities when scanning a verse; or, if we have been careless, the exigencies of the scansion will soon set us aright.

When we come to the very body of a word, we should know the quantity of the vowel or vowels as we know the spelling of the word itself; but it is here especially that the scansion comes to our aid. Virumque, in the first line, stands in a place where its i could only be short; on the other hand, in Georgics 1. 129:

ille malum virus serpentibus addidit atris,

the i of virus can only be long. So we learn from these lines, if from no other source, that the i of vir is short, the i of virus long.

As it is impossible to cover everything in so short a time, I am assuming that everyone here knows the pattern of the dactylic hexameter, with its last foot always a spondee (or a trochee -- the final syllable being indifferent in length), and with its permitted substitution of a spondee for a dactyl in the first four feet (and rarely in the fifth). For our present purposes the most important corollary of this pattern is that in such a line (ignoring always the final syllaba anceps, which may be either short or long) there can never be less than two short syllables together, nor more than two. When we start with the closed syllable ar at the beginning of the line, where the scheme in any case demands a long syllable, and follow it with the short syllable ma, we know that the vi must be short to complete the dactyl. Then rum, even if we could not see that it is long, would have to be so to begin the next foot; and the shortness of que makes it clear that the ca of cano is also short (an indication that should be corroborated in our minds by the thought of compounds such as recino, where the a

would not have become i if it were not short: cf.
facio, reficio). Similarly, after the initial long syllable of a foot, the sight of a short syllable coming up
in the third place will tell us that the second syllable
is also short. Exciderant, at the beginning of line 26
of Aeneid 1, is clearly a pluperfect, with the short e
of the pluperfect ending -erant. The ci must therefore also be short, and we have to do with a form not
of excīdo but of excĭdo. And so on and so on. This
requires, of course, that our eye should be in advance
of our voice; but all singing, in fact, all reading aloud
requires just this. It would be a poor singer, or a
poor reader, who while he was engaged with one note,
or one word, was not preparing himself for the next
to come.

We may now begin to indicate the scansion of the
hexameter graphically by lengthening the lines   of
syllabic division at the places where they also divide
the feet, and marking the first syllable of each foot
with an ictus:

$$\acute{-}\ \cup\ \cup\ /\ \acute{-}\ \ -\ /\ \acute{-}\ \ -\ /\ \acute{-}\ \ -\ /$$

lī/to/ra/ mul/t(um)_il/l(e)_et/ ter/rīs/ iac/

$$\acute{-}\ \cup\ \cup\ /\ \acute{-}\ \ -\ /$$

tā/tu/s e/t al/tō.

But the whole matter should not be regarded as a
puzzle to be worked out piecemeal on paper, and only
then, if ever, vocally rendered. It would seem to me
to be much better to start at the outset with pronouncing the syllables, each with its proper length, beginning in the natural way at the beginning of the line,
and striving to develop in ourselves the rhythmic
sense that will make us feel when we have "had it,"
so to speak. The first long syllable has been followed by a short; so we need another short, and that
is it. Or the first long syllable has been followed by
a long; and we are ready for another foot.

It is at this point that we must introduce another
matter of the greatest importance. As the words of a
line are variously distributed among its feet, it is
obvious that their endings must either coincide with
the ending of a foot, or else fall somewhere within a

foot, i.e., after the first long syllable of a dactyl or
a spondee, or after the first short syllable of a
dactyl. If word and foot terminate together, we have
what is called a diaeresis; if the word terminates
within a foot, we have what is called a caesura,
masculine if it comes after the initial long syllable,
feminine if it comes after the first short syllable of a
dactyl. (The expression "the caesura of a line" may
well be buried. There are as many caesurae as there
are word-divisions occurring within feet; their weak-
ness or their strength depends entirely on one's
estimate of their importance in the articulation of the
sense, and upon the rhetorical impetus of the passage.)
The caesura, in spite of its name, ordinarily has the
effect of binding the line together, as if the words
were, after the manner of brickwork, a course laid
over the cracks between the feet in the underlying
course. Even if the caesura (generally in this case
masculine) comes at a strong break in the sense, we
feel the rhythm, so to speak, held for an instant in
abeyance, and are not satisfied until we take it up
again. It is the diaeresis that constitutes a more
complete break in the rhythm. The well-known line
of Ennius:

$$\acute{-} \ - \ / \ \acute{-} \ - \ / \ \acute{-} \ - \ / \ \acute{-} \ - \ /$$
spar/si/s has/tis/ lon/gis/ cam/pus/

$$\acute{-} \ \cup \ \cup \ / \ \acute{-} \ -$$
splen/de/t e/t hor/ret,

marked throughout as it is by diaeresis, may perhaps
have been meant by the poet to represent in its
fragmented rhythm the scattering of the spears; we
need only compare it with the no less spondaic line of
Vergil (Aeneid 6.868):

$$\acute{-} \ - \ / \ \acute{-} \ - \ / \ \acute{-} \ - \ / \ \acute{-} \ - \ /$$
O/ gna/t(e) in/gen/tem/ luc/tum ne/

$$\acute{-} \ \cup \ \cup \ / \ \acute{-} \ -$$
quae/re/ tu/o/rum

where there is no real diaeresis, and where every foot
is marked by caesura, to feel the difference. In all

of this discussion we prescind from the question of
what really constitutes a word. It is obvious enough
that ne is not a word in the same sense in which
quaere is; somehow it is proclitic to quaere, and
there is no significant diaeresis between what we
continue to call, for the sake of convenience, the two
"words."

A brief consideration of the so-called penultimate
rule of Latin accentuation, over against the definition
of the terms diaeresis and caesura that we have just
given, will make it clear that wherever we have either
diaeresis or a feminine caesura, the accent of the
preceding word will coincide with the metrical ictus
on the first syllable of the dactyl or spondee, and we
shall have what is called concord between the two;
wherever we have a masculine caesura, the ictus will
fall on the last syllable of the preceding word, which
cannot in Latin (with very special exceptions) receive
the accent, and we shall have -- unless the word was
itself an emphatic monosyllable -- conflict between
accent and ictus. As both the metrical ictus and the
word-accent in Latin were characterized primarily
by stress (in contradistinction to the Greek, in which
the word-accent in classical times was purely one of
tone), this conflict was real; and as the poet could not
ignore it, he could only resolve it, or turn it to good
use.

Vergil's practice, in the Aeneid more especially,
may with some over-simplification be analyzed as
follows. Of the six ictuses in every line, the first
two may or may not coincide with the word-accent;
the second or middle two will ordinarily be in conflict
with the word-accent; the last two will almost always
be in concord with it. The rhythmical effect of this is
as of a gathering of tension between two stresses,
reaching a peak at what may be called the crest of the
line, where the wave breaks and rolls sonorously to
shore. To put it in another way, the middle of the
line, or even the first two-thirds, if the conflict has
begun so early, are raised above the tone of normal
prose by reason of the fact that every syllable, if the
rhythm is spondaic, or almost every syllable, if the
rhythm is dactylic, is sustained either by word-
accent or by metrical stress.

Sometimes the resolution may come, not as

ordinarily in the fifth foot, but rather in the fourth,
producing a longer cadence, which may be used by the
poet to mark the end of a period. It is only at the end
of what may be called the first paragraph of the
Aeneid, namely in line 7, that we have a resolution as
early as the fourth foot.

Only very rarely do we have concord throughout
the last four feet; and then the effect is a very special
one, which may find its physical analogue in the way
in which tramping feet on a swaying bridge may ac-
centuate the sway if they fall into the rhythm of it --
as in Vergil's line describing the heaving of the sea
(Georgics 1.357):

> aut freta / ponti
>
> incipi/unt agi/tata tu/mescer(e) e/t aridu/s altis
>
> montibu/s audi/ri fragor . . .*

Note here the shattering effect of the diaeresis after
fragor, at the exact middle of the line; one would have
to search through hundreds if not thousands of lines to
find another such example in Vergil. Horace will use
the same diaeresis in a passage of metrical prose
simply to point up a running this way and that (Epist.
2.2.75):

> (h)ac rabi/osa fu/git cani/s (h)ac lutu/lenta ru/
>
> it sus.

But to get back to the matter of concord and
conflict between ictus and accent: concord beginning
as early as the third foot (as in the example from the
Georgics given above) may also have a rocking,
lulling effect, as in Aeneid 2.9:

> et / iam noc/s umida / caelo

---

*From this point on we shall restrict our indication
of the scansion to the division of the line into feet and
the marking of the ictuses.

praécipi/tát sua/déntque ca/déntia / sídera /

somnos --

or we may feel in this long fall the downward sweep of
the stars toward their setting. It must be remembered
always that these rhythmical effects, like other sound-
effects in poetry, are facultative. A poet may use z-
sounds to indicate onomatopoetically the buzzing of
bees, or m-sounds to indicate their humming; but a
line may contain many of these sounds, and yet have-
no reference to either, or indeed to anything comparable.

Hexameters will show concord between ictus and
accent throughout only in styles that are essentially
prosaic, as in Horace's line (Epist. 1.11.29):

strénua / nos ec/sércet i/nértia: / navibu/ s átque

quadri/gis peti/mús bene / vívere . . .

written in a style which he himself would call sermoni
propior (if we were in doubt of the prosaic character
of the line, fine as it is rhetorically, the final atque
would assure us of it); or in a line of prosaic exposition in Lucretius (1.217):

nam si / quid mor/tál(e) e / cúnctis / pártibu/

s esset,

or a little further along (1.236):

immor/táli / sunt na/túra / praédita / cérte.

Such lines occur with great frequency in what may be
called the prosaic passages of Lucretius; they will not
be found in those passages in which his inspiration
soars, nor, to my knowledge, anywhere in Vergil.
Yet, so varied are the effects of any scheme in its
particular exemplifications that Horace can use
precisely this complete concord between ictus and
accent in a finely wrought line to suggest, in conjunc-
tion with a wealth of liquid sounds, the smooth flow-
ing of a stream (Epist. 1.2.43):

lábitu/r ét la/bétur i/n ómne vo/lúbili/s aévum.

(The et as here used is emphatic enough to deserve an accent.)

The regularity with which conflict between ictus and accent is found in the middle of the hexameter has an important practical corollary, namely, that even if we should be let down, so to speak, in the middle of a line, and alight upon a spondaic word like Troiae, for example, in the first line of the Aeneid, or terris in line 3, saevae in line 4, or bello and passus in line 5, we may assume, at least until we get our footing, that the ictus falls on the final syllable, in contra-distinction to the accent, which falls of course on the penult. The concord found in the word altae, in line 7, is, as we have already said, relatively unusual, and helps form the longer cadence that marks the end of the period. Anapaestic words like profugus (line 2), memorem (line 4), and Latio (line 6) should cause no difficulty; the ictus has to fall on the last syllable, which is the only long syllable the word contains, as over against the accent, which will fall on the first or antepenultimate syllable.

So, in practice, we start at the beginning of the line, carefully giving the proper quantity to each syllable, not knowing whether in this first third of the verse we shall have conflict or concord, both being here admitted. Then, as we get out into the deep, and our difficulties and uncertainties gather, we may trim our sails with a view to the rarely disappointed expectation that here in the middle of the line we shall find the ictus and the accent in conflict; and by that time we sight land, so to speak, and are carried in to shore by the breaking waves of a cadence marked by complete concord between ictus and accent. As this concord required either a feminine caesura in the fifth foot or a diaeresis at the end of it, there is room at the end of the line only for words of three or of two syllables; and the most casual check of any page of Vergil will show that the poet does in fact virtually restrict himself to trisyllabic and disyllabic verse-endings, reserving monosyllables and words of more than three syllables for very special effects.

So far we have been speaking of the dactylic hexameter, which is by far the most important meter

used by the ancient poets, both Greek and Latin. The
elegiac distich consists, as you know, of an hexameter followed by a so-called pentameter, really a
modification of the hexameter, which is so easy for
anyone to handle who has already mastered the hexameter that we must forego its discussion here, as we
must also omit, for lack of time, all consideration of
the meters used in the drama. But a word must be
said about the lyric meters, for it is in the lyric that
the beauty of the poem most inextricably inheres in its
musical qualities. There are odes of Horace whose
meaning seems so slight when loosed from the verse-
form in which the poet cast them that one might well
wonder, upon the basis of any translation, whether
they are worth reading at all; yet these same odes,
when experienced in their integrity, are among the
most charming of his works.

Students have a tendency to think that the lyric
meters, because of their diversity, are harder to
master than the dactylic hexameter; but rather the
converse is true. As the hexameter was used chiefly
for long epics, it was important that it should be
capable of a continual variation that would keep the
movement in accord with the sense and the tone of the
poem at each juncture. There are in fact no less than
thirty-two possible arrangements of dactyls and
spondees in the hexameter; and when we take into
consideration the number of permutations and combinations of conflict and concord between ictus and
accent that may be found with each of these, the number of rhythms possible to the line will be multiplied
many times. The lyric poem (at least as we have it in
Latin, which has nothing comparable to the Pindaric
ode) is short as a whole; and although one ode will
differ from another in mood as in rhythm, each ode
will consist of a standard strophe, repeated without
essential variation often enough to drive the rhythm
home, but not often enough to become tiresome. Only
in those strophes that contain a dactylic sequence,
like the Archilochian, the Alcmanian, and the
Pythiambic, are substitutions allowed, as in the
hexameter itself. In the commoner strophes, the
Sapphic, the Alcaic, and the several Asclepiadeans,
as well as in the rare but striking Ionics, the scheme
is fixed and invariable; once recognized, by careful

application of the rules for distinguishing long and
short syllables that we have already given, it needs
only to be kept in mind as the reading proceeds. The
best method of acquiring these rhythms is to memo-
rize a strophe, or better still an entire ode, in each
meter. This once done (and if the ode is carefully
chosen, it is worth doing for its own sake), the tentative reading of another ode will soon reveal its
pattern.

Careful reading and re-reading of the odes of
Horace, in their various meters, will bring home to
us the astounding delicacy of the poet's ear, the
great sureness of touch with which he chooses the
meter that will best accord with the tone that he wishes
to strike (perhaps all that actually happened was that
an effective sequence suggested itself to his trained
instinct, and formed the nucleus around which the
rest was built), and the extraordinary subtlety with
which he adapts the movement of his thought and of
his sentiment to the fixed scheme, once chosen. We
have here a splendid illustration of Goethe's dictum
about mastery showing itself in limitation. These
things, and more besides, make the study of the odes
a constant delight; but it would take another hour to
do more than adumbrate them.

It remains to touch upon the question of "accentual" verse. From what we have said about the
problems of adapting the quantitative meters of the
Greeks to a language like Latin, in which the accentuation was primarily one of stress, it is clear that the
classic prosody was (like the language itself, which
absolutely eschewed, for example, the word bellus,
which had been in early times, and continued to be in
the speech of the people, and was again to emerge
triumphantly in the Romance languages as the
universal word for "beautiful") a highly artificial
thing, capable of splendid effects in the hands of
masters, but at some remove from popular feeling.
(That the art of poetry should be in such case should
not really seem strange to us.)

The degree to which the early "Saturnian" verse
was accentual is still a moot question; and books have
been written on the ways in which the comic play-
wrights accommodated their meters to the spoken
word-accent. To trace the re-emergence of accentual

verse in later Latin would be entirely beyond our
scope; but one of the milestones in this development
is certainly the hymnology of St. Ambrose, who, as
St. Augustine tells us, introduced from the East the
custom of having the people sing together in church.
Himself a man learned in the classic tradition, he
wished to write hymns that even the humblest could
sing, yet without offending the ears of the cultivated.
With this in view, he chose of the classic meters the
one in which it was perhaps easiest to arrive at a
concord between ictus and accent, namely the iambic;
and he used it in short dimetric lines, each measure
being of the classic pattern, i.e., an iambic dipody,
with a spondee admitted as a substitution for the first
iamb. Such a strophe (cf. the Veni, creator Spiritus)
could be sung straightforwardly by those who had
never heard of quantitative scansion, or carefully
scanned by those who had learned all the rules; and the
only conflict between the two renderings would come
at the very beginning of certain lines, where it would
make no more difference than the substitution of an
initial trochee for an iamb in English blank verse.
This compromise was a real triumph for an apostle
who in his desire to be "all things to all men" must
have wished not to present Christian learning in too
unfavorable a light to those who had been trained to
older standards. Later, when the feeling for quantitative verse had quite died out, such compromises were
no longer necessary, and a St. Thomas could write
hymns in which the rhythm was determined entirely by
the word-accent.

In all of this talk of patterns and schemes we
should remember that the abstraction of a pattern
requires a dichotomy of opposites that do not exist as
such in any exemplification. We speak of syllables,
for example, as being "long" or "short," and say that
in our scheme one long syllable is equivalent to two
short; but syllables are really more or less long or
short, and a chronograph would reveal an unbroken
gradation between the longest and the shortest. So
also with the notions "stressed" and "unstressed."
It is these lively gradations that constitute the warm
flesh and the pulsing blood upon the bones of our ab-
stractions. The best reading, in Latin as in English,
will therefore be that which takes a mastery of the

basic metrical scheme quite for granted, without
ignoring it, and devotes its attention to larger matters.
In this connection we may let Quintilian have the last
word. "There is much," he says (1.8.1), "that can
only be taught in actual practice, as for instance when
the student should take breath, at what point he should
introduce a pause into a line, where the sense ends or
begins, when the voice should be raised or lowered,
what modulation should be given to each phrase, and
when he should increase or slacken speed, or speak
with greater or less energy. In this portion of my
work I will give but one golden rule: to do all these
things, he must understand what he reads." Ut omnia
ista facere possit, intelligat.

Passages chosen for demonstration:
    Vergil, Aeneid 1.1-7, together with the four
                  introductory lines; 2.1-13 and
                  6.264-72
        Georgics 1.231-51 and 322-34
    Catullus, 96 and 5
    Horace, Odes 1.11, 2.14, and 1.30
    St. Ambrose, Veni, creator Spiritus (first
        strophe).

THE CLASSICS IN TRANSLATION

by

Walter Allen, Jr.

Although I did not write the description of my remarks appearing in the workshop announcement, it is
a good outline of what I intend to say, except for one
item -- I am not going to talk about the decline in the
study of Latin. That study seems to be in a healthy
condition wherever teachers are applying themselves
industriously and intelligently, and their name is
legion.

I, therefore, am not going to speak about a substitute for courses in Latin and Greek, since there is
no substitute for them. Courses in ancient literature
in translation are to be regarded as another way of
continuing the tradition of Classical culture for those
students who for some reason are not competent in the
languages. I often teach them, for instance, to advanced students in other humanistic fields who must
know something of ancient literature but whose time is
chiefly occupied with their specialties.

It is obviously advisable that students in the
humanities should learn about the   ancient authors
from a specialist in the Classics. If we do not do it,
it will be done by professors in other departments,
and they lack our technical training that is absolutely
necessary for an accurate exposition and interpretation
of Classical antiquity. Certainly you have all had the
experience of correcting the false impressions which
have arisen among students from statements by
amateurs in the Classics. Can we be so heartless as
to allow a student to go into graduate work in English
who has never heard a professional Classicist say
what he sees in the Aeneid? Or to go into history
without a Classicist's discussion of the ancient
historians?

No one is a greater believer in mos maiorum
than I, but I pity my colleagues in some colleges and

universities who refuse to be even slightly adaptable.
The result in some cases has been the all-but-extinc-
tion of their graduate departments following the vast
reduction of their undergraduate enrollment and
offerings. It is foolish and selfish pride to allow
generations of students to walk past our classrooms,
and it is wicked and shameful for us to allow them to
graduate untouched by the Classics. There is more
than folk wisdom in the story about the French recipe
for rabbit stew. You recall the opening instruction:
"First catch your rabbit."

I should be the last person to suggest replacing
language courses or requirements with courses in
translation -- we should by all means and every effort
try to return to those requirements. But I do advocate
stiff courses in translation as a complement to offerings in the original languages. And I may add that I
have had a gratifying number of students develop an
interest in the original languages after taking courses
in translation.

It is also well to keep in mind the undergraduate
whose major is in the social sciences or the natural
sciences. By artful reading of requirements -- and
students may read little else but they do study cata-
logues -- many such students may avoid Classical
studies entirely. If they take one course with you, you
have the privilege and the responsibility of forming
their lifelong impression of Classical antiquity.

It used to be that I'd say I'd like to have the
students realize that something important happened
before 1920. Either undergraduates are growing
younger, or I am growing older, but now it is
necessary to be explicit about events before 1950!
World War II, for them, might as well have occurred
in the Dark Ages. They are astounded to discover
that the ancient Greeks and Romans were not
primitive, even 2,000 and more years ago. On such
a tabula rasa any teacher worth his salt feels compulsion to write.

I regard it as immensely important that we
create on each campus a favorable climate for the
study of the Classics, at least some knowledge of
their interest and value, two qualities which become
worthless unless the books themselves are read in
some form by each generation of students. Often the

students will come to realize the advantages of reading the material in the original, not that they are dissatisfied with the courses in translation, but because they can now envisage the rich feasts provided by the ancient authors. Perhaps, because of this understanding, the next generation will take its Latin and Greek in the original and earlier in school.

I presume that I was asked to speak on this topic because of my experience in teaching Classics in translation. By way of giving my own letters of recommendation, let me state that such courses have formed part of my teaching schedule ever since 1936, barring the years of World War II, of course, which were mostly devoted to the exposition of piloting and celestial navigation. Since 1936, I have taught these courses, in one form or another, at Princeton, Yale, Michigan, and mostly at North Carolina. Please note that I am stating that I have taught them extensively, and I believe with some success, but I am not claiming to know precisely what I have been doing or exactly how I have done it. One valuable result from this morning's discussion could well be the first principles of a philosophy for teaching the Classics in translation.

You might be interested in the courses I have been teaching for the last several years, all of them electives: Roman Civilization for juniors and seniors; and for graduate students and advanced undergraduates: Greek Drama; Greek and Latin Epic; Greek and Roman Historians. With us Greek Civilization is a course in archaeology.

You observe that all combinations are possible, depending on the amount of faculty time at the disposal of your department. One of the most enjoyable systems I have ever used was to allow individual students, or small groups of students, to do extensive reading in areas of their special interests, and to meet once a week with them severally for discussion. I really think that the division of literature by genre is more successful for the teacher than are the twin surveys of Greek and Latin literature, where the teacher is so apt to include too much in his desire to be comprehensive. I understand that the survey, however, is likely to be the first venture.

Precept number one: don't make these courses

easy -- not only is that poor educational practice, but the courses are good enough that you don't need to be easy to be popular. Therefore, leave that low device to disciplines that need it. I feel that students are paying for an education and that they should get one whether they want it or not. But seriously, these courses are definitely not easier than courses in Latin, for at least we make up in length what we lose in depth. The variety of the subject matter also places great demands upon both teacher and student.

I strongly advocate the most rigorous planning in the matter of the division of class time. Assuming that there will be available about forty-five fifty-minute class periods, there will be at least two hour tests, and one or two days will be used at the beginning for introduction. There may well be a day of review at the end, and, with those random excused absences that universities sometimes grant to students, it is prudent not to count on much more than forty class periods for serious discussion. Latin literature divides itself into Early Latin and Comedy, the Ciceronian Period, the Augustan Age, the Age of Nero, the Age of Pliny, and whatever you choose to do with post-Classical and Christian Latin.

It seems to. follow that one cannot allot an equal number of class periods to each of these great divisions, for you will doubtless regard some as more important than others. Then, when you have allotted the class periods to each division, you must decide how much you wish to grant each author within each division. There seems to be no alternative but to omit some authors entirely, for I have found that students retain very little from their reading of snippets of authors. There must be at least two days on an author for him to make a proper and lasting impression. The problem is not quite so forbidding if one asks himself which authors and which ideas he prefers the class to remember, and which authors and which ideas he regards as of secondary importance. It likewise seems fair to consider what authors and ideas a student can relate to classes in other departments, such as literature, philosophy, and history.

My method of teaching is the old-fashioned explication of the text. My classes are advanced classes but I regularly do the <u>Aeneid</u> in thirteen days, with a

fourteenth day for early Latin epic to start with. It
takes me two days to do Book I of the Aeneid. In
reading prose, an historian, for example, I estimate
that the class can absorb in the neighborhood of
twenty-five pages a day in a Modern Library text. Do
not, however, try to make a record by undertaking to
cover vast amounts of material, for that accomplishes
nothing if it merely means that the students have read
numerous pages that they have not comprehended.
After a year or two, it may be necessary to reduce
the assignments from your original plan. Perhaps it
is the professorial failing for becoming long-winded,
but I like to think it is because one comes to have a
better grasp of the subject which demands a fuller
class exposition.

I try to go over the text almost page by page,
carefully calling the attention of the class to the
important or puzzling passages. I cannot stress too
much the value of having the class examine the text
itself at places of paramount importance. The student
is likely to miss the passages that leap to our eyes,
and we tend to forget that some teacher long ago called
our attention to those very passages. I think poorly,
however, of the practice of reading large amounts
aloud to the class -- that wastes time.

Then it is advisable to make enough remarks to
clarify the broader significance of the assignment, as
well as its relation to the author's work as a whole.
Sometimes it is possible to make a contrast with the
works of other authors in the same or different
languages and, on a few fortunate days, you can dilate
on world significance.

Curiously enough, I have usually found it best to
make these general statements before I begin the
detailed analysis, which goes much better when the
students have a sense of direction. Sometimes it is
wise to give a few hints when you make the assignment, for then it can be read with a definite purpose
in view. And of course you will be careful to relate
each assignment to what went before and what comes
after.

There will be no difficulty if you lay out the
course completely in advance and then cling to a rigid
schedule. At the beginning of each author you may not
be able to cover all the first assignments as you give

them. Be satisfied if you have covered all the material by the time the class has finished its last assignment in the author. But allow yourself no greater
latitude than that. The clock is inexorable, and you
must stick to business in spite of student wiles cal-
culated to lead you up the garden path.

When you lay out the work for the semester or
year, do not stress your particular interest too much.
The students will appreciate hearing the opinions of an
authority, but they will appreciate them the more if
they do not hear too much of them. Then there are
bound to be disappointments in the reception accorded
some authors. It is very difficult to do lyric poets in
translation, and Lucretius does not always mean as
much to a class as he does to us. If an author does
not work out well with your class, next year do less of
his text, and supply the rest in lecture. Ancient
literature is so rich that you must make a selection
anyway, and I see no objection to practicality as one
principle behind the size of the selections from each
author.

I began teaching under the preceptorial system,
and I still prefer to discuss literature with my classes
rather than to undertake platform lecturing. My purpose is to discuss the text with the class, apportioning
time in relation to the importance or difficulties of the
passages. The first thirty-three verses of the Aeneid
demand extensive exposition, for example, with such
topics as the first four verses usually not printed in
our text; the deliberate allusion to Homer in verse
one; Aeneas as a Mediterranean legend; general con-
siderations of epic invocations and opening verses;
Vergil's attitude towards Juno; the reasons for Juno's
wrath and the Alexandrian way some of them are
stated; and so on. All rather old-fashioned, I know,
but how will the students learn these things unless
you tell them? And these fundamental points constitute
the basis for the study of the larger aspects.

You must teach the translation you use as complete in itself, for it is vital to teach the text the
students are using, not the Latin text. Yet the class
will welcome just a few verses, as it is rare to have
a class without a few quondam Latin students.

I have had considerable success with writing on
the board a few verses in the original, verses that are

essential to the understanding of the Aeneid and that
serve, when read aloud, to exemplify the majesty of
the Vergilian hexameter. I refer, of course, to such
cases as "Arma virumque . . ." for the Homeric
overtones of Iliad and Odyssey, "Tantae molis erat .
. ." for the national tone of the epic, "Sunt lacrimae
rerum. . ." for a touch of philosophy, and "timeo
Danaos . . .," which you may later hear your students
quoting. Not too many verses, but the class appreci-
ates occasional close contact with the original, and in
its own rhythms.

In teaching Plautus, I should use some passages
of verbal nonsense and word play, where the translation is often dreary by its literalness.

In Catullus I use poem 5, which some may take as
too naughty, but it is repetitious and close enough to
modern languages for the Latin-less class to follow
the Latin with your assistance. Then I use H. L.
Levy's article (American Journal of Philology 62
[1941] 222-224) which suggests that the numbers are
based on the use of the abacus, and R. Pack's further
and more reasonable suggestion (ibid. 77 [1956] 47-51)
that the Roman practice of finger-reckoning is a better
basis for this arithmetic. One can also talk about the
superstition of the "evil eye."

I have had the opportunity to observe the thinking
of numerous colleagues who have also taught the
Classics in translation. It is no surprising observation
to be able to report that each person has taken a highly
individual approach to his teaching, even where the
subject matter of the course was circumscribed and
specified. The conclusion appears to follow that
under these conditions a teacher must give more of
himself than he might in a course in an author in the
language. The danger is obvious. After a few years
the teacher must avoid giving a "personality course,"
for there certainly is the temptation to become overly
theatrical or opinionated. The requirement is to let
the class learn by seeing what the author means to the
teacher, always remembering that the class has
enrolled in a course in ancient literature rather than
in the professor's showmanship.

Yet showmanship must be there. The teacher has
to organize the material and its method and order of
presentation. His enthusiasm bridges the gap between

the original and a translation that does not equal the nobility and elevation of the original text. It is through his mind that the class will apprehend the qualities of the original that are necessarily rendered in imperfect form by the translation.

The first requirement is extensive knowledge, with thorough knowledge of the language and the author in the original. The emphasis for the class must be more on content and significance, etc., than on the language. The second requirement reminds one of Demosthenes' replies to the queries as to what came first, second, and third in successful oratory. He answered, "First, delivery; second, delivery; third, delivery." Perhaps this audience will forgive me if I say that a little blarney won't hurt.

While we have superb authors on whom to lean, it is you who will have to make the class workable each class hour. The students will always be waiting for you to take a firm lead, and, one way or another, you must create an atmosphere. I find it necessary, as I begin each author, to take a stand, to assume a specific point of view. Now that is not as scholarly an approach as I should like, but it is reasonable from the point of view of the student. I salve my conscience by making it clear to the class that there are other points of view, and by urging the students to some reading from the reserve shelf.

Be sparing of comparisons with the modern world. You may be well enough informed on antiquity, but do you feel you know enough about modern economics, politics, and sociology? I am sufficiently annoyed by the statements that students bring from other classes that I try not to offend by talking off the top of my head about non-Classical subjects.

Even in strictly undergraduate courses, the teacher must do his best to follow the most important of the newest scholarly works. If your course in epic includes Homer, naturally you'll have to speak about Linear B and about recitation and oral dictated texts, but you can look for help to any number of new books. When you come to the Aeneid and wish to discuss its larger organization, there are the two articles by G. E. Duckworth: "The Architecture of the Aeneid," American Journal of Philology 75 (1954) 1-15; "The Aeneid as a Trilogy," Transactions of the American

<u>Philological Association</u> 88 (1957) 1-10. That is the kind of subject you might not deal with in detail if you were reading in the Latin, so that here you too have learned something that you will find yourself using in your regular Vergil course.

Duckworth's articles will allow you to say more of the <u>Aeneid</u> than that it is two units of six books each. He explains the differences in tenor between the odd-numbered books and the even-numbered books. He gives an elaborate discussion of the relationship of Books VII-XII with the individual corresponding Books I-VI, and, in his later paper, adds that you can at the same time see a subordinate Vergilian plan of the twelve books as made up of three groups of four books each.

My demand for a very high level of instruction arises from my principle that the teacher's first concern should be for his own education. Otherwise, how can a student learn what a teacher doesn't know? From the studious but mute teacher a class can at least imbibe an appreciation of study. But let us be spared the glib and uninformed professor!

In short, it will be necessary to dabble in literary criticism, that noble but elusive discipline. The class will ask, or should ask, why a given work is a classic, and why it is considered so good. Those are legitimate questions, and it is up to the teacher to be ready with sound answers that command respect. But always remember that you are not alone in an unkind world -- the library is full of help. The critical efforts of the ages are at your command, beginning with such simple aids as the literary histories of Rome, but don't neglect to keep your scholarly reading up-to-date, for there are new discoveries in literary studies as well as in archaeology.

Students can absorb solid intellectual fare with as much gusto as they sit down to the dinner table. Let us not serve them Pablum! The students are the first to know a professor's scholarly limitations, but they respect the professor who is not content with his limitations. <u>Ars</u> may be <u>longa</u> and <u>vita brevis</u>, but life is still long enough to allow time for a determined attack upon one's own ignorance. If you undertake these courses, take the long view of acquiring as much useful material as possible each year, trusting that each year your performance will improve. I believe we all agree that we owe an apology to the students who took the first courses that we ever taught.

In addition to filling your copies of the textbooks with notes, use a loose-leaf notebook. Then you can add or alter pages as required without always rewriting your notes. The notes need only be a list of topics that you feel need discussion with regard to the day's assignment, but you will find that they can expedite your discussion to a marked degree. You will put your notes aside and lecture on some points without any aide-mémoire frequently enough that the class will see that you are using them as a help and not as a crutch. When examination time comes round, it is good to be absolutely sure as to what you have said.

The students like a class that doesn't ramble, and a professor who wastes no time in random digressions. Good solid notes mean that you have selected the significant items in advance, and that you will not lose time on minor points and then try to cram in the truly significant items after the bell has rung.

You will certainly need notes when you wish to present arguments from scholarly articles and books. Vagueness in this connection is abhorrent. You must phrase your ideas with clarity and authority.

For your own reading, for material that you absorb and then present to your students incidentally, don't neglect some of the new paperbacks. The University of California Press has republished some of the Sather Lectures in that form, and Tenney Frank's Life and Literature in the Roman Republic is ideal for your discussion of Roman orators and historians. Dover Publications has paperback editions of Cumont's classic works on Mithraism and Oriental religions, as well as J. B. Bury's Ancient Greek Historians (New York 1958). Some of the British books meant for popular consumption are superbly done. In the Oxford University Press's "Home University Library," in addition to W. W. Fowler's Rome (London 1947), there is also M. P. Charlesworth's admirable discussion of The Roman Empire (London 1951). Another British series, under the horrendous title of "Teach Yourself History" (The English Universities Press), has first-rate books written by specialists. Everyone knows the Penguin series, which produces Classical books at a prodigious rate, but a remarkable number of good translations of individual works are published by The Liberal Arts Press (153 West 72nd Street, New York 23, N. Y.). You need to put your names on the mailing lists of such publishers as Rinehart and Houghton Mifflin. Such books fill in those uncomfortable lacunae of knowledge from which we all suffer.

Don't worry about using the most modern translations. Undergraduates are by no means so up-to-date as they would have us believe, and the older translations may actually be easier for them to understand.

In the January, 1959, issue of the now Classical World L. A. Campbell brought out the latest list of "Inexpensive Books for Teaching the Classics," and I notice that CW's advertisers are busily trying to call our attention to books, slides, and other aids.

I also refer you to my own paper on "Teaching the Classics in Translation," in the then Classical Weekly 48 (March 7, 1955) 105-116.

While Campbell's list is admirable, he does not mention some British texts that are not stocked in this country. Since I need Livy, Bks. 1, 2, 21, and 22, totally unavailable in the U.S., I import the four little paper volumes put out by the University Tutorial Press, Ltd. (London). Once, when that edition was temporarily out of print, a British bookstore put me on to Brodie's Literal Translations (James Brodie, Ltd.). You might be able to solve similar problems for the price of an air letter. The great British booksellers are most obliging if you explain your needs, and none of these books need be expensive.

A minimum of history is a necessity. I recommend M. P. Charlesworth's revision of W. W. Fowler's brief book entitled Rome, the one published by the Oxford University Press in their Home University Library (London 1947). The book is divided into such chapters as to form excellent supplementary reading to the several periods of authors. It does enough of the political history for a skeletal background, and it also tries to speak of significance and larger issues. I demur only at its admiration for Julius Caesar, although it does reasonable justice to Cicero.

I tend to require the purchase of either Harvey's Oxford Companion to Classical Literature or the

Everyman Smaller Classical Dictionary. The former
is better for literary courses, the latter for historical
courses; and now the Seyffert-Nettleship-Sandys,
A Dictionary of Classical Antiquities, is again available (Meridian Books 1956). For Greek drama I use
as a reference book Edith Hamilton's Mythology (a
Mentor Book, published by The New American
Library). Everything the students can look up in
these books means time saved in class. Just as the
students can be required to read for themselves in
literary histories about the lives of the authors.

Your reference shelf for the class in the library
might well stress Roman achievements and civilization
as well as Latin literature. In addition to the handbooks of Latin literature, the students like The
Legacy of Rome (Oxford 1923; Oxford University
Press) and the new edition of M. Johnston's Roman
Life (Chicago 1957; Scott, Foresman and Co.), for
its magnificent illustrations, if not for the text as
well. I also make a good deal of use of the Guide-
Books to Museums and Monuments in Italy put out by
La libreria dello Stato, as on Pompeii, Herculaneum,
the Phlegraean Fields (for Aeneid 6). And why not
include W. W. Fowler, Social Life at Rome in the Age
of Cicero (New York 1909); J. Carcopino, Daily Life
in Ancient Rome, ed. by H. T. Rowell (New Haven
1940); F. F. Abbott, Roman Political Institutions
(Boston 1911); and G. Jennison, Animals for Show and
Pleasure in Ancient Rome (Manchester [England]
1937; Manchester University Press).

You can make a reserve shelf of Loeb Classical
Library volumes of minor authors, and, by a little
judicious assigned outside reading, you can give the
class a broader view of the ancient world than will be
obtained from a book of selections of Latin literature,
or from a handful of texts. Did you ever read Celsus
on medicine? Fascinating! And a student should at
least leaf through the first few pages of Frontinus to
learn about the water supply. H. N. Wethered's
selection from Pliny's Natural History, The Mind of
the Ancient World (London 1937; Longmans, Green and
Co.) presents enough of that compilation and in attractive form. A class should at least look at one of
the volumes of the military writers, either in Latin
or in Greek, just to see the ancient substitute for

training at West Point.

I have not solved the problem of maps, but my present procedure is to urge the class to buy Hammond's Historical Atlas, of which the first few pages are pertinent. It is imperative to make constant classroom use of maps, but the students also need them to study by, for most of the present generation is shockingly ignorant of Mediterranean geography. How can a student read Livy or Vergil intelligently without maps of Rome and Italy?

Next comes that miserable necessity, examinations! The novice soon abandons the use of just an essay question or two, for he discovers that he is grading the class, not on the material in the course, but on their ability to write English prose. While that is surely a noble and rare talent, such a procedure in examinations is subversive of the subject matter in the course. Next the novice flees to a list of identifications, dates, and similar specific items. But certainly that is not the purpose for which we study Classical literature.

There is, in short, no panacea. I am always experimenting. Sometimes I give twelve or thirteen questions, of which ten must be answered. Each of the dozen questions has two parts, deliberately compounded so that no portion of the assigned reading can have been safely omitted by the students, as might be the case if I asked them to answer twenty out of twenty-five questions. I try to keep an even balance between exact questions of factual matters and questions requiring interpretation of the facts.

This may seem mechanical, but at least it falls short of multiple choices and the use of machines to correct the papers. It also requires thought on the part of the teacher to correct the papers, and that alone bars automation. It has the further advantage of allowing the teacher to arrive at grades whose basis not too many students will dispute, as they will the grades on essay questions. A solid procedure is to decide first what answers you wish to the various questions, and then to frame questions that you hope will elicit those answers.

I even pass around my classes copies of the quizzes I gave the preceding year. That procedure always produces a gratifying flurry of study for the

coming exam. It also defeats the files of old exams
that students assiduously hoard.

Now for the trimmings.

In the literature courses one day of slides is
enough, just that portion of the first hour left after a
hurried organization of the class. For the epic, the
slides can illustrate the authors: Crete, Troy,
Mycenae, some Aegean islands, Ithaca, the Servian
Wall, the Roman Forum, the Forum of Julius, the
Forum of Augustus, Julius Caesar's coin showing
Aeneas and Anchises. Slides in color, of course.

In Roman civilization careful planning can sometimes produce double value. I do a slide lecture on a
few of the great men of the Republic and on a series
of Roman emperors just after I have been discussing
Roman sculpture. Since my course is not primarily
historical and since I prefer to devote more time to
the Augustan Principate than to the list of emperors,
this procedure gives a quick and vivid impression of
the Empire along with instruction in portrait
sculpture. And time is the great treasure which must
be jealously husbanded.

Use all the other visual aids in addition to
slides. Just a few coins can be of the greatest assistance. When you read the historians, you must
give a table of values and talk about relative pur-
chasing power. An Athenian coin when you do Greek
money, and a Roman coin when you do Roman money,
and you have the class's attention. Nero's coins are
handsome, and how appropriate to pass one around
when you read of Nero's fire in Tacitus! I shall not
dwell on this topic since you have already had a full
lecture on the subject of visual aids.

Since you must say something helpful about the
slides or coins, this again means more searching into
areas you had always intended to read up on. A first
book on Roman topography is certainly S. B. Platner,
The Topography and Monuments of Ancient Rome
(Boston 1911), and I still like a good many things
about the old J. H. Middleton, The Remains of
Ancient Rome (London 1892). For a quick knowledge
of all sorts of things, such as the army and medicine
and law, don't forget the old standbys like J. E.
Sandys, A Companion to Latin Studies (3rd ed.
Cambridge [England] 1921).

Material such as Dr. McGuire is presenting at the evening sessions is more than invaluable, it is essential. When a teacher is rapidly covering a large amount of material, he must be a ready mine of pertinent information. Unless you are omniscient, resort to the simple aids first, such as the Everyman Smaller Classical Dictionary and Harvey's Oxford Companion to Classical Literature, especially for those dates and details that give vigor and precision to a lecture. And I trust that you will have a good ancient history at hand, as C. A. Robinson, Jr., Ancient History from Prehistoric Times to the Death of Justinian (New York 1951).

If I were amplifying Dr. McGuire's series of lectures, I should insert a discussion of Roman economics and agriculture, two matters strikingly different from modern conditions, yet most useful to the teacher of literature in helping to explain the different circumstances of the ancient world. The best and most readable discussions are Tenney Frank, An Economic History of Rome (2nd ed. Baltimore 1927), and The Cambridge Economic History of Europe from the Decline of the Roman Empire. I. The Agrarian Life of the Middle Ages (Cambridge [England] 1942).

One word of advice in conclusion. If you are not interested in teaching the Classics in translation, especially after trying a course for a semester, my advice is: give it up! It requires a certain temperament, and some teachers, I believe mistakenly, are nevertheless constitutionally opposed to an approach for which they have not been specifically trained. The success of such courses will in large measure depend upon the teacher's enthusiasm, energy, and learning, and in that order. We all know better than to try to deceive an undergraduate, who can readily see through a teacher although he may never see through a subject.

The reward of careful teaching is the familiar one of the profession, i.e., more work. In each of my four courses I have in recent years seldom had fewer than twenty-five students, and in two of them we regularly, and vainly, try to hold the registration to thirty-five. I have no idea of how such courses are taught in the large Mid-Western universities, where enrollment in these courses is numbered in the hundreds.

But I wish you every success, even to classes numbered by the hundreds of students.

THE ORIGIN, DEVELOPMENT, AND CHARACTER OF MEDIAEVAL LATIN

by

Martin R. P. McGuire

The development of mediaeval studies, especially since the first decades of the present century, has been phenomenal. Yet in spite of this development as a whole, it is a regrettable fact that the Latin language itself as employed in the Middle Ages has not yet received the attention that is at all commensurate with its fundamental importance for all branches of mediaeval research. A large amount of excellent work has been published on Latin from about 150 to 500, and, thanks to the epoch-making investigations and evaluations of the School of Nijmegen, and especially of its leading representative, Dr. Christine Mohrmann, our knowledge of Christian Latin has been put on a new foundation.[1] Too many mediaevalists still fail to devote thorough study to the Latin in this period; they continue, in practice at least, largely to ignore Late Latin, and to make the great leap from Classical Latin into Mediaeval Latin. Yet it is precisely in the period from the second to the sixth century that what we call Mediaeval Latin took shape and assumed or began to assume its characteristic features in vocabulary, syntax, style, and pronunciation. Without a thorough acquaintance, therefore, with Late Latin, it is impossible to have any real understanding and appreciation of the Latin of the Middle Ages. Late Latin simply became Mediaeval Latin. There was no sharp break in linguistic continuity. Mediaeval Latin is essentially a continuation of the literary or written Latin as it was employed especially by Christian writers in the last centuries of Antiquity.[2]

Owing to the basic significance of Latin from about 500 to 800 for specialists in Romance, Celtic, and Germanic Philology, a great deal of solid work has

been done on Late Vulgar Latin and on Merovingian
Latin. [3]   In striking contrast to this generally favorable situation regarding Late and Early Mediaeval
Latin, the systematic and thorough investigation of
Latin in the period from about 800 to 1400 is still in its
early stages. The number of good linguistic studies on
writers of this period is still very small.

In the present paper, I propose to sketch, however
briefly, the history of Latin from the second century
A.D. to Cassiodorus, from Cassiodorus to Alcuin, and
from Alcuin to the Renaissance. In the process, I
shall discuss some of the characteristic features of
Mediaeval Latin, and the uniqueness of Mediaeval
Latin as a phenomenon in linguistic history.

The literary or written Latin of the early sixth
century may be regarded as consisting of or reflecting
the fusion of three basic elements: the traditional
"Classical" or profane, the popular, and the Christian.
We must analyse these elements and examine their
interrelationships.

As regards the Latin of the profane or pagan
literary tradition, marked changes are to be noted
from the beginning of the Silver Age. [4] The barriers
between the language of prose and poetry have broken
down; poetry as well as prose is dominated by
rhetoric. The periodic styles of Cicero and Livy are
superseded for a time at least by the aphoristic,
nervous style of Seneca and the highly wrought asym-
metrical style of Tacitus. The tendency towards
archaism which is so noticeable in Sallust and Tacitus
reaches its culmination in Fronto, Gellius, and
Apuleius. At the same time, Apuleius may be considered as the first and most famous representative of
the Second Sophistic in Latin. His rhetorical style,
much admired by his contemporaries and by succeeding generations, is not peculiarly African, but is
Asianism in Latin dress. Latin became more abstract
as it became more artificial. Hence we note a steady
increase in the Latin vocabulary, not only of compound
verbs, adjectives, and adverbs, but, especially of
abstract nouns of all kinds. The rhetorical schools
dominate the intellectual life of the last centuries of
pagan Antiquity, and style rather than content, as we
know from St. Augustine, was heavily stressed. [5] The
professor of rhetoric and the panegyrist enjoyed a

prestige which it would be difficult for us moderns to
exaggerate. With the exhaustion of real creative
effort in the pagan literary tradition after Apuleius,
the literary productions of that tradition became more
and more bombastic and empty of content. It is
enough to recall in this connection the Letters of
Symmachus, the rival of St. Ambrose in the controversy over the Altar of Victory. The great Roman
jurists of the second and early third century, it is
true, retained much of the terseness of the past in
their style, but their successors and the writers of
the imperial constitutions of the Codes of Theodosius
and Justinian were under the spell of a highly bombastic rhetoric. Yet, while not creative in significant
profane literature, this period is very important in
the history of Latin scholarship. It was the age of
Servius, Donatus, Marius Victorinus, Martianus
Capella, Nonius Marcellus, Macrobius, and Priscian,
editors, grammarians, and compilers who were
destined to play such an important role in the transmission of Classical texts and of a knowledge of the
Latin literary language to the Middle Ages.

The Latin literary language of the Classical
period was a more artificial language than is   ordinarily realized, differing in many respects from the
language of the masses.[6] As time went on, the
cleavage became ever wider. The literary language
tended, under the circumstances, to become more
and more conservative, artificial, and stereotyped,
while the living, racy Latin of the masses continued
to develop in relatively unhampered fashion. Thus,
living Latin could not escape completely the influence of the speech of the cultured elite and the school
tradition, but in the general cultural decline of the
last centuries of Antiquity it exercised a considerable
influence itself on the profane literary or written
language in pronunciation, vocabulary, and syntax.
Popular or Vulgar Latin, furthermore, played a
fundamental role in the development of Christian
Latin, as was indicated in some detail in my first
lecture.[7]

In the course of the fifth and sixth century,
Christian Latin became the common literary, written,
and spoken language of the West. The significance of
the achievement of the great Latin Fathers, especially

of St. Augustine and St. Jerome, in developing a truly
Christian humanism, can hardly be exaggerated. As
Werner Jaeger has acutely observed, Patristic
humanism was as creative as it was influential in the
history of civilization:

> There are still people who do not realize that
> what we had in both hemispheres of the late
> Roman empire at that time was one of the most
> creative civilizations which history has ever
> seen. The synthesis of Christian religion and
> classical Greek and Roman culture which it
> effected became classical in its turn for the
> following centuries of the Middle Ages, and for
> countless millions of people it still is. [8]

By the end of the fifth century the synthesis was
already completed; in fact it had become a tradition,
as is so clearly evident in Cassiodorus and later in
St. Isidore. That the tradition did not die, or at
least did not suffer greater damage than it did in the
sixth, seventh, and early eighth centuries, is to be
explained by the fact that the Church in the West,
having once adopted Latin as the language of her
liturgy, theology, and ecclesiastical administration,
persisted in maintaining it. In these first centuries
of the period we call mediaeval, the maintenance of
Latin was difficult, but, at the same time, definitely
successful, not only because the Church in the West
possessed and exercised a strong central authority
but also because she was practically the sole source
and vehicle of higher culture in this age in Italy,
Gaul, Spain, Ireland, and Britain, as she was destined to be later in Germany, Bohemia, Hungary,
Scandinavia, and Poland. The possible rise of a
liturgy in Gothic or Old High German vanished with
the triumph of Catholicism over Arianism.

From the last part of the fifth century, a marked
change took place in education, and one that inevitably
affected Latin. With the collapse of the western half
of the Roman Empire, the schools of the rhetors dis-
appeared, at first in Gaul and then somewhat later in
Spain and Italy. The Vandal invasion blighted the
culture of Africa from the middle of the fifth century
and the Islamic conquest destroyed it. The monastic

schools of the West, which began in the fourth century,
and later the episcopal and presbyteral schools along
with them, gradually became almost the sole centers
of education. 9 In outlook and practice they were exclusively Christian, and their pupils almost all pro-
spective monks and priests. Speaking and writing
Latin to meet the needs of the Church, and proficiency
in reading the Latin Bible and Christian literature in
general, were their primary and, at first at least,
their only intellectual objectives. In Italy in the first
half of the sixth century the situation was different.
Theodoric and Justinian restored and supported chairs
of grammar, rhetoric, law, and medicine at Rome,
and chairs of grammar and rhetoric at Milan; but all
this came to an end with the Lombard invasion beginning in 568. Cassiodorus had played an important part
in the restoration of these profane studies and he gave
an important place to profane learning in his Insti-
tutes.10 This phase of his work and outlook, however,
were not destined to bear fruit immediately, but in the
future. The more representative attitude of the age is
that rather of Pope St. Gregory the Great who, in his
lack of sympathy for profane literature, reflects the
characteristic point of view of the early monastic
schools.

The Latin from Boethius through Gregory the
Great is an unbroken continuation of the Latin of the
fifth century in all essential respects, and the same is
true of the Latin of Spain to the death of Isidore and
even later. As regards Gaul, a careful analysis of the
Latin of Gregory of Tours shows that, in spite of its
apparent or real divergences from the standard of
Avitus or Caesarius of Arles, it is much closer to
that standard than to the Latin of the Merovingian
charters. 11

The story of Latin in Ireland and of its reintroduction into Britain is quite different from that in
Romania, i.e., in Italy, Gaul, and Spain. St. Patrick
brought the Latin of the monastic schools of Gaul to
Ireland in the fifth century, and from St. Patrick to
Columbanus the Latin of Ireland was almost exclusively Christian in character. From Columbanus on-
ward, however, profane writers as well as Christian
were avidly studied for their content and employed as
models of composition. Latin for the Irish as well

as for the Anglo-Saxons, as later for the Germans and other peoples of northern and central Europe, was always a foreign tongue, and one very different from their respective vernaculars. St. Columbanus, his biographer Jonas, and Adamnan, and the Anglo-Saxons Aldhelm, St. Bede, and St. Boniface, all write a much more correct Latin by Classical standards than their immediate predecessors and contemporaries on the Continent. But their Latin style, with the exception of that of St. Bede, who writes in a clear, direct and readable manner, is involved, stiff, and artificial. It well deserves the label of "hot-house Latin" that was once given it by Ludwig Traube. [12]

The first real break in the continuity of the history of the Latin language was occasioned by the marked decline in culture which characterizes the Merovingian Age. As Norberg has observed, the Merovingian documents indicate that the literary or written Latin changed more within a hundred years after Gregory of Tours than in the whole 600 years before him. The Latin of these documents, however, should not be identified with the popular spoken language of the age, as is done by H. Muller and his pupils. [13] The Merovingian scribes were trying to write the traditional Latin in the strict sense, but their training was very poor and they could not avoid a considerable influence from the popular spoken Latin which by this time can be called Primitive Romance, at least in Gaul. The further decline of Merovingian written or literary Latin was brought to a halt by the radical reforms begun under Pippin and carried out to the full during the long reign of Charlemagne. Latin now enters a new phase within the period that we call the Middle Ages.

The purpose of Charlemagne's reform was not the revival of the study of ancient literature and learning as such but rather to create an educated clergy whose services were so badly needed in the Church and in the civil administration of his empire. [14] Alcuin, who had been trained at York, the leading intellectual center of Western Europe in the eighth century, served as his "prime minister of intellectual affairs." He was aided in effecting the reform of education by the Italians Peter of Pisa and Paul the Deacon, the Irishmen Clement, Dungal, and Dicuil, and the Spaniard

Theodulph of Orleans. It may be observed incidentally
that the important role of the Italians and of Theodulph
in the reform bears witness to the high state of Latin
and of Latin learning at this time in certain centers,
at least, in Italy and Spain as well as in Ireland and
England.

Under Alcuin's direction the ancient curriculum of
the liberal arts was restored. In actual practice, however, the chief emphasis was on grammar. Only quite
rudimentary instruction was given in the other arts,
but the foundations were laid for the eventual development of the full training in the remaining branches of
the trivium and quadrivium in the tenth and eleventh
centuries. The ancient grammarians, and especially
Donatus, were systematically studied, abbreviated,
expounded, and memorized, and the manuscripts of
pagan and Christian writers as copied and edited in the
last centuries of Antiquity were now recopied, studied,
and used as models for imitation in language and style.
The whole pagan and Christian literature of the past
from Plautus to the Merovingian Age was regarded as
an inheritance in the Augustinian sense and to be so
utilized. While the school curriculum was modelled,
as I have said, on that of the Late Empire, it should
be emphasized that it was now administered by
Catholic clerics in a Catholic environment and was
intended primarily to serve the interests of a closely
united Catholic Church and State.

In spite of the bent for imitation, Carolingian
Latin must not be thought of as rigidly Classical, but,
on the contrary, as flexible, or at least capable of
flexibility and further free development. The Christian element in the intellectual inheritance was regarded as the higher one, and the Carolingians with an
air of exuberant optimism and pride called themselves
moderni.[15] But from now on Latin in Gaul is a
language which, however thoroughly mastered, is
learned from books. There is now a sharp and conscious cleavage between Latin and the popular spoken
language. As is evident from a well-known passage in
the acts of the Council of Tours held in 813, the
people could no longer understand the reformed Latin;
bishops were commanded to have their homilies or
exhortations for the people translated in rusticam
linguam aut Thiotiscam, i. e., into the Romance and

German vernaculars. In Italy, however, and probably
in Spain, a similar situation did not arise before the
later tenth century.[16]

The revival of the study of profane authors in the
schools of the Carolingian Age, despite the fact that
the schools, as we have said, were now entirely
Christian in their teachers and in their environment,
established what Dr. Mohrmann has acutely called a
dualism in Mediaeval Latin.[17] There were two
tendencies partly in conflict, but largely dynamic and
fruitful. The school tradition tended, in general, to
emphasize -- sometimes even to overemphasize -- the
pagan authors. But this tendency was offset and sometimes completely overshadowed by the profound and
active influence exercised by the Christian tradition
in the strict sense. In this tradition emphasis was
placed on the reading and study of the Scriptures and
the Fathers, on the monastic life and monastic ideals.
Its greatest influence, however, was exerted by the
Liturgy, which permeated all phases of mediaeval
life, including, of course, language and literature.[18]
The old battle between profane and sacred studies --
particularly in respect to the question of the role of
the former in the training and intellectual work of
monks -- continues throughout the Middle Ages. The
quarrel is invariably solved in accordance with the
principles laid down in the Fathers, and, above all, in
St. Augustine's De doctrina christiana. In spite of
tensions, the profane element of the school tradition
and the religious element in the strict sense could not
help having many close contacts, and the harmonious
fusion of the two elements led ultimately to the full-
flowering of Mediaeval Latin and of Mediaeval Latin
literature in the Renaissance of the Twelfth Century.[19]

From the Carolingian Age to the Italian Renaissance, then, Latin as taught in the schools and as
developed by usage was the universal language of
Western Europe in the Church, in education, in administration and law, in philosophy, theology,
medicine, science, and technology, and it was the
vehicle of an international literature in prose and
verse. In spite of the cultural decline that was occasioned by the collapse of the Carolingian Empire and
the coming of the Northmen, Latin was assiduously
studied in the monastic and cathedral schools of the

tenth, eleventh, and twelfth centuries, and was forged
into a wonderfully flexible instrument of expression
in all domains of human activity. In the process
Classical, Christian, and Mediaeval elements came to
be more and more freely blended. It is in the course
of the eleventh and twelfth centuries in particular that
Latin assumed the full independence and the characteristic features which we undoubtedly have in mind when
we speak of Mediaeval Latin as such. This is the
Latin of St. Anselm, St. Peter Damian, St. Bernard,
John of Salisbury, Hugh of St. Victor, St. Thomas and
Duns Scotus, of imperial constitutions and royal
charters, of monastic records and business transac-
tions, of the canonists and the glossators of the
Roman law,   of the vast literature occasioned by the
Struggle over Investitures, but also that of the
sequences of Adam of St. Victor and ultimately of the
great hymns of St. Thomas and the Franciscan
School, as well as that of the disciples of Golias.[20]
This Latin, which was put to such myriad uses, was
learned in school, but it was not studied formally as
Early Latin, or Classical Latin, or Silver Latin, or
Late Latin, or Early Mediaeval Latin, but in practice
simply as Latin, which in the course of many centuries
had undergone many changes in vocabulary, syntax,
and style. There was some awareness, of course,
between what we call Classical and Late Latin and
between the Latin of the Bible and profane Latin, but
this knowledge did not have the radical effect upon
usage as was to be the case in the school tradition
inaugurated by the Italian Renaissance. On the contrary, with the application of dialectic to Latin
grammar by Peter Helias (fl. 1140-1150) and more
extensively, though more subtly, by Alexander of
Villa Dei in his Doctrinale (1199), for centuries the
most influential of Latin textbooks, the authority of
the ancient authors was weakened or even ignored.
Alexander reduces citations from the ancients to a
minimum and freely illustrates his rules by examples
of his own invention. As Bolgar well says in this
connection:

> Medieval culture was becoming conscious of its
> own value; and Alexander's work reflects this
> new esteem. Influenced by the idea that language

could be made into an exact instrument of
logical thought and encouraged by his conse-
quent admiration for contemporary writing
(which bore the stamp of the contemporary
love of logic), he went a long way towards
emancipating himself from the traditional
belief of the grammarians that the classical
authors were the only true guides to correct
Latin.[21]

To describe or characterize in definite concrete
terms the evolution or development, if always within
the broad framework of a language which from the
viewpoint of morphology, snytax, and even style, is
still strictly Latin, in the period from Charlemagne to
the Italian Renaissance, is not easy. It has been attempted, however, and, in my opinion, with conspicuous success and insight, by the Danish scholar Franz
Blatt, in an excellent article published in 1933, but
one that does not seem to have attracted the wide and
careful attention that it continues to merit.[22]

Blatt maintains that three main factors were responsible for what may be regarded as characteristic
changes in Latin from the close of Antiquity, but
particularly in the period from Charlemagne on.
These factors are:

(1) the continued influence of the vernaculars
     of Europe -- Romance, Celtic, Germanic,
     Slavic, Hungarian -- on the Latinity of
     writers using such vernaculars as their
     mother tongues;
(2) the transformation of society in the Middle
     Ages -- new political, social, and eco-
     nomic situations, etc., and the resulting
     need for and use of new Latin words or of
     old Latin words in new meanings; and
(3) the development of mediaeval philosophy,
     theology, law, science, and technology,
     and the necessity of creating an adequate
     technical or special terminology for these
     fields in Latin.

One of the most obvious influences of Vulgar
Latin, and later, of the vernacular languages, on the

Latin of the schools is seen in pronunciation and orthography. Latin in Romania was pronounced essentially as the emerging or fully developed Romance
dialects, and in non-Latin Europe -- Ireland, England,
Germany, etc., it was also pronounced pretty much
as the respective vernaculars. Mediaeval Latin pronunciation and orthography are directly and closely
connected. Instruction in the Middle Ages was of
necessity almost exclusively oral, and spelling by
habitual practice tended to be phonetic. Hence Mediaeval Latin exhibits features that are universal, like
e for ae and oe, the interchange of ci and ti, etc., but
likewise myriad spellings which are national or
regional in character. The ancient grammarians were
studied, but as Traube once observed, their rules in
orthography were not generally or systematically
followed in practice. In passing, it may be remarked
that even in the Renaissance there is still considerable
fluctuation in Latin orthography, and many problems
could not be definitely settled before the rise of comparative philology and the scientific study of Latin
phonology in the nineteenth century.

Given the international character of Mediaeval
Latin and its routine employment in all spheres of
human activity, it was only natural that words were
borrowed freely from the various vernacular
languages with which it had direct or even indirect
contact. The loan words were frequently not
restricted to the region of initial borrowing, but often
entered into general use, words, e.g., like prisonium
(France), baco (England), zabellinus (of Slavic origin).
A large number of such loan words fall in the general
sphere of government, administration, political, and
social institutions, like bannus, feudum, vasallus,
marcgravius, etc. Again, as in our own modern
languages, there was a marked tendency to retain the
native name for plants, animals, clothing, beverages,
etc. In the field of clothing, e.g., Blatt lists
almucium, birretus, tabardum, surcotium, roba,
hosi, sotulares. The native names of coins, weights,
and measures also pass into Latin, as francus, marca,
acra. The ancient Latin names for colors were often
replaced by loan words, as blavius, bruneus,
griseus, blaccatus, blondus. Loan words of the
various kinds indicated appear in greatest numbers in

private documents of a legal nature, in routine accounts of everyday activities, business transactions, etc. The writers of such records, especially in the later Middle Ages, have no scruples about employing the same word now in its vernacular and now in its Latinized form in the same passage. Finally, as Blatt has pointed out, a number of Greek words representing a wide variety of fields were borrowed in the course of the Middle Ages, e.g., dulia, emologos, elenchus, epikia, latria, homonimus, soma, etc.[23]

The influence of their vernacular idioms on writers of Mediaeval Latin could not be avoided except by those who through long school training had emancipated themselves from this perennial snare in Latin composition. At the lower levels of Latin proficiency, vernacular idioms often appear in Latin dress throughout Europe. Whole sentences as well as individual words and phrases can be affected. As typical examples may be cited: nulla ardens (candela) ... egrediebatur (German), discere sub genu alterius (Irish), a dorsu montis ... usque ad oculum Dinguarch (Welsh), rex ... tenuit, apud quem reliquie ... elevate sunt (apud = a after Irish la), amicus anime ("confessor", Irish), milleartifex (Tausendkünstler, German), quinta pars (Irish coiced), abbas de Esrom (Romance), curiam tenere (Germanic).[24]

Under his second main category of changes, namely, those resulting from changes in society and social institutions, Blatt lists, along with new words, a number of words which are found in Classical Latin but which acquired new meanings in the Middle Ages. Thus one finds consistorium in the sense of College of Cardinals, curia in that of the papal court, beneficium to designate a benefice, etc. In this group he might have included also the whole new vocabulary connected with mediaeval monasticism. In the civil sphere, the ancient Latin words comes, dux, miles, tribunus, advocatus, placitum, and many others acquired new meanings. Thus, senatus can mean a city council, consul, one of its members, proconsul, a burgomaster, etc.[25] Another important category that Blatt might have added is the entire vocabulary of new words and new meanings associated with mediaeval schools and mediaeval school life -- words like universitas in the sense of a corporation of masters or students, studium generale, baccalaureus, bejaunus, beneficiarii, bedellus, bursa and bursarius, camera, exhibitio, hospitium, Justiniani, librarii, pecia, peciarii, stationarii, lupi, vulgarisantes.26

Blatt's third main category comprises the rich and specialized terminology created by the Scholastics to meet their needs in philosophy, theology, and science.27 Perhaps no other phase of Mediaeval Latin was so ridiculed or scorned by the Humanists from the Renaissance to the late nineteenth century as this. But in the light of our more intimate knowledge of Scholasticism and of the deeper understanding that has come with the development of the science of linguistics, we now know that the terminology forged by the Scholastics was one of the truly great achievements in the history of Western culture. Classical Latin was inadequate as a precise vehicle of philosophical thought, as was clearly recognized by Cicero, the apologetic creator of qualitas and essentia. In the Silver Age a number of needed abstracts were added, but it remained for the Christian writers from Tertullian to Boethius to make Latin a more adequate instrument of philosophical and theological expression. While some new terminology was added before the twelfth century, the first great Scholastics found themselves embarrassed by a lack of technical words to express their rapidly developing speculation, and they were forced to create a large number of new words and phrases. So in the twelfth, thirteenth, and early fourteenth centuries, we find a large number of abstracts in -tas, which in part are formed on substantives and adjectives as in earlier times, as: actualitas, causalitas, corporeitas, intellegibilitas, materialitas, personalitas, realitas, studiositas; but also on verbs, as velleitas, on pronouns, as talitas, haecceitas, quidditas, and on pronominial and other combinations, as ipseitas, asseitas, perseitas. The suffix -ivus is employed to form a large number of new adjectives by being added to the stem of the perfect passive participle, and gives an active form beside a passive form in meaning: consummativus-consummabilis, disputativus-disputabilis, factivus-factibilis (a new form). There are also new formations in -alis and new adverbs formed in turn on

-alis, as: certitudo, certitudinalis, certitudinaliter;
and likewise, in -orius, as: aedificatorius, comple-
torius, contradictorius. Through the free use of prefixes (in-, con-, etc.) whole series of new words were
easily formed, and particularly negative opposites,
as: communicabilis-incommunicabilis, materialitas-
immaterialitas, iustificatio-iniustificatio, finitas-
infinitas. The prefix in- is regularly used in such
formations in its negative sense. The use of present
participles as substantives was greatly extended, but
there were common ancient examples to follow in this.
It was only natural also that many inherited words of
the general vocabulary should be utilized and given
technical philosophical meanings.

Without question, the study of Aristotle and the
problem of exact translation of his works and similar
works in the Greek philosophical tradition led to the
creation of the majority of the abstracts in -tas and of
the adjectives in -ivus, etc., of the types listed
above. The Schoolmen, out of necessity and with the
freedom justified by the logical approach to grammar
exemplified by Peter Helias and Alexander of Villa
Dei, created something new, a great technical vocabulary and a plain, clear expositional style capable of
expressing the finest shades of thought precisely and
directly. Latin under the Scholastics finally becomes
a truly adequate instrument of philosophical thought
that can be favorably compared in this respect with
the language of Aristotle.

Of the all-too-few studies that have appeared on
the development of mediaeval philosophical Latin
since Blatt's article, I should like to mention the following: M. Hubert, O.P., "Quelques aspects du latin
philosophique aux XIIᵉ et XIIIᵉ siècles," Revue des
études latines 27 (1949) 211-233; id., "Notes de latin
médiéval," ibid. 30 (1952) 307-317; M. D. Chenu,
"La langue. Le vocabulaire," in his Introduction à
l'étude de Saint Thomas d'Aquin (Paris 1950) 84-105;
A. M. Landgraf, "Die Sprache der frühscholastischen
Theologie," in his Dogmengeschichte der Frühscholas-
tik. I.1 (Regensburg 1952) 20-29. On the basis of the
lexica or indices of St. Thomas, Duns Scotus, and
other Scholastics,[28] and on that of the evidence furnished by the indices in the volumes of the Aristoteles
Latinus now in course of publication, it should soon

be possible to investigate the language of the Scholastics with the thoroughness that their achievement so
justly deserves.

Corresponding to the technical terminology in
philosophy and theology, elaborate special vocabularies were built up in Roman and Canon law, in science, medicine, popular remedies, and technology.
But apart from that in law, they were not strikingly
new or original, nor were they so narrowly technical
and exclusive. As time went on, of course, many of
the new terms in theology and philosophy spread into
wider circles, but many others remained confined in
use to their own field.

It remains to consider two most interesting and
important related questions, namely, the precise
character of Mediaeval Latin as a language and the
causes of its decline. Mediaeval Latin is a unique
phenomenon in linguistic history. From the Renaissance until the later nineteenth century it was almost
universally regarded as Latin that had steadily declined until it had reached a barbarous stage. The
title of Du Cange's lexicon, Glossarium mediae et infimae Latinitatis, reflects the judgment of his age on
the qualities of the Mediaeval Latin vocabulary. During the last seventy-five years, however, the beauties
of Mediaeval Latin poetry have come to be recognized
and enthusiastically admired, and with the revival of
Thomistic philosophy the great achievements of the
Schoolmen are now universally appreciated. But as
regards Mediaeval Latin itself, while modern evaluations are sympathetic, they are often somewhat con-
fused. Even some scholars who have made outstanding contributions in the Mediaeval field, as, e.g.,
Traube and De Ghellinck, have been inclined, consciously or unconsciously, to measure Mediaeval
Latin by the absolute standard of Classical Latin. A
different attitude has been adopted by Paul Lehmann,
Traube's successor at Munich, the late Einar
Löfstedt, by Franz Blatt, Ludwig Bieler, Richard
Meister, Dag Norberg, and Christine Mohrmann, but
these scholars are by no means in agreement on all
points.[29] My own views, I may observe, coincide
pretty much with those of Blatt and Mohrmann.

Late literary Latin had become not only the official language of the Western Church but also the

vehicle of a Christian culture, and Early Mediaeval
Latin was simply its continuation. Following the
Carolingian Reform, it was transmitted exclusively
through a school tradition. It was employed as the
official language of the Church, as the language of
civil administration and law, and as an international
language of literature and learning. It was mastered
so thoroughly by many that it was written and spoken
by them with the facility of a native tongue. Although
it was a school language, it was not static. Within the
broad framework of an inherited morphology and syntax, it showed amazing flexibility and capability of
development. It acquired a new vocabulary in words
and meanings to serve the needs of changing conditions
without losing its great inheritance from the past. For
those who wrote and spoke this Latin, it was a living
tongue.

But there is another side to the picture. It was a
school language and therefore was confined to a cultural elite in Church and State. It was not a language
of the masses. If it was spoken, men did not learn to
speak it from babyhood in the family circle but in the
course of its study in school. They pronounced it,
not in any uniform manner, but rather as they pronounced their own vernaculars. No matter how well
it became known, it was always a foreign tongue, and
especially so among those who were not in the Romance tradition. In this connection, it is well to remember, too, that there were varying degrees in the
knowledge of Latin in the Middle Ages, even when
measured by the standards of the same time and
place. There were not a few contemporaries of John
of Salisbury, e.g., whose Latin was probably not
much better than Friar Tuck's. Mediaeval Latin can
perhaps best be described as a Kunstsprache,[30] a
more or less artificial technical language employed
with varying degrees of proficiency by a relatively
small number of the total population. It was, however, a Kunstsprache which, while drawing heavily
upon its own inheritance and its internal potentialities,
as likewise upon the vernaculars of its own users,
was not a phase of a living language in the strict
sense. All literary languages are more or less artificial, and this was much more the case in the past
than in the present, when universal education and

mass media of communication are leveling so many
differences between the written and oral word. But
Mediaeval Latin can hardly be considered a living
literary or technical language in the sense of the
language of the Chansons de Geste beside the contemporary spoken Old French, or of the language of
Chaucer beside the spoken English of his time. On
the morphological side, one need only think of the
profound changes that took place in our own English
between Alfred and Chaucer as compared with the essentially fixed morphology of Mediaeval Latin. There
are no significant changes in Latin declension and
conjugation from the Carolingian Reform to the Italian
Renaissance.

In judging Mediaeval Latin as a language we
should not apply the old-fashioned and unscientific
standard of Classical Latin, but we should employ
rather the more objective criteria furnished by General Linguistics. If we examine Mediaeval Latin in the
light of these criteria, we can affirm without hesita-
tion that Mediaeval Latin was capable of expressing
the finest shades of thought in a precise, natural, and
economic manner. As a medium for sublime religious
poetry and prayer it has not been surpassed, and as a
vehicle for exact philosophical and theological expression it remains supreme.

The decline in the use of Latin, which began in the
late Middle Ages and has continued, is really not difficult to explain. Latin, as I have said, was the
school language of a relatively small cultured elite
and, however well known, was always a foreign
tongue. Hence, when the vernacular languages of
Europe had finally completed their apprenticeship
under Latin guidance, when they had thus begun the
progressive absorption of the common cultural inheritance transmitted by Latin into their own traditions
and were creating great formal literatures of their
own, it was inevitable that they should gradually replace Latin as a medium of communication in an ever
increasing number of fields. It should be noted that
mediaeval secular lyric poetry had exhausted itself
by the end of the twelfth century, and the great.
Mediaeval Latin hymns came to an end with St.
Thomas Aquinas, Jacopone da Todi, and Thomas of
Celano in the second half of the thirteenth. The

contemporary shift from the auctores to the artes is
not to be regarded, as it often is, as a major factor
in the decline, but rather as a symptom of change of
interests.[31]

Humanism and the Reformers unquestionably
hastened the decline of Mediaeval Latin, and both
contributed heavily, if in different ways, to the ultimate decline in the use of Latin itself. The Humanists
repudiated Mediaeval Latin and thus destroyed linguistic continuity in the development and use of Latin
as a living or quasi-living tongue. They replaced the
Late Mediaeval Latin by the polished Classical Latin
of Cicero, a language which, in the strict and rigid
form in which they employed it, was already dead in
the last centuries of Antiquity. The Reformers
hastened the decline of Latin by rejecting the traditional Latin Liturgy and the Latin Bible and by the
exclusive use of the vernacular in their Churches.
They also encouraged the use of the vernacular in the
new Protestant universities.

Latin remained the language of the Roman Catholic Church and of her ecclesiastical disciplines. But
even the Liturgy itself could not escape the influence
of the Humanists. The hymns of the Breviary and
Missal in their current form contain many hundreds of
changes which were made in the seventeenth century
under the misguided enthusiasm for Classical Latin as
the sole standard of correctness and elegance. Latin
prayers, hymns, and offices composed in modern
times often lack the truly Christian vitality and spirit
in their language that is so characteristic of the
liturgical texts of Christian Antiquity and the Middle
Ages.[32]

It may be observed in passing that, outside the
Church, Latin maintained itself longest as an international medium of communication in the field of
science, and that this scientific Latin retained some
of the freedom of its mediaeval counterpart.

In the last analysis, there is much to be said for
the theory advanced by R. B. Bolgar in his recent
book, The Classical Heritage and its Beneficiaries,[33]
namely, that from the end of Antiquity down to the
seventeenth century Latin served primarily a utilitarian purpose, and that it has gradually declined as
that purpose has been met -- or has been thought to

have been met -- through the medium of the vernacular
languages. From the seventeenth century to the latter
part of the nineteenth, Latin, it is true, occupied a
central place in the curriculum of the secondary
school and college, for it was considered the chief and
most effective instrument of intellectual training and
discipline. Since the last decades of the nineteenth
century, however, but particularly in our own generation, Latin has not only lost that central position in
the school curriculum, but it is finding it increasingly
difficult to retain any place at all, even on a restricted
and optional basis.

The marked decline of Latin in our Catholic secondary schools and colleges reflects the general
trend in respect to it and, at the same time, bears
witness to the powerful influence of contemporary
secular culture and educational values on the curricula
of Catholic schools. The utilitarian factor, however,
will inevitably operate to prevent the decline of Latin
beyond a certain point in Catholic education. As long
as Latin remains the official language of the Church
and her Liturgy, Latin must continue to be taught in
minor and major seminaries, and to some extent at
least in our Catholic secondary schools and colleges.[34]

FOOTNOTES

[1]See my essay, "The Origin and Character of
Christian Latin," and the pertinent bibliography
listed.

[2]See K. Strecker, Introduction to Medieval Latin.
English Translation and Revision by R. B. Palmer
(Berlin 1957) 20-21, and 35-37. P. Lehmann, "Vom
Leben des Lateinischen im Mittelalter," Erforschung
des Mittelalters (Leipzig 1941) 62-81. L. Bieler,
"Das Mittellatein als Sprachproblem," Lexis 2 (1949)
98-104. R. Meister, "Mittellatein als Traditions-
sprache," Liber Floridus: Mittellateinische Studien,
edd. B. Bischoff and S. Brechter (St. Ottilien 1950;
Festschrift in honor of P. Lehmann) 1-9. The latest
and best general evaluations of Mediaeval Latin are
by C. Mohrmann: "Le dualisme de la latinité
médiévale," in her Latin vulgaire. Latin des
chrétiens. Latin médiéval (Paris 1955) 36-54;
"Le Latin médiéval," Cahiers de Civilisation

médiévale 1 (1958) 265-294 (with valuable bibliography).

[3]See, e.g., the bibliography cited in Strecker-Palmer, op. cit. 21 ff. For Merovingian Latin, see, especially, A. Uddholm, Formulae Marculfi. Études sur la langue et le style (Uppsala 1954), with its copious bibliography.

[4]For a brief but good historical survey of the Latin language from the close of the Augustan Age to the fifth century A.D., see L. R. Palmer, The Latin Language (London 1954) 137-205.

[5]See, M. L. Clarke, Rhetoric at Rome. A Historical Survey (London 1953) 100-164. H. I. Marrou, A History of Education in Antiquity (New York 1956) 284-313; id., Saint Augustin et la fin de la culture antique (Paris 1938) 47-157.

[6]On this point see Palmer, The Latin Language 95-137.

[7]See especially, C. Mohrmann, Latin vulgaire ... cited supra in note 3.

[8]W. Jaeger, Humanism and Theology [The Aquinas Lecture, Marquette University] (Milwaukee 1943) 24. See also M. R. P. McGuire, "Mediaeval Humanism," Catholic Historical Review 38 (1952-1953), especially 401-402.

[9]On the early monastic schools, see H. I. Marrou, History of Education in Antiquity 330-350.

[10]See M. L. W. Laistner, Thought and Letters in Western Europe A.D. 500-900 (new ed. revised Ithaca 1957) 95-103. P. Courcelle, Les lettres grecques en Occident de Macrobe à Cassiodore (2nd ed. revised Paris 1948) 312-336.

[11]See D. Norberg, Syntaktische Forschungen auf dem Gebiete des Spätlateins und des frühen Mittellateins (Uppsala 1943) 11-12.

[12]See L. Traube, Einleitung in die lateinische Philologie des Mittelalters. Herausgegeben von P. Lehmann [Vorlesungen und Abhandlungen 2] (Munich 1911) 57, and 175-176.

[13]Norberg, op. cit. 12-22. He gives an excellent characterization of Merovingian Latin and refutes the views of H. Muller and his school.

[14]On the educational reforms of Charlemagne,

and, in particular, on the work of Alcuin, see:
Laistner, Thought and Letters 189-224. E. S. Duckett, Alcuin, Friend of Charlemagne (New York 1951).
On York as an intellectual center in the eighth century,
see especially W. Levison, England and the Continent
in the Eighth Century (Oxford 1946).

[15]The Chronicler of St. Gall employs this term in
referring to the work of Alcuin and its results. Cf.
MGH, SS II 731. The passage is cited and discussed
by E. Gilson in an essay, "Humanisme médiéval," in
his Les idées et les lettres (Paris 1932) 171-196.

[16]See Norberg, op. cit. 22-25.

[17]See especially her "Le latin médiéval," Cahiers
de Civilisation médiévale 1 (1958) 274 ff.

[18]See Mohrmann, art. cit. 273, and 280 ff. See
also the excellent book by Dom J. Leclercq, L'amour
des lettres et le désir de Dieu (Paris 1957).

[19]On the Renaissance of the Twelfth Century, see
E. M. Sanford, "The Twelfth Century-Renaissance or
Proto-Renaissance," Speculum 24 (1951) 635-642.
U. T. Holmes, Jr., "The Idea of the Twelfth-Century
Renaissance," ibid. 643-651. Mohrmann, art. cit.
277 ff.

[20]For the flowering of Mediaeval Latin sacred
and profane poetry in the eleventh, twelfth, and
thirteenth centuries, see the pertinent sections in
F. J. E. Raby, A History of Christian Latin Poetry
from the Beginnings to the Close of the Middle Ages
(2nd ed. Oxford 1953), and A History of Secular Latin
Poetry in the Middle Ages (2 vols. 2nd ed. Oxford
1957). Mohrmann, art. cit. 289-294.

[21]R. R. Bolgar, The Classical Heritage and Its
Beneficiaries (Cambridge [England] 1954) 208-210
(quoted passage on 210). Mohrmann, art. cit. 278-
279.

[22]F. Blatt, "Sprachwandel im Latein des
Mittelalters," Historische Vierteljahrschrift 28
(1933) 22-52.

[23]Art. cit. 24-30.

[24]Art. cit. 30-34.

[25]Art. cit. 38-40.

[26]See, e.g., the technical Latin words (printed in

italics) in the Index of Volume III of the new edition of
H. Rashdall, The Universities of Europe in the
Middle Ages, edited by F. M. Powicke and A. B.
Emden (Oxford 1936). See also the technical Latin
words listed in the Index of A. L. Gabriel, Student
Life in Ave Maria College, Mediaeval Paris (Notre
Dame, Indiana, 1955).

[27]Blatt, art. cit. 40 ff.

[28]See R. J. Deferrari, Sister M. Inviolata Barry,
C.D.P., and J. I. McGuiness, O.P., A Lexicon of
St. Thomas (Washington 1953). Deferrari-Barry, A
Complete Index of the Summa Theologica of St.
Thomas Aquinas (ibid. 1956). M. Fernandez
Garcia, O.F.M., Lexicon scholasticum philosophico-
theologicum ... a B. Joanne Duns Scoto (Quaracchi
1910).

[29]C. Mohrmann has dealt critically with the
views of the scholars mentioned in her article, "Le
Latin médiéval," Cahiers de Civilisation médiévale 1
(1958) 265-273. This is the best evaluation that has
been published to date.

[30]See Mohrmann, art. cit. 272-273.

[31]On the decline of Latin in the Late Middle Ages,
see M. R. P. McGuire, "Mediaeval Humanism,"
Catholic Historical Review 38 (1952-1953) 405-407.
Raby, Secular Latin Poetry in the Middle Ages II
341 ff. J. de Ghellinck, S.J., L'essor de la littérature latine au XIIe siècle II (Paris 1946) 312-321.

[32]See, especially, the last part of C. Mohrmann's
article, "Die Rolle des Lateins in der Kirche des
Westens," Theologische Revue 52 (1956) 1-18. See
also J. Connelly, Hymns of the Roman Liturgy
(Westminster, Md., 1957) XVII-XVIII.

[33]Op. cit., especially 380-393. See also G.
Ganss, S.J., "A Historical Sketch of the Teaching of
Latin," in his St. Ignatius' Idea of a Jesuit University
(Milwaukee 1954) 208-248.

[34]On official ecclesiastical concern over the
decline of the knowledge of Latin among priests and on
the measures to be taken to remedy this situation, see
the Letter of the Sacred Congregation for Seminaries
and Universities addressed to local Ordinaries on the
study of Latin, Acta Apostolicae Sedis 50 (1958) 292-

296. The Letter also lists a series of papal pronouncements on the subject, beginning with the Encyclical Singulari quidem issued by Pope Pius IX in
1856. An English translation of this Letter, with
accompanying observations, by M. R. P. McGuire,
was published in the Bulletin of the Committee on
Affiliation, The Catholic University of America
(March 1959; SC 39:59; HC 39:59). It is reprinted as
one of the appendices in the present volume.

ST. AUGUSTINE AND HIS PLACE
IN LATIN LITERATURE

by

Roy J. Deferrari

St. Augustine's contribution to Latin literature, especially in his earlier literary activity, is so closely bound up with his religious experiences that something must be said about his conversion and his surroundings before we approach his writings specifically. For example, it is important to be well informed about the nature of Augustine's conversion to appreciate at all adequately his great work the Confessions, and also the so-called minor works or Cassiciacum dialogues. It is valuable also, in order to understand and evaluate all his works, but especially the sermons and the letters, to have some knowledge of the language of the people, as well as of the people themselves, to whom he addressed himself.

On Augustine's spiritual and intellectual development, we are informed with unparalleled accuracy by his Confessions and by his philosophical dialogues. For the incidents of his life, besides his Confessions, his other writings, but especially his Letters , are sources of prime importance. For the events following his conversion until his death, particularly his literary activity, we are indebted chiefly to a biography written by his fellow country man and friend Possidius, Bishop of Calama, and to his own unique composition the Retractations.

The question of Augustine's spiritual development, his conversion if you will, has been one of the most fascinating studies for Patristic scholars of the last sixty years. An ever increasing number are being attracted to it, allying themselves to the various schools of opinion, and anything like unanimity of opinion among them seems quite impossible at present.

Previous to about sixty years ago, the autobiography which Augustine gives us in his Confessions was accepted in complete confidence as the most reliable source for the story of his life and the details of his spiritual evolution. One exception, however, should be noted in the person of one Jean Pherephon (pseudonym of Jean LeClerc), 1657-1736, who in his annotations on the writings of Augustine, particularly on the Confessions, expressed doubts as to the credibility of various statements contained therein. No one expressed a similar opinion until more than a century later.

During the past three generations, especially since the wide spread of the new historical method of research, the writings of Augustine have been interpreted with all the scrupulous exactitude that is connoted by the term "historical method." As a consequence, many of the opinions previously based on the Confessions have been changed in the minds of some scholars. Possibly the most noteworthy change of opinion is seen in the development and growth of the so-called "recent theory" on the conversion of Augustine. The exponents of this new notion no longer regard Augustine's conversion to Christianity as having taken place at the time and under the circumstances which he himself ascribes to it in the Confessions. They maintain that it was only later, after his sojourn at Cassiciacum, after his baptism even, that he returned to the faith of his youth and really accepted Christian doctrine. In the meantime, he was completely under the influence of Neoplatonism.

This new evidence counter to that of the Confessions was found chiefly in Augustine's philosophical dialogues. They were written just before Augustine's baptism, while he was sojourning at Cassiciacum, a suburb of Milan, and are entitled Contra Academicos, De vita beata, De ordine, and Soliloquia. They are imaginary dialogues of the kind so successfully cultivated after Plato's time, and in form are modeled directly on those of Cicero. Their content is supposedly taken from the conversations on serious subjects, which Augustine frequently had with his friends just before and at the time of his conversion. Their interest to modern scholars lies chiefly in their value as source material for the study of the question now under discussion.

The "recent theory" assumed a definite form in

1888. Almost simultaneously Gaston Boissier in an article which appeared in the Revue des deux Mondes for January 1, 1888, and Adolf Harnack in his Augustine's Confessionen expressed the opinion that the Dialogues and the Confessions are not in harmony with regard to the story of the conversion; that the Dialogues, contemporaneous with the facts, hardly consider it, and that the remote Confessions exaggerate it.   Since 1888, there have appeared in various degrees of vehemence other advocates of this theory. A chronological list of the outstanding followers of Boissier and Harnack include: F. Loofs, L. Gourdon, H. Becker, W. Thimme, and P. Alfaric.

Although this theory is still being affirmed with great confidence, it is constantly being met with opposition. Of those who accept the story of the Confessions and have attacked the new theory, the most prominent are F. Worter, J. Martin, E. Portalié, L. de Mondalon, W. Montgomery, O. Bardenhewer, P. De Labriolle, and C. Boyer. The one school of opinion believes that the spiritual evolution of St. Augustine can be explained satisfactorily by a critical exegesis of his writings and a study of the various environments in which he lived. In the opinion of the other, such an accomplishment is impossible, since it cannot account for the inner and personal motives of Augustine, without a thorough understanding of which, they maintain, no study of his spiritual evolution is complete. Moreover, they believe that no critical study can fathom the inner personal motives of Augustine; only he himself can explain them. This he has done. Therefore, they say, to comprehend the spiritual development of Augustine we must read the Confessions.

Still a third group of scholars quite reasonably urges a harmonizing of the evidence of the Confessions and the Dialogues. They feel that much in the dialogues can be explained only with the Confessions, and vice versa; that the two are complements, one of the other. Among these are A. Hatzfeld, T. Bret, G. von Hertling, J. Mausbach, J. Hessen, and P. Courcelle. This seems to us the most reasonable. As a matter of fact, there is nothing in the Confessions and the Dialogues which can be said to be contradictory in fact.

Considerable confusion exists in the popular mind as to the racial origin of Augustine himself and of the people among whom he labored. As for Augustine, nothing more is known by way of direct evidence than the following brief statements. In the Confessions (2.3.5), Augustine speaks of his father as municeps Thagastensis admodum tenuis, and in the Confessions (9.8.17), he says that his mother was reared in domo fideli, bono membro ecclesiae. In the Confessions (2.3.6), Augustine says further about his father, that he was adhuc catechumenus et hoc recens, while he (Augustine) was in his fifteenth year. Possidius in the Vita (1) speaks of Augustine as having been born de numero curialium parentibus honestis et christianis. This is the sum total of our actual knowledge of Augustine's origin. He was born of a Christian mother and a pagan father, both of whom were of families of some official colonial rank. Anything more than this is conjecture based on what is known of Augustine's upbringing and later life. In all probability, he was of Roman colonial stock.

The base of the population of Hippo Regius, the see over which Augustine was made bishop, and its adjacent territory was Libyan, a race like the modern Berbers. Upon them came the colonists, invaders, and conquerors, who, as they mingled to some extent with the native population, accomplished many changes in economic conditions, in government, and in religion, and erected imposing monuments. The later-comers were successively the Phoenicians, the Romans, the Vandals, the Byzantines, and the Arabs. In addition to these, there were a certain number of Greeks in North Africa. Although the Greek sphere properly speaking did not extend west of Cyrenaica, even in the western or Punic districts, the all-pervading influence of Hellenism was felt, and some account must be taken of the Greeks as a factor in the development of North Africa. The negroes and the Jews also were present in these regions from early times, but their influence was not very great. But judging from the characteristics that prevail today in the people of North Africa, and bearing in mind that generally recognized principle in the field of anthropology, that regardless of the number and intensity of migrations, the native and subdued peoples usually

succeed in maintaining their racial qualities, I would
say that Augustine lived and labored among men who
were for the most part Libyans, or like the Berbers
of today.

The language, which was Augustine's native
tongue and which he employed in his teaching, was
Latin. Latin was introduced into North Africa by the
Roman conquerors, and came into general use probably at the beginning of the Empire. The exact nature
of this Latin, however, has been one of the interesting
problems of the study of Late Latin. Of course, we
may say in a general way that it has a Classical base
with very slight ingredients of Libyan, and much influence from Greek and Punic, the latter through normal
contacts with the Greek and Punic speakers. But
what relation does it hold to the stream of Latin that
preceded and was contemporary with it? Was it in
direct line of descent from the language of Cicero,
and like the Latin in general use throughout the Empire at Augustine's time, or was it in the nature of a
local dialect, distinct enough to bear the name
Africitas which some have given it? Scholars today
for the most part agree that these questions are
satisfactorily settled. We know much more today
about the language of St. Augustine's contemporaries,
his predecessors, and of Augustine himself than we
did a generation or two ago, so that we can speak with
considerable confidence on the subject. We can say,
I think, that Africitas in the strict philological sense
of a dialect does not exist, but in the sense of a
slight local coloring, particularly with reference to
style, exactly as we speak of Pativinitas in the
language of Livy, it is quite evident. Moreover, we
would say that the Latin of North Africa was a lineal
descendant of the Latin of the Golden Age, marked
very conservatively, chiefly as to style, by local
conditions.

Of Augustine's literary activity, we are informed
more accurately than is the case with any other man
of antiquity, Cicero himself not excepted. We owe
this detailed and reliable information to a work in two
books, called the Retractations, which Augustine
composed in the year 427, when an old man, indeed
only a few years before his death. The Retractations
contains a chronologically ordered account of all his

works, with the exception of his letters and his sermons, to which should be added about ten other works written after that date. He seems to have looked upon his consecration as bishop as an important turning point in his literary career, for he assigned to the first book of his Retractations the works which antedated his election as bishop, and to the second book all his later works.

As literature, the Retractations is quite unique. It aims to record for all of Augustine's finished works any change of opinion which he might have undergone in the course of his life, information which, of course, Augustine alone could give.

The nature of these changes of opinion do not involve any serious matters of dogma, as is commonly supposed. They do, however, reflect interesting traits of Augustine's character. The work also furnishes us with an authentic list and résumé of Augustine's genuine works. It does not contain, as has been said, any treatment of the letters and sermons, for the reason that death intervened. That Augustine fully intended to do this is evident from the definite statement which he makes at the very end of the existing portion of the Retractations. The lack of this sort of a discussion of the sermons is in all probability responsible for the fact that over 300 spurious sermons came into circulation in the course of time under the name of Augustine. The value of the Retractations, however, is confined chiefly to the field of literary history.

Sufficient mention has already been made of Augustine's dialogues written at Cassiciacum, which have been called more philosophical than Christian. So we shall proceed at once to consider briefly Augustine as a theologian. There is scarcely a field of scientific theology or dogma which Augustine did not enter to produce important and often pioneer works. Not to mention many sermons and letters, which often grew into detailed treatises, the polemico-dogmatic writings against the Manichaeans (among which the twenty-three books against Faustus deserve special mention), and those against the Donatists and the Pelagians represent in bulk more than half of his works. His dogmatic masterpiece is the De Trinitate in fifteen books. It required, with interruptions,

almost seventeen years for completion, and is remarkable for its original treatment of a problem already endlessly discussed. This treatise and the
City of God were the only works of Augustine which
were ever translated into Greek, a high tribute for
the originality and intrinsic worth of any work in any
period of Latin literature. This was done in the
thirteenth century by a Byzantine monk, Maximus
Planudes. Besides a number of minor and unimpor-
tant treatises, the Adversus haereses, although almost exclusively a compilation from various sources
still extant, achieved lasting fame because of its detailed treatment of the subject.

Augustine was also active sporadically in the
field of Biblical exegesis. The fruit of his work in
this field is represented by the three last books of the
Confessions, some of his sermons, and numerous
special treatises. He was enthusiastically praised
as an exegete far into the Middle Ages, but this was
due to his great name rather than to his true scientific worth. For St. Augustine was entirely ignorant
of Hebrew, and, as he himself says, had only a very
superficial knowledge of Greek, and without these he
was shut off from a vast body of important literature
on the subject.

As a practical interpreter of Holy Writ -- witness
his sermons -- he does not, according to some, rank
high, but as a theorist thereon he has produced in his
four books of the De doctrina Christiana one of his
most excellent works. This treatise is divided into
two parts: Books 1-3, dealing with the discovery of
the true sense of Scripture, and Book 4, treating of
its expression. The fourth book is of special interest
to Classicists, because in it Augustine has made free
use of the material of Cicero's rhetorical works, the
Brutus, the Orator, and the De oratore. It was used
as an unerring model of Christian hermeneutics
throughout the Middle Ages and even later. Furthermore, in it the author spoke in defense of the so-called
worldly studies of eloquence, rhetoric, and dialectic,
because he saw in them an invaluable means to a
practical religious purpose. Unconsciously, perhaps,
Augustine thereby is ultimately responsible for the
preservation and dispersion of no small part of
Classical literature. Baldwin's estimate of the

fourth book sums up the values of the treatise as follows: its repudiation of Sophistic, its reintroduction
of the Classical standard, and its presentation of the
Christian ideal.

The sermons[1] of St. Augustine are perhaps the
most neglected of his works: "Their study leaves
much to be desired." (Cf. Schanz-Krüger,
Geschichte der römischen Litteratur IV[2] [Munich
1920] 458). It is true that popular editions of the sermons are numerous; but the feeling persists among
scholars that their study is not of much value, since
what Augustine says in his sermons often does not
represent his final opinion on the subjects discussed.
As a matter of fact, we have express statements of
St. Augustine (Retractations 2.93.2) and his biographer
Possidius (Vita 28) on the unrevised character of the
discourses. The great number of clearly spurious
sermons which came into circulation after the publication of the Maurists also acted as a deterrent to those
who would make special studies in this field of literature. But in comparatively recent years, the investigations of Dom Germain Morin, Dom de Bruyne, Dom
Wilmart, and Dom Lambot have most convincingly
distinguished the genuine from the false. The following table shows the various collections of sermons
published by and after the Maurists and the numbers
identified as genuine.

THE SERMONS OF SAINT AUGUSTINE

MAURINI

Migne PL 38	183	Sermones de Scripturis
	90	Sermones de Tempore
	67	Sermones de Sanctis
PL 39	23	Sermones de Diversis
	32	Dubii
	317	Spurii
PL 35	124	Tractatus in Joannis Evangelium
	10	Tractatus in Epistolam Joannis ad Parthos

Migne PL 36   207 Enarrationes in Psalmos
and 37

POST MAURINOS

The genuine Sermones post Maurinos are col-
lected in "S. Augustini sermones post Maurinos
reperti," edited by Germain Morin in Miscellanea Agostiniana I.

	published	genuine
M. Denis (Vienna 1792)	25	23
F. Fontani (Florence 1793)	4	0
O. Frangipane (Rome 1819)	10	9
A. Caillau and B. Saint-Yves (Paris 1836, 1842)	269	7
F. Ravaisson (Paris 1841)	2	0
Cardinal Mai (Rome 1842, 1852)	206	26
J. P. Migne (Paris 1849)	2	0
F. Liverani (Florence 1863)	10	1
H. Bordier (Geneva 1866)	6	0
Editores Bibliothecae Cas. (Monte Casino 1873 ff.)	46	4
G. Morin, Revue Bénédictine 1890-1929 passim;	17	17
Munich 1917)	34	34
A. Wilmart, Revue Bénédictine, Revue d'Ascétique, Journal of Theol. Studies (1912-1930) passim	13	11

Since Dom Morin's edition of 1930 twelve new
sermons have been published by Cyril Lambot
in Revue Bénédictine (1933-1939) passim.

By a dissertation published in 1928 and by an ex-
haustive article in Miscellanea Agostiniana ("Die
Chronologie der Sermones des hl. Augustinus"),
Adalbert Kunzelmann has partially established the
chronology of the sermons. As a result of his work
and of a compilation of findings prior to 1928, about
two-thirds of the sermons can now be dated with

certainty, though at times only by decades. Thus, the
material of the sermons is in a condition to invite
detailed studies of their content. The fact of the professed unrevised nature of the sermons should not
give scholars pause, since St. Augustine in the revision of his other works has indicated no striking
change in his thinking.

Without doubt, the sermons of St. Augustine
would repay serious study. Kunzelmann considers
them essential for an understanding of Augustinian
thought and of the culture and liturgy of the age that
produced them. ("Augustins Predigttätigkeit,"
Aurelius Augustinus. Festschrift der Görres-
Gesellschaft [Cologne 1930] 167). A few examples
will indicate the kind of witness provided by the discourses. In Denis 3, occurs a rare statement of the
form of consecration employed in the African Church
at the end of the fourth century. Denis 6 contains
material for the history of the Eucharistic doctrine,
a clear and eloquent exposition of the words of consecration as the cause of consecration, beginning thus:

> Tolle verbum, panis est et vinum; adde
> verbum et iam aliud est. Et ipsum aliud,
> quid est? Corpus Christi et sanguis Christi.
> Tolle ergo verbum, panis est et vinum; adde
> verbum et fiet sacramentum.

Denis 19 contains mention of the appeal of the Donatist
Crispinus to the emperor. At times, as in Frangipane
2, there are references to local customs; here it is
the banquet for the poor on the occasion of the Bishop's
birthday. Denis 24, against the Manichees, furnishes
a valuable passage on the virginity of the Blessed
Virgin Mary. Contemporary events are often mentioned incidentally in the sermons, for example,
the royal edicts of 399, Alaric's capture of Rome in
410, the earthquake of 419, the barbarian invasion of
Africa.

Despite the impressive number of the extant
sermons (some 800 plus many fragments), they must
represent only a fraction of the total. St. Augustine
preached regularly on Sundays and on all special
feasts. We have instances of sermons on five successive days (Sermones 153-156; Tractatus in

Joannis Evangelium 19-23), and on three (Sermones 320-322); there are, besides, numerous references to sermons preached on two successive days. Forty years of preaching, even at the rate of two sermons a week, a low figure when one considers the evidence, would involve more than four thousand addresses. And since St. Augustine often spoke outside his episcopal see, in Carthage, Bulla Regia, Hippo Diarrhytus, Utica, and elsewhere, we may believe that the number was considerably larger. Of Augustine's extensive preaching in the cities of North Africa, Possidius (Vita 9) says:

> Et episcopus multo instantius ac ferventius maiore auctoritate, non adhuc in una tantum regione, sed ubicumque rogatus venisset, verbum salutis aeternae alacriter ac gnaviter, pullulante atque crescente Domini ecclesia, praedicabat, paratus semper poscentibus reddere rationem de fide et spe quae in Deum est.

St. Augustine himself (Retractations, Prol. 2) indicates that preaching was almost constant in his life:

> Tantumque mihi tributum est, ut ubicumque me praesente loqui opus esset ad populum, rarissime tacere atque alios audire permitterer et esse velox ad audiendum, tardus autem ad loquendum.

In Sermo 94, there is an indication, whether intended humorously or not, that the burden of delivering speeches was heavy.

As for the subject matter of the sermons, it was, as Father Hugh Pope (St. Augustine of Hippo [London 1937] 151) says, the Bible all the time. Its words and expressions flow almost unconsciously from his lips; his stories and illustrations are taken from it. There is not a book in the Bible that he has not commented on in some form or other; it is the quarry for all his doctrine. At first sight, it might seem strange that an audience apparently so uncultured as that at Hippo could appreciate sermons which demanded an

intimate acquaintance with the text of Holy Scripture.
Yet they must have had such an acquaintance; and it is
likely that it was from Augustine's sermons that they
had gained it, for very many of them could not read.

Next in prominence to Biblical exegesis rank the
sermons against the heresies of the age. Possidius
(Vita 7) testifies to these discourses:

> Et docebat et praedicabat ille privatim et
> publice in domo et in ecclesia salutis verbum
> cum omni fiducia adversus Africanas haereses,
> maximeque contra Donatistas, Manichaeos et
> paganos, libris confectis et repentinis ser-
> monibus, ineffabiliter admirantibus Christianis
> et collaudantibus, et hoc ipsum ubi poterant non
> tacentibus et diffamantibus.

Some ten sermons inveigh more or less openly
against the Manichees. A fourth of all the sermons
show traces of his strife against Pelagianism; more
than fifty, his efforts against the Donatists. Less
weighty problems, topics which he has been handling
in his treatises and letters, come up repeatedly.
There are, for example, passages like that on the use
of the body after the resurrection; on whether man can
see God with bodily eyes; on apparently contradictory
passages in the Scriptures.

An interesting feature is St. Augustine's custom
of holding the same sermon each year on a given occasion, as in Mai 128 and Sermones 248-252 on our
Lord's appearance to the Apostles on the shore of
Lake Tiberias. In Guelferbytanus 15, the preacher
refers with self-satisfaction to this repetition.

Every sermon contained a great deal of doctrinal
exposition, but this always had its moral application,
couched in brief and pithy form. We call attention
here to his fondness for allegorical interpretation and,
a phase of it, his preoccupation with the symbolism of
numbers. The sermons have their share of this
characteristic. In all his moralizing, Augustine is
simple and sure, tender and strong, exhibiting in his
manner the qualities of the medicus, a comparison of
which he was fond (cf. Denis 24). Some call attention
to the modern tone of Augustine's sermons, going so
far as to call him "the modern man," (cf. Denis 20

and Morin 18), but we would probably be more accurate if we said that we are ancient in our human weaknesses rather than say that St. Augustine is modern.

The rough external form of the sermons, which
has often been severely criticized, as well as on the
other hand their intrinsic historical value, is due to
the manner in which they were delivered and preserved. On examining the sermons, evidence appears
on every hand to substantiate the belief that they were
delivered extemporaneously, without any serious
preparation, and were taken down by shorthand
writers (notarii) present in the church, later to be
transcribed and offered to the public without further
attention from Augustine.[2] All this, while it gives the
sermons a very rough exterior, lends them all the
spontaneity and freshness of dictographic reports,
and, as we have said, adds much information about
the habits of the people of North Africa which we
would never have known otherwise.

In content, St. Augustine's letters belong to the
most valuable of all literature in the field of ancient
epistolography. The Christian writers of the first
centuries found this tool, the epistle, at hand and apt
for their purposes. It was by letters as the medium
of publicity that Athanasius, Basil, Gregory, and
others of the Fathers braved the persecutions of the
Arian emperors. The epistolary tool was similarly
used in the West. The letter remained the means of
publicity, often the only means, and for the Christians
letters became a bond of union between churches and
between individuals. They were a means of exhortation, of rebuke, of encouragement, as well as an
instrument of defense.

It is important to note that such letters varied
greatly in their destinations. They were sometimes
addressed to one individual, sometimes to several.
At times, they were posted up so that many might
know them or they were transcribed and copies circulated. In the case of an individual addressee, it often
happened that the letter would pass from hand to hand,
and finally end up as public property.

St. Augustine's letters were dictated, and, for
the most part, written on papyrus. There are sufficient references to indicate that copies of letters
were kept. This appears definitely in the letters

between Augustine and Jerome and in many other instances.

If, by some misfortune, St. Augustine's other works had perished and there had remained only his letters, we would still have all his doctrine, all his genius. The letters of St. Augustine are the whole St. Augustine. While we have the Confessions to tell us of Augustine's life up to the time of his conversion, for the later period we are dependent on Possidius' Vita and on the letters. In addition, the letters are particularly valuable for their vast store of evidence bearing on the contemporary life of Augustine's day. After speaking of the letters as the expression of the author's self, the Benedictine Preface states:

> But this, in addition, adds dignity to the
> letters of Augustine, the fact that, although the
> holy Bishop was occupied with the heavy burdens
> of the Church, his collection of letters not only
> embraces his private life but almost the entire
> ecclesiastical history of his time. .

The correspondence of St. Augustine covers the period from 386 to 429. The 270 letters of the Benedictine edition contain fifty letters addressed to Augustine and 220 written by him. In general, the subject matter of the letters falls in one of the following divisions: theological, polemical, exegetical, ecclesiastical, moral, or philosophical. The range of subject matter again recalls the fact that the letter was for St. Augustine as for others of the Fathers an instrument of response to the definite needs of the time. Thus, in terms of literary criticism, if letters are divided according to the purpose of the writer, Augustine's are non-literary, inasmuch as they are letters in fact and not primarily intended as literature which merely assumed a letter form.

St. Augustine's correspondents range from personal friends to bishops, government officials, pagan philosophers, Christian scholars, wealthy landowners, poor widows, heretics, schismatics. Perhaps the department of personal friendship is least well represented. Though Augustine is ever the scholar, philosopher, theologian, ecclesiastic, pastor, citizen, ascetic, the letters constantly show that with it all he is a friendly and helpful human being.

To many, the most interesting of Augustine's letters is the correspondence with St. Jerome. Much of this interest, I fear, has been aroused by a morbid delight in witnessing two saints quarrel bitterly. As a matter of fact, if the controversy is followed carefully and understandingly, it appears for what it is -- a serious and earnest discussion of scholarly problems in the course of which misunderstandings arose through tampering with the correspondence by unscrupulous trouble-makers. That Jerome came to have full trust and confidence in Augustine, though not apparent in his direct correspondence, is evident in a letter which Jerome wrote to Marcellinus (Ep. 120.1). Marcellinus, just as St. Augustine, had written to Jerome about the problem of the origin of the human soul. Jerome states that an answer is to be found in his work against Rufinus, but he adds:

> Surely, you have there [in Africa] a man of
> holy life and learned, Augustine the Bishop,
> who can teach you with the living voice, as
> they say; who will explain to you his own
> thoughts on the subject; even more, through
> him you will have my judgment.

Letter 211 has interest for many because of its content and because of its history, for it has played its part in the 1500-year-old problem of determining whether St. Augustine wrote a Rule and, if so, which one of the several at hand.[3] Although some scholars of our time reject Letter 211 as being no essential part of Augustine's true and complete regula, it still retains its supreme importance as one of the major sources for Augustine's monastic doctrine; since, reflecting his other monastic creations, it serves as an excellent synthesis of his long monastic experience and, in a measure, even of his entire ascetical doctrine.

The modern student of letters usually studies and stresses the letter as a means of insight into the personality of the writer. But the reader who seeks to find the Augustine of the Confessions in the letters will, for the most part, be disappointed. The idea we form of him from his correspondence is of a tremendously vital and powerful mind, able to treat with penetrating insight of widely diverse subjects, but at the same time willing to admit the possibility of error and to confess ignorance.

There still remains for me to say something about Augustine's two most impressive works, literary accomplishments both of which have carried his name far beyond professional theological circles, and to which because of their unique and almost unprecedented influence must be accorded a very high place in the literature of the world. I mean, of course, the Confessions and the City of God.

Attention has been called to the importance of the Confessions for an understanding of Augustine's spiritual development. As literature, we would classify the Confessions as an autobiography of a very unique sort. It is confessions primarily in the sense of glorification, i. e., a glorification of God, who in His infinite mercy has led the author out of a life of sin. The details of the author's life are introduced not as parts of a narrative for its own sake, but only insofar as they contribute to the glorification. It should be stated emphatically, however, that these details of Augustine's life have all withstood the test of accuracy. Not one can be shown to be contrary to the facts of the case as presented elsewhere in Augustine's works.

At any rate, these life-confessions are heart-gripping and touching, and appeal to every man who has experienced the struggle between good and evil. The author does not attempt to scale lofty peaks of holiness, but he reveals to us the heart of a passion-tossed youth, and of an ambitious man wrestling with temptation common to all mankind. Hence, the great power of the Confessions. On this account, it belongs to the literature of the world, and has been read more than any other Latin work with the exception of Vergil's Aeneid, and has been translated into the language of every cultured people.

Strangely enough, too, little serious attention has been paid to the Confessions from the point of view of its literary structure and style. The reason for this is probably that the Confessions, like the Bible, has attracted readers entirely by reason of its content, which in turn has distracted them from any

consideration of externals. Yet, an opinion prevails
that Augustine wrote his Confessions under tense
emotions, with a soul so stirred that it but seldom
permitted any thoughts of an aesthetic-literary nature,
and that, as a result, his style in this work is sloven-
ly; his sentences and phrases are often choppy and
arbitrary of structure; countless quotations from the
Bible are scattered about in a manner to destroy all
unity of style; and these quotations are often dragged
in quite inappropriately.

Personally, I cannot believe that St. Augustine, a
man of such a great intellect and soul as he reveals
himself to be in all his voluminous works, thirteen
years after his conversion, would suffer such a complete case of "jitters" as these critics would have us
think. A careful analysis of the Confessions will
show that Augustine followed strictly a very well
layed out plan; there are few if any digressions; the
presentations move steadily toward their objectives
and then stop. We have already seen in the sermons
and in the letters that Augustine had a keen dramatic
sense. He instinctively adapts his presentation to the
audience for which it is intended. This he exhibits
most skillfully in the Confessions. He conceives of
God as his solitary auditor, and he confides to Him
without interruption his innermost experiences,
thoughts, and feelings. At the same time, he is
conscious of those who will read the Confessions, and
he keeps this notion before their minds by continued
apostrophes to God. St. Augustine was quite aware at
all times of what he was doing, and intentionally gave
the Confessions an apparent rough exterior, a very
clever and skillful composition. He might well have
felt that a public sensitive to the rhetorical devices of
sound would be diverted by a highly finished style
from the devout and serious content. Furthermore,
the more intelligent of his readers would feel, as he
himself probably felt, that such an exterior would be
quite foreign to the nature of his subject, indeed, even
in bad taste.

If the mighty effect of the Confessions rests upon
the power of feeling, the epochal importance of the
City of God rests on its deeply conceived philosophical
and historical content. Its fundamental thought is that
the earthly order is decaying to annihilation, while a

heavenly order is constantly growing and following
upon it. Paul Janat, over a hundred years ago (1856),
in the Revue des Deux Mondes (p. 388) eloquently
said:

> What an occasion and what a theme! Rome
> taken, paganism imputing to the new faith this
> last downfall, this irreparable overthrow of all
> the grandeur of the past; in its turn, Christianity
> throwing back these misfortunes upon the entire
> ancient civilization, and to that frail city which
> had been vaunted as eternal opposing another
> city which was really eternal and could only ac-
> complish her destiny in the bosom of God, but
> which was beginning already in the souls of those
> who believe and pray.

This idea in itself may have existed before Augustine's time, and Augustine may be found to be dependent to a certain extent upon his predecessors, but
Augustine's comprehensive development of the idea in
his City of God is entirely independent, and is an
original work of the first rank both for its profundity
of thought and its inexhaustible fullness of material.
It is, of course, Augustine's masterpiece.

The author took almost fourteen years, from 412
to 426, for its completion. In fact, Augustine himself
tells us that he published it in installments. But this
circumstance of its growth and development, however
strange it may appear, was more advantageous than
harmful, because it made possible the reading of
separate parts of this great work without incurring any
difficulty in understanding the whole. Augustine says
further that he planned to divide the work into two
great parts. One of these, the first (Books 1-10)
bears in the main a polemic-apologetic character,
Books 1-5 refuting the assertion that the plurality of
gods is necessary for existence here below, Books 6-
10 refuting the idea that pagan gods are also useful for
the life after death. The second part (Books 11-22)
contains the speculative establishment of the earthly
and the divine cities, Books 11-14 treating the beginning of the two communities, Books 15-18 their further development, and Books 19-22 their end.

Ideas differ as to how well Augustine carried out

his original plan. Here again, many general statements have been made, some of them contradictory,
others vague, and all of them incomplete. On the
basis of an investigation made some years ago ("St.
Augustine's City of God: Its Plan and Development,"
AJP 50 [1929] 109-137), we may say with certainty
that Augustine in writing the City of God conformed to
his original plan in its main outlines. But we must
admit that St. Augustine in his City of God writes in a
rather rambling style. He reaches his end indeed but
only after frequent pauses on the way, and after
several lengthy wanderings from the main road. His
goal is ever before him, and he keeps pushing on
towards it, but he seems to take it as a matter of
course that he will stop now and again to answer supposed objections, to give numerous and unnecessary
examples, and to explain difficulties often with weary-
ing details, even if they are foreign to his main
theme. A conservative estimate is that one-fifth of
the whole, 247 out of the 1234 Teubner pages of the
City of God, contains material which has no immediate
or essential connection with the subject.

     The influence of the City of God upon succeeding
generations was tremendous. The religious outlook on
the world as laid down in it predominated throughout
the Middle Ages. Papacy and Empire alike drew upon
Augustine's City of God in support of their opposite
views and claims regarding the powers of Church and
State.

     I would like to bring together these more or less
random remarks on St. Augustine's contribution to
Latin literature by a brief summary of what we may
call St. Augustine's greatness. As his writings, which
embrace the whole field of theological science, enjoyed
an almost canonical authority, his influence upon his
own and later generations has been immeasurable.
Even today he holds among the Latin Fathers an in-
contestable first place. In the whole history of
theology, he has no superior, and St. Thomas Aquinas
is the only one who can be regarded as his equal. And
St. Thomas for the most part built on the foundation
laid by St. Augustine. However, it cannot be denied
that in dialectical skill Tertullian and St. Jerome are
Augustine's equals, as they are also in general erudition, particularly in their knowledge of Greek

literature. Again, as an exegete Augustine produced
no scientific results of pioneer importance. Finally,
as a literary artist, while he may be said to be the
foremost of his period, he cannot be said to tower
greatly above Cyprian, Hilary, or Lactantius.

The following characteristics of his works as
literature are at the same time the outstanding features of all the literary efforts of the Patristic
Period. First, they are almost without exception
written under the immediate demands of some individual or the Church. There is really no work of any
importance by any one of the Fathers which was
written consciously and solely as a serious literary
accomplishment. St. Augustine once started work on
what was to have been an encyclopedia of the liberal
arts, but he did little with it. This was his nearest
approach to writing for its own sake. His works, like
all Patristic literature, are characterized in the
second place by a general indifference to externals.
The Fathers were so engrossed in their serious
utilitarian purpose that they cared little about form.
To be sure, they might be more or less lavish with
rhetorical figures of speech, and this more or less
unconsciously, but their works, with one possible
exception, lack what may be called "finish." Now the
possible exception which I have in mind is the
Confessions of St. Augustine, and this view, which I
have already discussed, is considered by some
critics as an idiosyncrasy on my part. The third
characteristic is by nature closely allied to the other
two. I have said that the literature of the Fathers is
essentially serious and utilitarian. Now the great
questions of the early Church were preeminently
philosophical and theological, and accordingly it is not
easy to find Christian literature in this period which
has not a philosophical and theological trend. From
Augustine's works, I would select as possible material
in this category parts of the Confessions and of the
City of God, certain of the Letters, and the fourth
book of the De doctrina Christiana. However, we
must bear in mind, when considering the literary
qualities of the works of St. Augustine and his contemporaries, that the Latin language of this period
was a living language, and the natural vehicle of expression for the Christians who used it. Moreover,

the Classical genius is still living in St. Augustine and his contemporaries just as much as in their pagan rivals, and they are all patriotic citizens of the Roman Empire of the Caesars. All this lends a special attraction to their works for those of us who have been brought up in the old strict Classical tradition.

I have not yet touched, however, upon the real secret of Augustine's surpassing greatness. It rests primarily upon his originality, his fullness of thought, and the magnetic power of his general and sympathetic personality. Everything about which he attempted to write, regardless of the frequency of its previous treatment, he made distinctly his own by these striking qualities. Finally, as a result of all this, to Augustine alone belongs the glory of having given to the Western Church, once and for all, a trend independent of the Oriental-Greek world of thought, an influence which had dominated all his predecessors. This intellectual achievement can hardly be overestimated in its results.

FOOTNOTES

[1]When we speak of St. Augustine's sermons, we have reference to the Sermones ad Populum, Tractatus, and Enarrationes. Any attempt to make some distinction in these terms has been most unconvincing. They are all sermons.

[2]Roy J. Deferrari, "Saint Augustine's Method of Composing and Delivering Sermons," American Journal of Philology 48 (1922) 97-123; 193-219.

[3]A thorough treatment of Augustine's complete ascetical doctrine for all classes of people, religious and non-religious, clerical and lay, remains to be done.

VERGILIANA NOVA ET VETERA:
A 'LANX SATURA'

by

Bernard M. Peebles

If, in connection with my title, some apology is needed, it would not be for the propriety of the title itself -- for what I present is indeed "a medley, full of different things," and of things of different dates, too, late and early -- but rather, perhaps, for my decision to let this miscellany be what I would offer you, instead, perhaps, of an overall study of the poet himself, set against the background of his times, together with a balanced judgment of his achievement. While I should have been proud to attempt to direct your thoughts along these lines, I feel no shame at undertaking a humbler task, wherein I bring you these fruits of pleasurable reading and study in the poems of Vergil and especially around them, hoping that here and there may be found things -- more likely borrowed from others than of my own devising -- that will lead you in turn to the solid delight and satisfaction that such reading can produce.

In further preamble it would seem to be well to bring at once to the fore a few publications relating to the study of Vergil that will be mentioned hereafter, as well as others that have appeared recently and may not yet have won the place on school and college library shelves that they deserve.[1] Well known surely to all of us is the survey of recent work on Vergil published serially in 1958 in several numbers of the Classical World by George E. Duckworth, of Princeton University, and most usefully reprinted as a unit by the Vergilian Society of America. This report is based on a study of not fewer than 1300 items -- books and articles -- published during the years 1940 to 1956. For those who can use it one publication listed by Professor Duckworth will have the value of many score, the monumental article on Vergil by Karl Büchner in the Classicist's principal

encyclopedia, Pauly-Wissowa-Kroll et al., comprising
a total of 466 solidly printed columns and likely to
provide to Vergilian specialists a point of departure
for many, many years to come. Less formidable is
what seems to me, among books in print, the most
thorough and most valuable English monograph on our
poet, the Roman Vergil of Mr. Jackson Knight, of
Exeter University, dating from 1943. The work has
had its critics, and continued use will surely be found
for the earlier monographs of Sellar and Glover, of
H. W. Prescott, Tenney Frank, and E. K. Rand; but
I know of one lover of Vergil -- a poet but not a professional Classicist -- who told me a few years ago
that it was Jackson Knight that had made Vergil and
his verse come alive for him. Available to some
would be certain outstanding monographs published on
the Continent: the Virgile of Mlle Guillemin, the
Dichtkunst Virgils of Pöschl, the Virgilio of Paratore.
Our chief need is perhaps for editions of Vergil's
poems with full and up-to-date English commentary.
New work of this kind includes R. G. Austin's Fourth
Aeneid (published soon after Professor A. S. Pease's
monumental commentary) and Sir Frank Fletcher's
Sixth Aeneid. For the rest of Vergil's production we
still go, when we can find it, to Conington's three-
volume commentary or to that, later yet still old, of
T. E. Page -- kept in print in this country through the
zeal of the St. Martin's Press. For the study of
Vergil's influence on later literature we have been
given admirable provision in recent works by Highet,
Thomson, and Bolgar. The delver in ancient commentary on Vergil was greatly aided thirteen years
ago by the publication of the first volume (Vol. II) of
the Editio Harvardiana of Servius, containing Servius's treatment of the first two books of the Aeneid;
pupils of E. K. Rand, the founder of the project, are
shortly to bring out a second volume (III), embracing
the commentary on Aeneid III-V. No less welcome is
Colin Hardie's new edition of ancient vitae of Vergil.
Finally, I would reinforce Dr. Siefert's recommendation of C. G. Cooper's Introduction to the Latin
Hexameter.[2]

Sed iam tandem ad propositum.
    Vergil's end is my beginning. From Donatus'

Life of the poet, unless the work should rather be
called that of Gaius Suetonius Tranquillus, we learn
that after Vergil's remains had been transferred
from Brundisium, where he had died, to Naples, and
there buried where he had lived so long and so
happily, a distich was carved upon his tomb composed
by the poet himself in the last stages of his illness,
the familiar lines:

> Mantua me genuit, Calabri rapuere, tenet nunc
>   Parthenope: cecini pascua, rura, duces,

or, in a free English version:

> Mantua gave me birth; Calabria hurried me
>   deathward;
> Now I am held asleep here by Parthenope's
>   shore.
> Shepherds I sang, and rural tasks, and the doing
>   of heroes.

We may not tarry here to consider the long series of
imitations that this couplet has generated, except to
mention the single line on Lucan, "Corduba me
genuit, rapuit Nero, proelia dixi," and Dante's re-
handling in the Purgatory (5.133f.), "Siena mi fe';
disfecemi Maremma," which, more closely than the
original, stands back of T. S. Eliot's adaptation in the
Wasteland.3 For the time being, it is my purpose
simply to use the several segments of the epitaph as
headings under which to subsume the material that I
would bring before you. In its own place the distich
itself will return, along with other matters relating to
the poet's burial and to the history, especially the
legendary history, of his tomb.

Mantua me genuit...
      Many have written with charm and learning of the
Mantuan country and of the village of Andes, the
poet's birthplace, fixing this where they judged best,
but mostly, with local tradition itself, near the town
of Pietole. We could with pleasure follow Professor
Gilbert Highet as our guide or else listen to E. K.
Rand's account of his Quest of Virgil's Birthplace,
made in company with Mrs. Rand in the summer of

1929, just on the eve of the bimillenium of the poet's
birth.[4] Let us hear, rather, some perhaps tantalizing
excerpts from what purports to be an account of a
pilgrimage that occurred not long before 100 A.D.
The pilgrim is the well-schooled amanuensis and
freedman of a certain Marcus Mutius, himself named
Marcus Mutius Palio. Both Marcuses are friends of
the younger Pliny, and it is to Pliny that Palio writes,
the client for his patron, for the patron is ill with a
quartan fever. The only available text -- later, this
will not seem surprising -- is in English blank verse.
Palio, returning from beyond Tridentum, where he had
journeyed to inspect a porphyry quarry, had stopped at
Mediolanum, musing upon the studies the boy Vergil
had made there well over a century before and recalling his own earlier visits to the nearby lakes:

> Your own fair Larius [writes Palio to Pliny] like
>   a turquoise gem
> In her green coronal of hills; Benacus,
> Whose billows lift them like the ocean waves,
> Roaring to match the surf. -- Stop, stop my pen!
> I must not here retail the Georgica, --
> To you of all men, poet as you are
> Yourself, and poet lover.

And then from Milan Palio went [he writes]:

> To Mantua, uprising from her lake
> Amid the water-lilies and the reeds,
> Breasting the ripples like a dreaming swan;
> His birthplace, -- they have put it on his tomb,
> Like some proud title in the Honour Course,
> Consular, Legate, or the Cure of Roads!
> "Mantua gave me birth"; even so it stands.
> It was the season of the ripened vines,
> October Nones, when I to please my fancy
> Walked, pilgrim roughshod, on the winding road
> That leads to Andes, -- such the hamlet's name,
> But Mantuan soil, that gave our Poet birth.
> O golden day, that I shall ne'er forget!

Palio inspects the vintage, where [he continues]:

> the well-worn, farmstead vats

Reeked with the honeyed juices, where young
    men,
Splashed knee and thigh, and scanty-garmented,
Trod out the spurting must.
                        Then from my lips
Ay, from my heart, welled forth the Master's
    lines:
"O all-too-happy swains, could they but know
Their happiness! Care-free their life is spent,
Untroubled by the feverish demands
Of wealth or rank or offices; ...

With more from that gem of the Georgics, the "O
fortunatos nimium, sua si bona norint, agricolas ...,"
Palio passes to the crossroads of the village, where
already there is a monument, "a pillar-crowning
statue to the poet." A village priest nearly persuades
him to stay into the night, witness the vintage festival,
and hear the vintage hymn, the priest's own work, in
septenarii, with a curiously reminiscent refrain --

Drink to-night who ne'er hath drunken; who hath
    drunken drink to-night,

but the visitor must make for the footpath to the
Mincius, and gets his directions to it from the priest
as he takes his leave. Along this track, "all the
landscape spoke one name alone, The name of
Maro ..."

                  He too [writes Palio]
Heard yon cicala's hot stiletto-voice
Stabbing the noontide to a fiercer heat; ...
               He seemed
Here but this hour to pass, -- the gawky lad,
With hesitant speech, and shy, and awkward
    bearing,
Of which rusticities no polishing,
No contact with the world, nor intercourse
With the world's great, could ever free him
    quite.
How many times, a little boy, he passed
Along this road holding his father's hand,
With steps "not equal," (you recall that touch)
Like young Ascanius with his sire. I wonder,

Did he remember that? Or were his eyes
So clear, his heart so loving quick, to note
Whatever marked the frail, the small, the weak,
The tender ones of the earth? ...
But who was Vergil's father, who can tell?
Some say a hireling, with the luck to rise
Wedding his patron's daughter; some assign
The potter's trade. (Your good friend
    Tranquillus,
In his "Illustrious Men," will not decide.)
But what a judgment his! ...
He had the wit to estimate his son,
This swarthy stripling, as more precious clay
Than served to make the jugs of Andes. Here
Was one that might be fined to rarest gold
To daze the eyes of gods and men; his care,
To him by some Fate thus committed! What,
One asks, persuaded him his son was not
As other sons born on the Mincius shore? ...
Could his father see a poet in the bud?
What did he know of poets? What was proof
That his boy was a poet? Surely not
That trifling epigram: "Beneath these stones
Ballista buried lies," and so forth; lines
That many a schoolboy equals when the rod
Lies close beside the magisterial hand;
Such as proud mothers hoard with the last curl!

  His mother! Was it she who had the eyes,
The wit, to separate between her sons,
The genius, and the two of common clay?
She had -- so runs the talk among folk here --
More than mere human power. Her father's
    name,
Magius, forsooth! a mage! And she from him
Derived some wizard force! Well, be it so.
It were no stranger than the truth exact;
Where genius is, there is some magic always
That is not to explain. So Vergil went
A different road from those his brothers' feet
Followed to goals obscure. From Mincius'
    shore
Mantua took him; then Cremona next;
Then Mediolanum, ere he went to Rome
To hear Epidius lecture (O ye gods!

Can you not hear his flowery periods
Wind in slow convolutions on their way?)
And end among the mightiest of the world,
Augustus' friend, Maecenas' intimate.
        But all this to you! 'Tis carrying owls
To Athens! -- Where was I on my journeying
From Andes to the Mincius? ...

In this further passage we have not time to follow
our pilgrim, for all the fascination of the farmer-
fisherman in whose boat he crossed the Mantuan lake,
the present owner (so he held) of what was once
Vergil's farm, his very own, and of how Palio bought
from him a papyrus carrying a copy of a pastoral
poem composed in far-off Libya by the farmer's
soldier-son, a legionary. To this pastoral we shall
return when we briefly glance at Vergil's Eclogues.
But now must come an accounting for the blank verse
I have been reading. It was, I hope, familiar to not a
few of you, for I think it bears re-reading and has, I
believe, given us here today a sensitive account of
Vergil's origins. The author of these fictional letters
in verse to Pliny is George Meason Whicher, born in
Iowa in 1860, for twenty-five years Professor of
Latin and Greek in Hunter College (1899-1924),
Professor in Charge of the School of Classical Studies
of the American Academy in Rome in 1921, and in the
following year created Doctor of the University of
Padua, fifteen years before his death in 1937 after an
extended retirement. The letters, twelve in all (I
have quoted from two), form a volume by themselves
entitled Vergiliana and published in Amherst,
Massachusetts, in 1931. 5
        Whicher's Palio has brought us well into Vergil's
maturity, perhaps to the very time when four men of
letters, Vergil himself, the two poets who were later
to be his literary executors -- Lucius Varius and
Plotius Tucca -- and Horace, who describes the trip
(Satires 1.5), kept their patron Maecenas company as
he journeyed from Rome southward to negotiate the
"treaty of Tarentum" with Antony in the year 37 B.C.
In the field of studies Vergil had passed from rhetoric
to philosophy, especially the Epicurean philosophy,
while in literary composition he was already well
established. After various early essays in verse,

such as the poems of the Appendix Vergiliana in part
may either represent or reflect,[6] Vergil had produced
his first definitive work, the ten pastoral poems, the
Bucolics or Eclogues. These were begun when he was
twenty-eight and were three or more years in the
writing. The state journey of 37 B.C. fell early in the
next period of Vergil's career as poet, the seven years
that brought forth the four books of the Georgics, an
account of the farmer's life and his occupations.[7]
From this he was to pass definitively to what appears
to have been attracting him for years -- a plan to
compose an epic on Rome. Like the composition of
the Georgics, the work of the epic was mainly carried
on in or near Naples, though parts may have been
produced in Sicily, or even in Greece -- for in these
years may fall Vergil's voyage to Greece that Horace
sings of in the Third Ode of the First Book. In the
eleven years that Vergil devoted to the composition of
the Aeneid, the last of his life, he was in frequent
touch with Augustus, even when the latter was absent
in Spain (26 and 25 B.C.). The poet declined, however, to send him a draft of the parts of the poem
already completed. Some three years later Vergil
was more obliging. Much of the poem was then in all
but final shape, and from this Vergil read to Augustus,
Donatus tells us,

> three books in all, the second, fourth, and
> sixth. The last of these produced a remarkable
> effect on Octavia, who was present at the reading,
> for it is said that when he reached the verses
> about her son [who had recently died], 'Tu
> Marcellus eris...,' she fainted and was with
> difficulty revived.[8]

...Calabri rapuere...

The second segment of Vergil's epitaph brings us
to his death, and Donatus gives us here again the
basic evidence:[9]

> In the fifty-second year of his age [that is,
> in 19 B.C.], wishing to give the final touch to
> the "Aeneid," [Vergil] determined to go away
> to Greece and Asia, and after devoting three

entire years to the sole work of improving his
poem, to give up the rest of his life wholly to
philosophy. But having begun his journey, and
at Athens meeting Augustus, who was on his
way back to Rome from the Orient, he resolved
not to part from the emperor and even to return
with him; but in the course of a visit to the
neighbouring town of Megara in a very hot sun,
he was taken with fever, and added to his dis-
order by continuing his journey; hence on his
arrival at Brundisium he was considerably
worse, and died there on the eleventh day before
the Kalends of October, in the consulship of
Gnaeus Sentius and Quintus Lucretius.

From Donatus's Vita Vergilii I pass to quite another
text:

Of the seven high-built vessels that followed
one another [toward the harbor of Brundisium],
keels in line, only the first and last ... belonged
to the war-fleet; the remaining five ... were of
an ornate structure in keeping with the Augustan
imperial rank, and the middle one, the most
sumptuous ... bore under the purple sails,
festive and grand, the tent of the Caesar. Yet
on the ship that immediately followed was the
poet of the Aeneid and death's signet was graved
upon his brow.

A prey of seasickness, held taut by the
constant threat of its outbreak, he had not dared
to move the whole day long. ... So he lay there,
he the poet of the Aeneid, he Publius Vergilius
Maro, he lay there with ebbing consciousness,
almost ashamed of his helplessness, at odds
with such a fate, and he stared into the pearly
roundness of the heavenly bowl: why then had
he yielded to the importunity of Augustus? why
then had he forsaken Athens? Fled now the hope
that the hallowed and serene sky of Homer
would favor the completion of the Aeneid, fled
every single hope for the boundless new life
which was to have begun, ... fled the hope for
the miracle of knowledge and the healing through
knowledge. Why had he renounced it? Willingly?
No!

Then a few pages on:

> He assured himself that the chest with the
> manuscript of the Aeneid stood undisturbed
> near him, and, blinking into the deeply-sinking
> western day-star, he pulled his robe up to his
> chin; he was cold.

These English words are those of an American
poet, Jean Starr Untermeyer, and they are found near
the beginning of her translation, published in 1945, of
a then new novel -- "poem" is what she called it -- by
the Austrian poet and dramatist, Hermann Broch,
entitled The Death of Virgil.[10] Here is a work that
seems as yet to have little affected our thinking about
the poet Vergil and the man Vergil and yet, for all its
massiveness and intricate involvement, may have a
good deal to tell us -- us especially, Broch's own
contemporaries, older and younger. The book contains nearly 500 large pages; through no fault, I feel
sure, of either author or translator, it is hard to
comprehend. In one, quite hurried reading, I have by
no means grasped well its force or its message, but
I think that some of you would want to try, as I mean
to try again.
    To state it very superficially, the book is about
the last hours of the prostrate poet and of what happened to the chest with the manuscript, until after
an extended interview with Augustus the poet abandons
his decision to have the manuscript burned and yields
it to Varius and Tucca, fixing in his will the terms
which will govern the editing. The emperor and these
two fellow poets, along with a physician, Charondas of
Cos, are the leading clearly human figures. Prominent, though entering only as a part of the poet's
"tidal remembrance of things ... past,"[11] is the one
woman whom Donatus mentions as having had a
liaison with Vergil, Plotia Hieria, who here -- if I
read aright -- represents the forces that would lead
Vergil away from concern for poetry. Over against
her is set a boy, sometimes quite clearly present in
body (for example in the compelling scenes in which
he sees to conveying the poet from the piers to the
imperial palace in Brundisium, he himself carrying
the manuscript), sometimes, like Plotia, a voice and

in memory or imagination a form without a body, but
in either case -- again, if I read aright -- the impulse
to poetry and a poet's life, present and future. Of the
four parts into which the book is divided -- Water,
Fire, Earth, Air -- the third, "Earth -- the Expectation," would be the most interesting to a Classicist,
embracing as it does the long interviews between the
poet and the emperor and between the poet and his
future editors and executors of his will. The will
itself is dictated in our very hearing.

To a suggestion from Vergil that Lucius Varius,
himself a poet, will find it hard to limit himself in
preparing the Aeneid for publication "to merely
textual corrections," Lucius replies:

> "I would fight shy of wanting to correct any
> verse by Virgil ... not a word should be added,
> not a word struck out, for I see clearly that this
> is your wish, and that only in this way can one
> meet it."
> "So it is, my Lucius."
> "... but, Virgil, what are we to do about the
> verses that you once called waiting-stones?"
> The waiting-stones indeed! They were still
> there, those parenthetical verses which were
> later to be replaced by perfected ones -- ah
> now they would never be replaced. It was not
> good to think of it, and speech had again become
> labored: "Leave them as they are, Lucius."[12]

... tenet nunc Parthenope...

The grave at Naples now stands before us, and the
epitaph itself, the latter suggesting the old question
whether Vergil himself did indeed compose it,[13] the
former inviting a history of the site of the tomb --
whether the real one which long ago was submerged
(because, says Whicher's Palio[14] --

> Amphitrite and her watery train
> Covet the tomb of Vergil for their realm
> And strive to wrest it from the solid earth),

or the columbarium of post-Vergilian date which for
at least 500 years has been identified with the burial
place of Vergil. I leave aside both the literary

question and the topography, and come instead to a
legendary event of Nero's reign located at Vergil's
tomb and to certain reflections of that event in
mediaeval literature. In passing, however, we may
note that at one time other inscriptions marked the
site. The antiquarian Cocchia, in 1888, in the
course of a richly documented account of the tomb
area, [15] was pleading for governmental ownership
and for making the site generally available to the
public. Perhaps then, he wrote, we would see rise
again an inscription that once had invited the passer-
by to pause for a moment before the poet's grave:

SISTE VIATOR QVAESO PAVCA LEGITO
HIC MARO SITVS EST

This inscription, in 1685, was seen -- or at least
reported as found recently (nuper repertum) -- by the
Benedictine scholar, Jean Mabillon, who remarks
upon the brevity and elegance of the text. Thinking
of the verbosity of the tomb inscriptions of his own
time -- and by such memorials he was himself to be
honored -- Mabillon observed: "These days no
epitaph has a fine ring unless it forms an entire
book."[16] Entering, albeit with difficulty, into what
was regarded as Vergil's tomb-chamber, the Benedictine visitor saw an urn with the "distichon vul-
gatum." Whether the couplet Mabillon saw was our
own "Mantua me genuit" or an adaptation likewise
ending "Pascua rura duces," I cannot say. [17]
    No epigraphical problem attaches to the story to
which we now come, part of the legend of Vergil the
Magician, Vergil the Necromancer. [18] We learn from
St. Luke (Acts 28.13f.) that St. Paul the Apostle
landed in Italy near Naples, at Puteoli, and there
tarried seven days before setting out for Rome, his
journey's end. While in those parts, legend has it,
the Apostle visited Vergil's tomb and sadly voiced his
regret that he had come some years too late to convert him to Christ. While there may be yet older
traces of this story in Celtic hagiography, [19] the
oldest expression of this legend known to me is a
highly influential Old French work of the thirteenth
century, assigned now to Maitre Gossouin (formerly
to Gauthier of Metz); entitled Image du monde, it

comprised a popular encyclopedia of general knowledge.[20] The text that concerns us we have not only in
more than one form of the French original but also in
a Middle English version published by Caxton, in his
Mirrour of the World, the first illustrated book to be
printed in England. I'll here adapt and modernize the
Caxton text:[21]

> Certain philosophers there were that through
> their knowledge and understanding prophesied
> the holy time of the coming of Jesus Christ,
> such as Vergil, who lived in the time of Caesar
> at Rome ...; for he said that a new lineage had
> come down from high heaven [Ec]. 4. 7], that
> would perform wonders on the earth and by
> whom the devil would be overcome. These
> words Saint Paul had seen and highly valued,
> and it was of Vergil that he spoke when, with a
> heart sorrowing because he had not been a
> Christian, he said, "Truly would I have rendered
> and given thee over to God, hadst thou been living
> when I came to thee."

The tomb is only implicit in the words, "came to
thee," vouched for by both the Old French and Middle
English texts, but it is plainly mentioned in what may
well rank as the classic expression of the legend --
six verses in Stabat mater form that I feel sure are
familiar to everyone here:

> Ad Maronis mausoleum
> Ductus, fudit super eum
> Piae rorem lacrimae;
> Quem te, inquit, reddidissem
> Si te vivum invenissem,
> Poetarum maxime.

John Addington Symonds, in 1877, gave us this
rendering:[22]

> When to Maro's tomb they brought him
> Tender grief and pity wrought him
> To bedew the stone with tears;
> What a saint might I have crowned thee,
> Had I only living found thee,

Poet first and without peers!

Among other resemblances, the contrary-to-fact
condition has its counterpart not only in Caxton's
Mirrour but in the Old French source of that work,
the Image du monde. While, then, it seems likely
that the idea embraced in the six verses goes back to
the Image or to its sources, we are left uninformed as
to the frame in which these isolated lines immediately
fit. Nearly two hundred years ago, when the single
stanza was published by Saverio Bettinelli, authority
was adduced declaring that the lines were drawn from
a sequence formerly sung at Mantua in the Mass of
St. Paul. Since then, however, Bettinelli's source
-- a d'Este manuscript of a work by one Giovanni
(Francesco) Piccinardi of Cremona[23] -- has been
rarely mentioned and never, it would seem, hunted
down, even when there may be a chance that the work
that gave Bettinelli one stanza might yield others, if
not the sequence entire, and thus perhaps give
further indication of honor once paid Vergil by the
Church in his native Mantua.

Investigation of the "Ad Maronis mausoleum" was
discouraged, it appears, through a suspicion, voiced
by influential writers, that the lines are spurious.
Here enters a Catholic jurist of the early and middle
nineteenth century, poet and friend of Goethe's,
Johann Friedrich Heinrich Schlosser, who, in 1851,
wrote that he had learned the lines in 1812 from the
mouth of his brother, since deceased. Of Mantua the
brother must have said nothing, for Schlosser states
that, in an attempt to trace the "Ad Maronis" to its
source, he made enquiries in 1835 at Naples and
Pozzuoli (the ancient Puteoli), only to find nothing to
confirm the actual existence of the sequence.[24] Five
years after Schlosser's publication of the verses along
with a disheartening report of their genuineness, the
hymnologist, H. A. Daniel,[25] reprinted the stanza
from Schlosser and made this suggestion: "Fortasse
stropha deprompta est ex illa sequentia, quae
Bettinellio teste (Del resorgimento d'Italia tom. II.
p. 18. not.) per non nulla medii aevi saecula apud
Mantuanos decantata est in honorem Virgilii." Given
the virtual identity of Schlosser's lines and those
published by Bettinelli,[26] Daniel's "fortasse" almost

suggests that he had not read Bettinelli, of whose
source, at any rate, the Piccinardi manuscript at
Modena, he has not a word to say, any more than has
Domenico Comparetti, in whose Vergil in the Middle
Ages the "Ad Maronis" is perhaps most frequently
read.   The handling given the piece by Schlosser and
Daniel has led to its virtual neglect by hymnologists
-- it has no place in the fifty-five volumes of the
Analecta hymnica medii aevi -- while Vergilian
scholarship tends, in this case, to ask no questions.
These remarkable lines stand, then, in an ambiguous
position, a position from which an attempt should be
made -- first at Modena or Cremona or, if such
there be, in the papers of Saverio Bettinelli -- to
disengage it.

...Cecini[27] pascua rura duces.
    Under this final segment of the epitaph will fall
a few remarks prompted by Vergil's poems themselves or by work done directly on them.
    First the Eclogues, which for all their occasional
quality have exercised a strong influence on European
poetry. Professor Duckworth's report of Vergilian
scholarship records a particular emphasis on the
Eclogues, especially the Fourth.   Recently Professor
Courcelle of Paris has taught us that the Christian
exegesis of this poem is not single but manifold.   His
intricate study of the Messianic Eclogue in development of this thesis matches an earlier analysis he
made of the reaction of the Church Fathers to the
Vergilian underworld.[28] New mediaeval texts
relevant to both of these enquiries will soon be
brought out from this University in the editio princeps
of a long Biblical poem from eleventh-century France,
the De nuptiis Christi et ecclesiae of Fulcoius of
Beauvais.[29] And twentieth-century America, both
North and South, has its contribution to make as well,
for I must not forget that we were to come back to the
Palio of George M. Whicher's fictional letters and to
a papyrus that Palio purchased from the ferryman on
the Mincius. The roll, Palio tells us, contained a
bucolic poem written by the ferryman's elder son, a
soldier campaigning in distant Libya. With its
double refrain it is an amoebaean poem, in which two
shepherds tell of their longing for a third, who had

left the Mantuan countryside, Micon his name in the
poem, but (whispers Mr. Whicher) in fact Vergil himself.

> Sweet-gliding Mincius! hear thou my strain
> And bear it southward where my love is gone.

This is the refrain sung by Menas, alternating with
that of Damon:

> O Echo! Echo! listen while I sing;
> Repeat my longing till my love return.

Mr. Whicher's charming poem[30] met with unexpected
fortune, a Spanish verse rendering in 1937 by the
distinguished Ecuadorian Jesuit, Father Aurelio
Espinosa Pólit,[31] and from the same talented hand a
second version, in which the English plaint of Menas
and Damon rings now with the full resonance of
Latin:

> O Minci tacite labens, has suscipe voces,
> Quoque Micon, me cura, latet, cito perfer ad
>   austros!

> O Echo, cantum exaudi! Echo, disce querelam,
> Perque auras itera, donec coniungar amanti!

Among the established imitators of the Eclogues
in English stands John Milton, both in various English
poems and especially in his Latin Epitaphium
Damonis, a lament for his dear friend Charles
Deodati, who died in London when Milton was
travelling in Deodati's native Italy. Here too we may
note the refrain, this one adapted from the line with
which Vergil closes the Eclogues:

> Ite domum saturae, venit Hesperus, ite capellae.

Milton's imitation is close:

> Ite domum impasti, domino iam non vacat, agni --

translated by Miss Helen Waddell[32] as

> Away, my lambs, unfed; your shepherd heeds you
> not!

But it is, of course, not primarily with the Eclogues
in mind that we associate Milton with Vergil. J. W.
Mackail showed how in weighing the influence of
Vergil upon another writer of epic we must bear in
mind four separate elements -- the epic structure,
the ornament, the rhythm and phrasing, and the
diction -- and added: "It is in Milton, and perhaps in
Milton alone, that all these four together are absorbed
and re-created."33 This close relation of the two
poets lies behind much of a course of lectures given
in 1941 by Mr. C. S. Lewis, Fellow of Magdalen
College, Oxford, and published (Oxford 1942) under the
title, A Preface to Paradise Lost. Not emphasized by
Professor Duckworth or perhaps even overlooked in
his survey, this little book is a capital introduction to
the Aeneid -- and to Homer too -- bringing out with a
charm and clarity hard to match the stylistic differences between the "secondary" epic (which Vergil,
like Milton, represents) and the "primary" epic of
Homer and Beowulf.

The mention of one Oxford scholar of our time
suggests another -- the late Monsignor Ronald A.
Knox, whose contributions to the Vergilian tradition
include his autobiography, A Spiritual Aeneid, and a
delightful edition (Oxford 1924) of Books VII-IX of the
Aeneid, now out of print, I fear. We shall doubtless
look not in vain for Vergilian traces in an edition of
some of Knox's own Latin verses that will soon be
reaching us from England. -- A posthumously published volume of essays by Msgr. Knox, Literary
Distractions (1958), contains, along with one of his
excellent studies of English Translation, a paper
called "A Neglected Poet (James Grainger)."
Grainger, who remarks Knox (p. 99), "served Apollo
with the lyre and lancet indifferently," migrated from
England to the West Indies, where he found the
material for a work in verse, The Sugar-cane: A
Poem in Four Books (published in 1764). "The
selection and grouping of the matter is bad Virgil.
The style is bad Milton." So affirms Msgr. Knox·
(p. 100) and proceeds with his characteristic wit and
skill to prove it. But Grainger, with his four long

books in blank verse on Some Art or Other or How to
Do Something or Other, is characteristic of eighteenth-
century English didactic, which could moreover,
among these late descendants of the Georgics, produce
poems that rise to the level of all but first-class
poetry. A venture more successful than Grainger's
was the earlier work of John Philips -- Cyder (of the
year 1708). The opening lines follow almost exactly
the arrangement of the proem of the Georgics:

> What soil the apple loves, what care is due
> To orchats, timeliest when to press the fruits,
>   etc.

The finest examples of this eighteenth-century English
didactic are Thomson's Seasons and Cowper's Task.
"There may be little or no deliberate imitation,"
writes J. A. K. Thomson of these works;[34] "but it is
not credible that a classically educated poet of their
century who wished to describe natural scenery and the
procession of the seasons would not think at once of
the Georgics as the great classic example of how to
treat such themes. And it is evident that Thomson and
Cowper had it often in their thoughts." Our own
century has also seen an English poet, Victoria
Sackville-West, produce a work after this order, The
Land, published in 1926,[35] and divided, like
Thomson's masterpiece, into four parts corresponding
to the seasons. Vergil is present, especially in the
indirect way in which he stands behind Thomson and
Cowper. The last page, however, opens with an
apostrophe to Vergil:

> O Mantuan! that sang the bees and vines,
> The tillage and the flocks ...

which leads, after a few lines, to the very end of the
poem:

> Nature, tender enemy, harsh friend,
> Takes from [man] soon the little that she gave,
> Yet for his span will labour to defend
> His courage, that his soul be not a slave,
> Whether on waxen tablet or on loam,
> Whether with stylus or with share and heft

The record of his passage he engrave,
And still, in toil, takes heart to love the rose.

Then thought I, Virgil! how from Mantua reft,
Shy as a peasant in the courts of Rome,
Thou tooks't the waxen tablets in thy hand,
And out of anger cut calm tales of home.

"Out of anger" -- may I ask you to bear that
phrase in mind in connection with a judgment of Vergil
to be presented now in the single paragraph that my
space permits me to devote here to the "duces" of our
epitaph, the Aeneid. The last fruit left in our "lanx
satura" is an unorthodox paper which I had lost for
more than a decade until Professor Duckworth's
survey brought it once more to my attention. It is the
work of Francesco Sforza and, dated from Nicosia in
Cyprus, was published in the Classical Review for
July, 1935 (49. 97-108). It maintains the thesis
("impossible" Duckworth calls it) that the Aeneid
was nothing other than a bitter attack on Rome and
Augustus, that Vergil portrayed Aeneas and the
Trojans as treacherous and despicable and the Italians
as loyal and chivalrous -- all this as one of the ways
in which the poet showed his angry resentment at
Augustus for the seizure of his and others' farms at
Mantua and the murder of his friend, Cornelius
Gallus. Sforza has more recently resumed the theme
in an Italian monograph, and at least one English
scholar has written to defend him.[36] I mention the
matter here for this reason. When I read Sforza's
article some ten years ago I could not produce for
myself an adequate refutation; yet a refutation was
needed, and some day, I said, I'd try again. Now,
the Sforza thesis may be yet stronger than it was
before, but that only increases the challenge. I invite
you to see, along with me, whether the challenge can
be successfully met. There could be worse ways to
test our understanding of the heart and mind of
Vergil.

FOOTNOTES

[1] The essential bibliographical detail not found in
the text will be given in note 2.

[2]Professor Duckworth's Recent Work on Vergil:
A Bibliographical Survey, 1940-1956 is sold by the
Secretary-Treasurer (currently Professor Charles T.
Murphy, Oberlin College, Oberlin, Ohio), The
Vergilian Society of America, for 75¢ (for 50¢ to
members of the Vergilian Society). -- Büchner's
article, "P. Vergilius Maro" in the Pauly-Wissowa-
Kroll Realencyclopädie, 2te Reihe, 8 (1955/8) 1021-
1486 (also published separately). -- Publishers
of W. F. Jackson Knight, Roman Vergil, are Faber
and Faber of London (2nd ed. of 1945 has appeared in
several printings). -- For Sellar and most of the
other older books listed see J. A. Nairn's Classical
Hand-list (3rd ed. Oxford 1953) 69-71. -- A. M.
Guillemin, Virgile: Poète, artiste et penseur (Paris
1951); V. Pöschl, Die Dichtkunst Virgils: Bild und
Symbol in der Aeneis (Innsbruck 1950); E. Paratore,
Virgilio (2nd ed. Florence 1954). -- The Oxford University Press published R. G. Austin's Fourth Aeneid
(1955) and Sir Frank Fletcher's Sixth Aeneid (1941);
the Harvard University Press, A. S. Pease's
Fourth (1935). -- R. S. Conway's edition of Aeneid I
(Cambridge 1935) and H. E. Butler's Aeneid VI
(Oxford 1920) are, unhappily, out of print. Just
published (in England) is R. D. Williams' Aeneid V. --
T. E. Page's Vergil with commentary makes up
three independent volumes in Macmillan & Co.'s
Classical Series (American agents, New York's St.
Martin's Press): Buc. and Georg., Aen. 1-6, Aen.
7-12. -- G. Highet, The Classical Tradition (New
York 1949; also paperback from original publishers,
Oxford Univ. Press); J. A. K. Thomson, The Classical Background of English Literature (London 1948);
id., Classical Influences on English Poetry (London
1951); R. R. Bolgar, The Classical Heritage and its
Beneficiaries (Cambridge 1954). -- The Editio
Harvardiana of Servius, ed. E. K. Rand et al.
(currently the chief editor is A. F. Stocker) is published by the American Philological Association;
vol. II, 1946. -- Colin Hardie (ed.), Vitae Vergilianae
antiquae (Oxford 1954), forming with R. Ellis's
Appendix Vergiliana (which precedes) a volume in the
series Oxford Classical Texts. -- A convenient guide
to much of the pre-Bimillenium literature is Felix
Peeters, Bibliography of Vergil, published by the

American Classical League as Bulletin 28 (April
1933). -- Macmillan & Co. (London) and St. Martin's
Press (New York) publish Cooper's Introduction
(1952).

[3]Donatus, Vita Vergilii 36 (lines 138-9 Hardie).
The epitaph is also given in the Vita Probiana of
Vergil (lines 20-21 Hardie) and in St. Jerome's
Chronica (the seventh of Hardie's excerpts). The
English version is G. M. Whicher's, incorporated in
Vergiliana (cited at n. 5) 95. For a variety of imita-
tions see A. S. Pease, "Mantua me genuit," Classical
Philology 35 (1940) 180-182; the line in Lucan, A.
Riese, Anthologia Latina 2 (2nd ed. Leipzig 1906)
No. 486c; Eliot, Wasteland 293f. ("'Highbury bore
me. Richmond and Kew / Undid me.'").

[4]Gilbert Highet, Poets in a Landscape (London
1957) 56ff.; Rand, Quest (Cambridge [Mass.] 1930).

[5]See Who's Who in America, vols. 19 and 20.
Permission to quote thus extensively from Mr.
Whicher's book, now out of print, was most kindly
granted by the widow of his son, Mrs. George F.
Whicher (collaborations of father and son: On the
Tibur Road, a Freshman's Horace [Princeton 1911];
Roba d'Italia [Amherst 1930]). The quotations are
from pp. 38, 39 ("the well-worn ..."), 50-54 ("He
too ..."); the Vintage Hymn appears on pp. 42-45.
For the epitaph of Ballista, see Donatus (Vita Verg.
17; lines 52-56 Hardie) and Servius (Vita Verg.,
lines 10-13 Hardie).

[6]See Duckworth, Recent Work, sect. 3. For a
delightful discussion of one poem of the Appendix, see
E. Fraenkel, "The Culex," Journal of Roman Studies
42 (1952) 1-9.

[7]It is refreshing to note that one admirable
critic -- L. P. Wilkinson, to whom we owe excellent
monographs on Horace (1945) and Ovid (1955) -- has
recently maintained that the poem was not written to
support a "back to the land" policy: "The Intention
of Virgil's Georgics," Greece and Rome 19 (1950) 19-
28.

[8]Donatus, Vita Vergilii 32 (lines 110ff. Hardie);
trans. J. C. Rolfe (Loeb Classical Library
Suetonius II 475).

[9]Ibid. 35 (lines 125ff. Hardie); Rolfe's Suet. II

475, 477. On this passage and other related texts, see the valuable discussion of W. T. Avery, in Classical Journal 52 (1956/7) 225-229.

[10]Permission to quote from the book (pp. 11f., 16, and infra 430) was generously granted by the publishers, Pantheon Books, Inc.

[11]The phrase is Hamilton Basso's, used in his review of Broch's novel in the New Yorker (June 23, 1945) p. 64f. See also Orville Prescott, in the Yale Review 35 (Sept.-Jan. 1945/6) 190f.; Leonard Bacon, in the Saturday Review of Literature (June 30, 1945) p. 11.

[12]The "waiting-stones" seem to be the "tibicines" of Donatus, Vita Vergilii 24 (line 88 Hardie).

[13]Brief discussion by Pease, op. cit. (n. 3) 180, with further references.

[14]Vergiliana (cited at n. 5) 93, in the course of Epist. 8. The tomb (cf. Statius, Silvae 4.4.51-55) figures also in Epist. 2, 3, 10, while these letters and others also (Epist. 6, 9, 11, 12) deal with Silius Italicus, thus serving as commentary on Pliny, Epist. 3.7 (on the death of Silius) and Martial 11.48f.

[15]E. Cocchia, "La tomba di Virgilio," Archivio storico per le provincie napoletane 13 (1888) 511-557, 631-744, esp. 725. Cocchia, while giving no evidence, says the inscription was erected shortly after Vergil's death, but T. Mommsen ignores the item in the relevant volume of the Corpus inscriptionum latinarum, 10 (1883), even among the "falsae." Mommsen may well have regarded the inscription as mediaeval or modern work that did not pretend to be anything else. If, however, Mabillon had so thought it (see the following note), he would hardly have paid special attention to it in a work like his "Iter Italicum." -- John Eustace, who visited Naples in May/June 1802, quotes a certain Eugenio, "an author of 1625," as saying that a stone bearing the inscription "SISTE ... SITUS EST" had been found in a neighboring villa (A Classical Tour through Italy, chap. XXIII).

[16]J. Mabillon, Museum Italicum I (Paris 1687), Iter p. 113, quoting the text with the opening "SISTITE VIATORES, QUAESO PAUCA LEGITE. HIC ..." Mabillon adds the remark: "Nihil brevius, nihil concinnius. Nunc non belle sonat epitaphium,

nisi librum efficiat."

[17]The adaptation runs as follows:

> Qui cineres? tumuli haec vestigia; conditur olim
> Ille hic qui cecinit pascua rura duces.

Cf. Pease, op. cit. (n. 3) 181; Guida d'Italia del Touring Club Italiano, Italia meridionale II (Milan 1931) 306; Cocchia, op. cit. (n. 15) 513 n. 2.

[18]In addition to Comparetti's invaluable work (cited n. 19), we have J. W. Spargo, Virgil the Necromancer (Harvard Studies in Comparative Literature 10; Cambridge [Mass.] 1934). -- For Vergil the Prophet of Christ as a figure in the mediaeval religious plays, see Chap. XXI in Karl Young, The Drama of the Medieval Church (Oxford 1933) II 125ff., esp. 132, 143, 151, 164; also 456.

[19]D. Comparetti (trans. E. F. M. Benecke), Vergil in the Middle Ages (London 1895) 98 n. 6 (new edition of the Italian text, I [Florence 1937] 121 n. 1).

[20]See O. H. Prior, L'image du monde de Maître Gossouin: Rédaction en prose ... (Lausanne and Paris 1913) 1-13. Prior dates the three recensions (two of them in verse) in the years 1246-1248; names Gossouin as author of the first redaction in verse and of that in prose (Gauthier may have authored the second redaction). Cf. Spargo 310, 324f.

[21]Caxton's Mirrour of the World (ed. O. H. Prior; Early English Text Society, Extra Series 110 [1913 (for 1912)]) 25. For the Old French verses see Carl Fant, L'image du monde: Poème inédit du milieu du XIIIe siècle (in Uppsala Universitets Årsskrift 1886) 12. Of the text-form reported by Fant, lines 737ff. (and especially lines 745ff.) are relevant here; Fant in part summarizes, in part transcribes. "v. 737. Au moyen âge [Virgile] était ... considéré comme magicien, voire comme prophète, prédisant l'arrivée de Jésus Christ. Saint Paul, ayant vu ses écrits: (v. 745ss.) "Dist de lui a cuer irascu: / Ha! quel ge t'eüsse rendu / A Deu, se tu fusse vescuz / Tant que ge fusse a toi venuz!'" A variant form of the verse redaction is given by Fant 12 n. 2. For the Old French prose (Part I, chap. 5) see Prior, L'image 73 (with remarks p. 32-33). See also

Spargo 20, 61, 115.

[22]Renaissance in Italy: The Revival of Learning
(new ed. London 1912) 46 n. 1.

[23]Saverio Bettinelli, Delle lettere e delle arti
mantovane ... Discorsi due accademici ... (Mantua
1774) 19f., the first printing of the "Ad Maronis."
The verses had been included in the author's Del
risorgimento d'Italia (Parte I, Capo quinto: "Mille
trecento"), but this work was not printed until 1775,
at Bassano (2 vols.; I 194 n. a for the "Ad Maronis").
An inadequate reference has been given in Comparetti
(cited n. 19; first published 1873, 1896[2]), even in the
new Italian edition (loc. cit. supra n. 19). "II,
p. 18," a reference, though Comparetti does not say
so, to the 4-vol. edition, Milan 1819 (owing to an ill-
advised reworking of the footnotes our passage does
not appear in the Bassano printing of 1786). In the
Mantua Discorso, "Francesco" is not included as part
of the name of Piccinardi, whose identity I have not
established.

[24]J. F. H. Schlosser, Die Kirche in ihren
Liedern durch alle Jahrhunderte (1st ed. Mainz 1851/
52) I 416, (2nd ed. Freiburg im Br. 1863) I 382
(No. 48), 474. -- Schlosser composed additions to
the poem "O Roma nobilis"; cf. B. M. Peebles, in
American Benedictine Review 1 (1950) 82f., 92.

[25]Thesaurus hymnologicus 5 (Leipzig 1856) 266f.
(No. 534).

[26]The verses that Schlosser had orally from his
brother show line 4 in the form "Quantum, inquit, te
fecissem," and this is repeated by Daniel (loc. cit.)
and J. Kehrein, Lateinische Sequenzen des
Mittelalters (Mainz 1873) 282 (No. 393). -- In
Bettinelli, Del risorgimento (loc. cit.), a variant,
"Oh te qualem reddidissem ...," appears in a form of
the lines reported as found "nelle loro [of the Mantu-
ans] storia di Paolo Florio").

[27]In the oral version of this paper there followed
here a brief treatment of Vergil in music, based
largely on an article by W. O. Strunk, Musical
Quarterly 16 (1930) 482-497. School and college
groups may find a practical interest in a plainsong
setting of Aen. 2.274-286, given by F. Liuzzi, in
Studi medievali 5 (1932) 78-80, who refers also (67ff.)

to 10th/11th-century MSS (Florence, Bibl. Laur., Ashb. 23; Berne 239) containing similar settings of Aen. 2.42-49; 4.424-436, 651-658; 12.945-946), with a warning (71, 77) that such transcriptions of the neumatic notation of these manuscripts are only approximately accurate. -- Earlier bibliography in Peeters, Bibliography (cited n. 2) 74f. (music), 69-74 (art).

[28]P. Courcelle, "L'exégèse chrétienne de la quatrième Eglogue," Revue des études anciennes 59 (1957) 294-319; "Les pères de l'Eglise devant les Enfers virgiliens," Archives d'histoire doctrinale et littéraire du moyen age 30 (1955) 5-74.

[29]The editor is Sister M. Isaac Jogues, S.S.N.D. (Mt. Mary College, Milwaukee 10, Wisc.); the edition, her Ph.D. dissertation, will appear as Vol. 23 of The Catholic University of America Studies in Medieval and Renaissance Latin.

[30]Vergiliana (cited at n. 5) 60-64 (for the narrative of the purchase of the papyrus, 54-59).

[31]La pastoral vergiliana de Whicher (Quito: Editorial Ecuatoriana 1937); copy in the Library of Congress.

[32]Lament for Damon ... (pp. 12; Privately printed 1943).

[33]Virgil and His Meaning to the World of Today (in series, Our Debt to Greece and Rome; Boston 1922) 137f.

[34]Classical Background (cited n. 2) 78.

[35]London: Heinemann (a number of printings since 1922). Mr. Jackson Knight may well be right in calling The Land "probably the most Vergilian of all recent poems" (Roman Vergil viii).

[36]Duckworth, Recent Work, sect. 6A. F. Sforza, Il più prezioso tesoro spirituale d'Italia (Milan 1952); W. S. Maguinness, "Some Remarks on the Aeneid" (a Virgil Society lecture, 1951; cf. Proceedings of the Classical Association 48 [1951] 23). Cf. Jackson Knight, Roman Vergil 300f.

PART II

SUMMARIES OF SEMINARS

ON METHODS OF LATIN INSTRUCTION
AT THE HIGH SCHOOL LEVEL

Sections A, B, and C

Sister M. Francis McDonald, O.P.; Sister M.
Aquinata Britz, I.H.M.; and Sister Claire Helene
Taylor, S.S.J., Directors

Seminar 1, Methods of Latin Instruction at the
High School Level, was divided into four sections,
three of which were concerned with the problems of
Latin teaching in high schools and academies, and the
fourth, with the teaching of Latin at the high school
level in minor seminaries. This résumé concerns the
work of the first three.

At the first meeting a tentative outline of topics
for discussion, suggested by the workshop announcement and also by the requests made by the participants
at the time of their registration, was presented to the
members. Added to this basic outline on the following
days were the specific suggestions for discussion
which had been made by the members of each section
at the first meeting.

Appropriately, the first issue was the preparation
of the teacher of Latin for the work of the high schools
of today, where it is more important than in any
other area of Latin teaching, perhaps, that teachers
be adequately trained to teach students Latin, to teach
Latin in such a way that it may fulfill its role in the
modern world and be a vehicle of the liberal tradition,
as it has been in the past, and that it may thus provide
a safeguard against the overwhelming imbalance which
threatens our entire educational system. Successful
teaching comes from enthusiasm, breadth and depth of
preparation, and skill in communicating. The ideal
preparation, four years of high school Latin, a college
major, and a Master's degree, cannot, of course, always be attained. It is possible, however, for
teachers to compensate for lack of formal school and
college courses by intensive personal study. The

members of each section were unanimous in upholding
this objective of continued personal study.

The secondary school curriculum was next discussed. Attention was confined to Latin, but it is
hoped that improvement in the status of Latin will
provide an impetus to approach the problem of Greek.
Several suggestions were presented concerning the
introduction of changes into the traditional curriculum,
and many members advocated greater fluidity in
syllabus requirements. The major divisions of
course-content into vocabulary, grammar, translation, composition, and background were retained,
however, and several members prepared a summary
of the scope and content of a four-year program. A
copy of one of these proposed programs, which was
accepted by the other members and which adheres to
the standards of a sound, cultural, and feasible
program -- at least for average and better students --
but which also admits of modification when applied by
reliable judgment, is submitted with this report.

It was decided that new texts for teaching some of
the traditional authors are needed. During the course
of the workshop each member analyzed a particular
text or series of texts. Some of the texts in use require revision. Dissatisfaction is quite generally experienced in the matter of the second year course.
Discussion shifted to the matter of the first year work.
Recommendations were made in each section that the
work of the first year program be intensified. If
students are advanced more quickly and more thoroughly to the stage of reading connected Latin passages
and perhaps some of Caesar (or appropriate substi-
tutes) during the first year, the transition to the
literary selections of the second year, which are
predominantly Caesar, will be made more effectively.
As a consequence, the staples of Cicero for the third
year and Vergil for fourth, with additional selections
from other authors, are acceptable because they will
have been adequately prepared for.

The question of method in general and its role in
the art of teaching was next considered. Caution was
urged against the overemphasis of methods and devices which must ever be ancillary to the fundamental
process of learning.

Discussion of methods in particular followed.

Inasmuch as the formal or "traditional" approach had been considered in connection with the treatment of scope and content, at this point attention was paid chiefly to the newer forms of the inductive or direct method and the approach of structural linguistics. Neither the old, tried method should be declaimed because it is old; nor are the new methods to be accepted simply because they are new. In this whole matter care must be taken that the objectives of the Latin program in our high schools be clearly stated and that our teaching aim to achieve them. Since the main objective of the Latin courses is the comprehension of the literary passages that are read, it follows that everything which contributes to this comprehension must be included in the method of teaching and learning. From the very beginning, aspects of the oral-aural technique for learning sounds, formations, and structure are to be used, but it is essential that from the beginning also there be definite, systematic training in formal grammar and analysis. In each section discussion was held on the three phases of comprehension: reading, translation, and analysis.

Testing programs were next considered. Matters of reliability of standard tests were merely mentioned, but most schools participate in general or standardized programs of some authoritative worth. Criteria for good classroom testing were discussed, and a select bibliography was presented. General dissatisfaction with and evident disapproval of the purely objective type of tests were expressed.

Some attention was given to the questions of correlation of the Latin course with other subject areas and to the matter of integration within the course itself. Extra-curricular or club activities are to be for enrichment purposes, not for entertainment. Several profitable suggestions, with emphasis on reading, creative writing, and related phases of an advanced or "honors" type of work were received.

Throughout the course of the meetings additional problems on selectivity and grouping of students were considered, as were also some which dealt with program arrangement, such as the general two-year terminal course, the regular academic, and the advanced placement programs. The question of Latin in the upper grades in grammar school was considered

quite favorably and the introduction of such a course
was urged, provided that the work be introduced by a
competent teacher of Latin. The current trend of
Latin's giving way to the modern language course in
the first year was also discussed. Most of the members felt that it is not advisable to have the beginning
Latin follow the beginning course in modern language.
Selective grouping was strongly urged wherever this is
practicable. It was indicated also that in the whole
matter of the Latin program in the high school sound
policies of administration must be preserved, and
wholesome "public relations" assistance ought to be
secured.

The enthusiasm and generous spirit of cooperation
manifested in each of the sections made for profitable
discussions and for an exchange of problems and suggested solutions; and Sister Aquinata, Sister Claire
Hélène, and I are grateful for the opportunity that was
ours and for the help and inspiration that the seminar
has been to all of us. We wish to mention particularly
the contributions of the secretaries in each section
and those of the summary-making committees on
content, textbooks, testing, and enrichment activities.

ON LATIN IN THE MINOR SEMINARY
AT THE HIGH SCHOOL LEVEL

Section D

Reverend Hermigild Dressler, O.F.M., Director

The discussions of this seminar differed considerably from those outlined in the report just submitted.
Two specific reasons will explain these differences.
Objectives of the teaching of Latin in the minor
seminary have been clearly defined in many ecclesiastical directives over a long period of time, and the
University has regularly sponsored the Minor
Seminary Conference which carefully planned a
curriculum to achieve the objectives.

The Latin program of the minor seminary at the
high school level in the light of more recent statements
and directives from the Roman Pontiffs and Congregations was the broad topic of discussion in the early
meetings of this seminar. The Enchiridion Clericorum,[1] the Apostolic Constitution Sedes Sapientiae,[2]
and the Letter to Local Ordinaries[3] of the Sacred
Congregation for Seminaries and Universities of
October, 1957, served as source books.

The first meeting of the seminar considered in
some detail the vital importance of properly qualified
Latin teachers even at the very beginning of instruction in Latin. There seemed to be unanimous support
for the proposition that the general seminary program
which prepares candidates for the priesthood is not of
itself adequate teacher training for instructors in the
minor seminary. In fact, the spirit of the most recent
Roman directives seems to call for the Master's
degree, or equivalent training, as the minimum
standard of proper qualification.

The seminar next discussed textbooks and methods
to be used in the teaching of Latin. In both these
areas there seemed to be considerable divergence of
opinion among this group of dedicated teachers.
Consequently, the seminar discussion was limited

primarily to the textbook and method for the first year
of the Latin program; the remaining parts of the program were covered in written reports submitted at the
final meeting. An analysis of the first-year text used
by the members of this seminar showed that, apart
from minor differences in vocabulary and syntax,
most of the textbooks were uniformly poor in the area
of "home-made Latin." Very many textbooks actually
introduced the students to much they will have to un-
learn eventually if they are to gain any appreciation of
Latin literature. Textbooks which seek to introduce
the student to Latin by way of the so-called "easy
Christian and liturgical Latin" have, in addition to the
failing already mentioned, another serious defect.
They invert the historical order and generally engen-
der in the student a false sense of achievement and
mastery of a Latin he really does not understand
precisely because he does not grasp one of its basic
component elements, Classical Latin.

As to the amount of vocabulary and syntax to be
mastered in the first year, the difference of opinion
was not so great as it appeared in the early stages of
the discussion. A rather interesting fact, however,
came to light at this point. Almost all the teachers in
this group admitted that the achievement level of the
class was geared to the pace of the slowest learners.
While all admitted that this situation called for
remedial measures, only one minor seminary[4] actually had procedures which took cognizance of this
matter. In all fairness, however, it must be stated
that practically every teacher was generously doing
much on his own initiative to exploit the full potential
of the rapid learner.

In regard to the method of teaching Latin there
seemed to be a sharp difference of opinion. Perhaps
it should be stressed once more that all agreed upon
the ultimate goals and objectives, but some thought the
objectives could be achieved more easily by newer
methods. The discussion on this point did not arrive
at any definite conclusion, but even the most partisan
members of the group admitted that some methods are
as yet too new and too narrowly tested to yield any
valid data for a sound conclusion. On the other hand
there was some evidence that there is a tendency,
particularly among the less experienced and poorly

trained teachers, to lay the blame for poor results at
the door of faulty method.

Little time remained for the discussion of the rest
of the Latin program in the minor seminary at the
high school level. The majority, however, of the
participants wanted the traditional Caesar (not in
simplified version) in the second year, Cicero in the
third, and Vergil in the fourth. All strongly urged
Latin composition based on the author being read in
class.

FOOTNOTES

[1]Enchiridion Clericorum (Rome [Typis Poly-
glottis Vaticanis] 1938) p. 172; 341; 445; 603-612;
671-683.

[2]Sedes Sapientiae (editio altera Rome 1957),
Articulus 43, pp. 66-68. An English translation of
this Apostolic Constitution was published by the
Catholic University of America Press in 1957.

[3]Acta Apostolicae Sedis 50 (1958) 292-295. An
English translation published in the Bulletin (March
1959) of the Committee on Affiliation, The Catholic
University of America, is reprinted as Appendix C in
these Proceedings.

[4]The members of this seminar group came from
13 states: California, Connecticut, Florida, Illinois,
Louisiana, Massachusetts, Michigan, Minnesota,
Missouri, New Jersey, New York, Oklahoma,
Pennsylvania, and are teaching in twenty-one minor
seminaries.

ON THE COLLEGE PROGRAM IN LATIN

Section A

Josephine P. Bree, Director

The seminar on the teaching of Latin in college included representatives from twenty-one colleges, four of which were junior colleges. They represented thirteen states, from New Hampshire to Minnesota, and south to Maryland and Missouri. Thirteen members had studied previously at Catholic University, six having obtained advanced degrees here. The impressive thing about the group was the desire to be honest and face up to the facts involved in the difficulties each college had with its Classics curriculum. They were present seeking answers, and willing to share their experiences in helping each other. All were obviously dedicated to their field of teaching and highly sensitive to its value and worth in the sum total of humanistic education.

Since many had expressed an interest in specific problems, the discussion of the seminar was centered on these focal points. Each day, however, a short time was spent in discussing questions raised by the excellent lectures we were privileged to hear.

The first point of discussion was the planning of the curriculum, and the choice of authors to be studied. For those students entering college with four years of Latin, the questions raised were chiefly the order in which various authors should be studied, and whether the freshman course should be based on selections from different authors, or on a few authors studied in greater depth. The anthology approach seemed advisable to those thinking of this course as terminal for the majority. Some of those using an anthology preferred a semester of prose and the other of poetry. Others found it more satisfactory to read selections chronologically. Teachers concerned with students likely to concentrate in Latin perhaps favored the reading of single authors. There was no pressure

for agreement, as everyone felt that local conditions
and the teacher's own knowledge of the situation determined the decision. Ten colleges were fortunate
enough to have students majoring in Latin, and all but
one of these required a comprehensive examination at
the end of the senior year. Six offered a seminar
course in the senior year for the purpose of coordi-
nating work done by students in class and by independent reading.

In planning the curriculum there was general
agreement on the inclusion of Cicero, Catullus, Vergil, Horace, Pliny, Tacitus, and some comedy. Other
authors most often included were Lucretius, Sallust,
Ovid, Seneca and Juvenal. Not all colleges offered
Christian Latin. Of those which did, seven gave more
than one semester. The most popular course in this
field was St. Augustine's Confessions, though a few
offered Mediaeval Latin including various authors, and
some favored a course in Liturgical Latin.

All favored the inclusion of prose composition
either as a separate course or concurrently with a
prose author. Only one teacher was trying the writing
of Latin verse. Fluency in conversational Latin was
not a usual goal, but two members of the group
favored conducting advanced courses by speaking Latin
in class.

All agreed in wanting their students to gain both
comprehension and appreciation of the great works of
literature studied. Difficulty lay in finding a proper
balance when insisting on a good translation showing
comprehension of the text, and also when discussing
style, background, and literary value. We recognized
the danger of talking too much about our individual
enthusiasms and prejudices, yet felt the need of
carrying the student beyond comprehension of the text
itself.

There was general agreement on the necessity of
requiring some course in Greek for a Latin major,
but most were limited by local conditions from offer-
ing more than two years, and often from giving more
than one.

It was also felt that there should be a course in
Ancient Civilization as a supplement to the study of
works in the original language, and that courses in
ancient literature in translation should be taught by the

members of departments of Classics. The general
principle was established that a course in literature
in translation must be conducted by a teacher who had
read the works in the original. Though this principle
seemed obvious to us, it had apparently been often
overlooked by those planning the curriculum.

The problem of the student entering college with
two years of Latin (and usually after a lapse of two
years) involved the question of placement examinations
and a review of elementary forms and syntax before
entering into a reading course. Providing that the
students were of good mental calibre, it was thought
that they would soon overcome their handicap and
move into appropriate college courses.

Since an increasing number of students are beginning Latin in college, we spent quite a bit of time,
outside the seminar and in it, examining new textbooks written for this purpose. Some seemed to move
too rapidly, some too slowly, some deferred the
reading of connected passages too long. Several books
were rated very highly, however. More important
than the choice of textbook, we agreed, was the quality
of the teacher, who should be able to adapt a good book
to his own purposes. Most preferred the traditional
approach, but were willing and eager to borrow new
good ideas as they appeared. Almost all, but not all,
favored the learning of Ciceronian Latin before
Christian Latin.

The perennial problem of teaching the student to
read Latin at sight and of freeing him from being a
slave to the dictionary was left unsolved as usual.
Classroom procedure varied according to individual
differences in the teachers.

The members of the seminar did become acquainted with new books and new methods, and seemed
to gain insight into the quality of their own teaching by
comparing their ideas with others. I strongly suspect
that the best work of the seminar was accomplished by
reading in the library, and by discussion in small
groups in the dining rooms and dormitories. Many
were relieved to find their problems not unique and not
without solution.

The attitude of the members of the seminar, undoubtedly good teachers already -- though some were
very young, speaks well for the future of the study of

the Classics in our Catholic colleges throughout the
country.

ON LATIN IN THE MINOR SEMINARY
AT THE COLLEGE LEVEL

Section B

Reverend Simon P. Wood, C.P., Director

Seminar 2B was composed of a group interested solely in the teaching of Latin on a college level in minor seminaries. We came from various parts of the country and represented different dioceses and religious orders; yet we soon realized, from our discussions in and out of the seminar, that we shared to a high degree common outlooks, ambitions, and a very real concern to improve our teaching of Latin. The following remarks are an attempt to summarize the more salient conclusions of our work during the past twelve days.

At the very beginning, we defined the course of our discussions:

(1) the precise objectives the seminary Latin course should have;

(2) the general scholastic quality of the students who come to us;

(3) the curriculum best adapted, and the classroom technique best suited, to achieve our objectives; and

(4) the kind of course, or courses, to be given to students with little or no Latin.

While we were not able to cover all these topics with the same thoroughness, we did touch on them all in a general way. While we did not always find answers, certainly not simple answers, still we believe that we did raise at least many of the right questions.

There are many documents from the Holy See insisting on the results it expects seminary professors to achieve. Therefore, in common with the seminar conducted by Father Dressler, we decided to investigate carefully at the very start just what these documents say, especially Pius XI's <u>Officiorum Omnium</u>

(Aug. 1922), the Apostolic Constitution Sedes Sapientiae (May 1957), and the Letter to Local Ordinaries of the Sacred Congregation for Seminaries and
Universities (Oct. 1957). We also referred to the
helpful papers given at the Minor Seminary Conferences conducted under the auspices of The Catholic
University of America in 1951, 1952, and 1953.

From these documents, it became clear that the
primary objective we must have is a practical one of a
high order: to equip our students with a real facility
in handling Latin, so that they can use it with ease in
their future studies. At the same time, it also became
quite clear that the Holy See insists that this seminary
course must be a cultural, liberal arts course consisting of a literary study of Classical authors and
civilization so important for an appreciation of
Western culture, and also of Christian authors whose
literary qualities and importance give them a place
beside the best Classical writers. An interesting
point was then raised. Does the Holy See expect the
speaking of Latin and the writing of Latin to be an
objective of our course as equally urgent as the reading of Latin? Most of our students, we agreed,
reach us without knowing how to speak Latin, and few
will be called on, in practice, to speak Latin after
they leave us. After some interesting observations
and discussions, the majority of us felt that the
central objective of our teaching must be to develop a
facile reading of Latin, difficult as that is, while we
should also do what we can, in the circumstances in
which each of us is placed, to cultivate a speaking and
writing facility as well.

After establishing the objective, we turned to the
concrete problem of why it is that we get results so
little commensurate with the efforts expended, both by
ourselves, and also -- perhaps -- by the students.
The first answer that suggested itself was that the
students who come to us are in fact seldom sufficiently
trained to achieve in two years of seminary college the
fluency that the Holy See requires. College sopho-
mores who have majored in Latin, we observed, do
not usually have anything near such an ideal fluency
after their two years, and they presumably have a
special ability in Latin. We felt that, among many
reasons, the main one is that in outside schools, as

far back as grammar school, too little stress is put
upon a solid grammatical and literary foundation
even in English; and that in secondary schools, Latin
especially is seldom taught carefully enough or with
proper intelligent emphases. Even in seminaries,
again, teachers are appointed to teach Latin who are
poorly trained, and burdened with so much other work
that they do not have the time to improve their own
abilities.

Then we turned to our respective curricula.
Comparing our courses with those of colleges of
liberal arts, it was gratifying to us to recognize that,
despite the difficulties, our course offerings are, in
general, on an adequately advanced level. There was
some discussion, however, of the common over-
crowding of the seminary curriculum. It is difficult
for our students to find the time to do the advanced
work asked of them, that is, the college standard requirement of at least two hours of study for every
hour of class. Someone pointed out, however, that the
seminarian usually studies with more discipline and
efficiency; and the consensus of opinion was that, in
fact, we are able to cover approximately as much in
quantity and quality as typical colleges. We then discussed the criteria by which to select the proper
authors, Christian and Classical. We concluded that
these criteria were, first, the need of promoting
facility in reading Latin -- which demands writers
whose style is challenging enough to keep the students
working, yet not so difficult as to be beyond their
current ability -- and, secondly, the need of acquaint-
ing the students with the whole of Classical civilization
by studying a sufficient number of representative
authors. There was little difficulty about the majority of our curricula, except that, in some places,
there was too much stress on too easy and non-
representative Ecclesiastical Latin. We agreed that
this type of Latin has a most appropriate place in our
curricula, but a subordinate one, as side-reading or
sight-translation. We concluded that the usual
authors met our criteria: Horace, Livy or Tacitus,
Cicero or Seneca, and selections from the Fathers or
St. Augustine's Confessions. Some advocated also a
course in Mediaeval Latin. There was a division of
opinion about the practicality of anthologies instead of

concentration upon some one author in a semester. It was agreed, however, that as long as the selections from any one author were of sufficient length for the student to get used to his style and to obtain some real understanding of its characteristics, such anthologies were useful. In fact, in teaching the Fathers, almost all did make use of selections. There was then brought up for discussion the growing tendency to turn the closing semester of the liberal arts course into a pre-philosophy course, with concentration almost exclusively on the terminology of works that the student will study in the major seminary. We all regretted this tendency keenly, as it is clearly opposed to the explicit instructions of the Holy See. Furthermore, in the opinion of those who had had experience with such a course, this procedure did not accomplish its purpose, but only wasted the students' time. Surely, we felt, if the student can be given an intensive enough course in good Latin, he can adjust to another type of Latin in a short time; but if he is given such a practical sort of course, he cannot master the terminology apart from the science, nor continue to gain the real proficiency in Latin a Classical course could give.

Shortly after we began to discuss the curriculum, the question arose of what to do about composition. All felt the need of some sort of composition; many used a standard work such as Bradley's Arnold, revised by Mountford, although some felt dissatisfied with the results. We could not resolve our differences here, for some thought that composition should be taught as a separate course, aimed mostly at a review of grammar, while others thought more would be achieved if it were based on the author being read, reviewing only current syntactic weaknesses, and aiming as well at appreciation of word-order and style.

We then discussed various classroom techniques: assignments, recitation -- oral and written -- sight-translation, lectures, and term-papers. In all of this, we felt we should be guided by the proper hierarchy of seeking first thought-content, then appreciation of literary style and historical background for better understanding of what is read.

Finally, we discussed the students who come to us with little or no Latin. The difficulty is that so often

these students are deficient, not only in Latin -- that's
bad enough -- but also in basic linguistic or literary
training, and have hardly more than the barest minimum talent for Latin. There were different ways of
handling such students. Most required them to spend
a special year of intensive study of Latin before being
admitted to the regular freshman course, while a few
felt it was sufficient to have them take most of the
regular freshman course along with their classes in
elementary Latin. We were divided, too, about the
advisability of having these students continue in a
second year adapted to their needs and perhaps at a
slower pace. Even with these students, however, it
was agreed that they should be given as much of a
Classical course as possible, to conform to the mind
of the Holy See. We had an interesting discussion on
the various textbooks available. It was definitely
agreed that the beginning text should not be one on a
first-year high school level, but one written for more
mature students. Of the five or six discussed, several
stood out as especially promising, both theoretically
and on the basis of the results gained by those who had
used them. As for modern structural or functional
approaches to beginning Latin, there were the usual
differences of opinion. In substance, we agreed that
it would be much safer to keep essentially to the more
common, tried methods of the so-called traditional
variety, stressing fundamentals and translation. At
the same time, we should continue to investigate and
weight the merits of any new techniques or methods
that could freshen and invigorate the fulfillment of our
most important work: the training and development of
effective, articulate, well-educated future priests.

ON AUDIO-VISUAL AIDS IN LATIN INSTRUCTION

Sister M. Melchior Beyenka, O.P., Director

In résumé, the seminar on audio-visual aids will be considered under three headings:

(1) the equipment, materials, and other resources at the disposal of the workshop members;

(2) the students' use of materials and equipment in the A-V laboratory; and

(3) the formal instruction by the director of the seminar.

Sources of supplies of A-V material are listed at the end of my report.

EQUIPMENT

For the seminar in A-V aids in the teaching of Latin, Room 208 of Mullen Library was made available as a laboratory and storage room. Its supply of bulletin board material was also left for the use of the members. Equipment belonging to The Catholic University of America and put at the disposal of the workshop consisted of an Ampro movie projector, a Webcor tape recorder, a Rek-o-Kut record player, an American Optical 2x2 filmstrip and slide projector, and an American Optical 3x4 slide projector.

Wilson Gill, Inc., of Washington, provided the workshop with the free loan of an RCA movie projector, two RCA record players, a Beseler opaque projector, a Vu-Graph overhead projector, a Wollensak tape recorder, a Da-Lite screen, and an Instructomat console and language laboratory booth. This last item was demonstrated by Mr. Wilson Gill and an associate.

Viewlex Company of New York loaned two slide and filmstrip projectors for the duration of the workshop.

Mr. George W. Frid of American Optical

Company, Silver Spring, Md., furnished the loan of a 3x4 slide projector and an opaque projector.

Mr. A. H. Evans, president of Electronics Language Laboratory, Washington, gave a demonstration of the Monitor language tape recorder. The unit remained in the A-V laboratory for the balance of the workshop.

The Pentron Company of Chicago also furnished us with tape recording materials.

A. J. Nystrom Company loaned a set of 32 maps.

The Department of Greek and Latin of Catholic University made available its sets of maps covering the Ancient World.

The loan of an Argus 3 camera and a Brownie Kodak was made by one of the members of the Dominican House of Studies.

Mr. Joseph Popecki of the Catholic University Library staff was most generous with his equipment and help.

MATERIALS

Materials for the classes and laboratory periods were loaned (*), rented (**), or purchased (***) from the following companies or individual owners:

(1) Films: Encyclopedia Britannica (*), Coronet (*), International Film Company (*), Eastman Kodak (*), Eternal Films (**), and National Educational Television (NET) (**).

(2) Tapes: EMC (*) and Waldo A. Sweet (*).

(3) Filmstrips: Roa Films, Inc. (*), Jam Handy (*), Basic Skills (*), Richard Walker (*), and Waldo A. Sweet (*).

(4) Slides: Rev. R. V. Schoder, S.J. (*), Jacronda (*), Sister Winifred Mary, O.P. (*), Catholic University of America art department (*), and Argo Slides (***).

(5) Records: Richard Walker (*).

OTHER RESOURCES

A reserve shelf in Room 211 of the Education Library provided texts on the subject of A-V

instruction in general. The Catholic University of
America bookstore sold copies of Wm. M. Seaman's
Guide to Audio-Visual Materials in the Classics
(American Classical League [Oxford, Ohio, 1956]). A
selected supplementary bibliography for materials
available since 1956 was furnished to the members of
the class by the director of the seminar.

Literature from A-V manufacturers was received
in great quantity upon request and was distributed to
the members of the workshop.

Sincere thanks is due the Director of the Latin
workshop, Dr. Martin R. P. McGuire, who channeled
the materials and equipment until the arrival of the
members. Gratitude is also due the Reverend Leo R.
Lynch, who made his car available to bring materials
and equipment to and from Caldwell Hall for the afternoon sessions. I am also very grateful to the many
unnamed persons who helped project materials at
class time and who assisted generously in the
laboratory each day. I wish to acknowledge also the
services of Sister M. Vivien Jennings, O.P., careful
keeper of the minutes of each day's proceedings.

STUDENTS' USE

The members of the workshop received the above-
mentioned illustrative materials at class meetings or
found them available upon request in Room 208.

Each member was also given an opportunity during
the hours 10:30 a.m. - 2:30 p.m. each day to learn to
operate the various projectors and recorders, to hear
recordings, or to see the many materials. They were
encouraged to become proficient in the operation of
the movie projector, slide projector, filmstrip
projector, opaque projector, and tape recorder. For
this purpose, two witnesses were required to attest
their successful performance of these skills on form
sheets. These records, when completed, were given
to the respective seminar directors. Frequently as
many as thirty persons used Room 208 during the
arranged hours. Many members became proficient
operators of machines they had previously eschewed.
Several items were purchased by the members.

Bulletin boards were made available in the Mullen
Library for the use of the workshop. The following

themes were illustrated by class members: The A-V
Laboratory, Coming Events of the Workshop, Op-
portunities for Study at Home and Abroad, Paper
Backs on Classical Subjects, Projectors in A-V
Instruction, and Donald Honz's Stimuli.

FORMAL INSTRUCTION

Classes for the Seminar in A-V aids in the
teaching of Latin were held each afternoon at 4 p.m.
in Room 101, Caldwell Hall. At the introductory
lecture audio-visual instruction was defined as the
carefully planned and integrated use of films, slides,
pictures, maps, posters, records, chalk boards,
radio, etc. Several principles were outlined for the
effective and efficient use of these aids: namely, the
use of materials significant in the light of the
teacher's purpose; the appeal in teaching to as many
senses as possible; the use of a variety of A-V
materials; the preparation of teacher and students
beforehand; the conditioning of the room for proper
light, air, and seating; and the careful guiding of the
students' thinking before and after the presentation by
well placed remarks, questions, or other means.
Subsequent lectures discussed and illustrated the
use of chalk boards, flash cards, maps, opaque
projectors, bulletin boards, pictures, posters,
photography of colored and black and white pictures,
slides, filmstrips, movies, recordings, and tapes.
It was emphasized that if a teacher had all of the
so-called modern visual aids but lacked a chalk board
in her classroom, she would be seriously hampered in
her teaching. That very old visual aid is still the
most universally valued. Flash cards of desk size or
of classroom size can heighten interest and proficiency in the learning of vocabulary, paradigms, etc.
These and posters and maps are essential for the
teaching of elementary Latin, but may be used, if
less extensively, in more advanced courses. Bulletin
boards have a place in the Latin teacher's classroom,
and whenever it is possible, the Latin teacher and her
students should arrange bulletin boards on Classical
subjects in more frequented parts of the school where
they will attract favorable attention and interest. The
opaque projector can serve to project maps, graphs,

pictures, or entire pages of a text or test. Its use was
demonstrated in the seminar when the text of the
Carmina Burana was projected during the playing of
the record. The overhead projector allows the teacher
to face the class while she projects materials at the
front of the classroom.

Slide projectors were recommended chiefly to en-
rich the Latin program by occasional talks on Roman
life, ancient art, mythology, etc. The excellent illustrated lecture by Msgr. Patrick A. Skehan on the
Dead Sea Scrolls gave proof of the worth of this
device. Its possibilities are quite extensive. Filmstrips are available in the field of ancient history,
mythology, antiquities, and language arts. Several
filmstrips were shown to the class, notably one on
Roman coins, which was synchronized with a tape
recording. Movie films which might be used to en-
rich the Latin curriculum are available to a limited
degree. This area of A-V aids in Latin is less well
supplied than several others.

Tape recordings of language drills, dramatic
readings of passages from literature in Latin or in
English, and simple Latin conversations were
demonstrated at the seminar. To many teachers this
aid is new, but it deserves to be more widely used. A
student's translation, for example, can be taped and
then played back for comment or correction. Teachers
have administered or corrected a test during an en-
forced absence from class. Tapes for help in drill
work may be purchased from the publishers of textbooks or made by the teacher herself.

An outgrowth of Dr. McGuire's talk on the pronunciation of Latin is of interest here: tapes on the
Italian pronunciation of Latin, which are available at
present, are more suited to teach the pronunciation
for singing rather than speaking Latin. There is a
real demand for tapes or recordings for classroom
use which will demonstrate the Italian pronunciation
of spoken Latin. Several members expressed the
hope that this need would be met by Dr. George J.
Siefert of the Department of Greek and Latin at
Catholic University.

Some materials for the teaching of Latin are
available on recordings and were utilized. These are
chiefly passages from Latin literature in English or

Latin, and drills from Richard Walker's series,
"Tutor that Never Tires," and "Texts that Talk."

   Seminar 3 endeavored to keep the spirit of its
title, "Audio-Visual Aids in the Teaching of Latin."
Its role was that of auxiliaries, helpers of the
magistri.   Like the auxiliaries of the ancient Roman
army, the armor is somewhat foreign, somewhat
peculiar among the regular ranks, but the day is
envisaged when more and more auxiliaries will fight
side by side with legions of veterans and tyros in the
effective teaching of Latin.

SOURCES UTILIZED

   The following materials were used during class
periods in Seminar 3 (sources are given in parentheses).

Slides

Athens, the Holy Land, Rome, Italy (Argo Slides)
Book of Kells, Lindisfarne Gospel, St. Sever
      Apocalypse (Sister Winifred Mary, O.P.)
Selected slides of ancient sites (Rev. R. V. Schoder,
      S.J.)

Filmstrips

Apollo and Phaethon (Jam Handy)
City of Rome (EBF)
Diagramming of Sentences (SVE)
How to Use a Teaching Film (Basic Skills, Inc.)
Roman Coins (EMC)
Tutor that Never Tires (Richard Walker)
Wanderings of Odysseus (Educational & Recreational
      Guides)

Movies

Mediterranean North Africa (EBF)
Pompeii and Vesuvius (EBF)
Noble Roman Letter (NET)
St. Peter's Excavations (Eternal Films)
World's Great Religions (EBF)

Tapes

Herbert Abel's radio play, Phaethon, by Rosary
  College Players (Sister M. Melchior, O.P.)
Cicero vs. Catiline (EMC)
Quis Sum? (EMC)
Vergil's Aeneid VI (EMC)

Recordings

Carmina Burana, arranged by Carl Orff (Angel
  Record)
Tutor that Never Tires (Richard Walker)

The following items were used out of class hours
by members of the workshop:

Slides

Felt Boards (Jacronda)
Views of Europe (Sister M. Melchior, O.P.)

Filmstrips

Effectiveness of A-V Materials (Basic Skills, Inc.)
English Grammar (SVE)
Glory that was Greece (Eye Gate)
Grandeur that was Rome (Eye Gate)
Heroes of Greek Mythology (Jam Handy)
      Daedalus and Icarus
      Golden Apples of the Hesperides
      Jason and the Golden Fleece
      Orpheus and Eurydice
      Pegasus and Bellerophon
      Ulysses in the Cave of the Cyclops
Hellenistic Greeks (SVE)
Julius Caesar (Educational & Recreational Guide)
Lesson in Mythology (Educational & Recreational
  Guide)
Life in Ancient Rome (Museum Extension)
Life in the Middle Ages (Eye Gate)
Myths of Greece and Rome (Jam Handy)
      Apollo and Phaethon
      Atalanta's Race
      Baucis and Philemon

    Ceres and Proserpina
    Minerva and Arachne
    Prometheus and Pandora
Odyssey (SVE)
Roman Empire (SVE)
Roman Republic (SVE)
Rome the City (Museum Extension)
Using Charts and Graphs (Basic Skills)

Movie Films

Art and Life in Italy (Coronet)
Chaucer's England (EBF)
Clear and Sharp (Eastman Kodak)
Facts about Films (International Films)
Facts about Projection (International Films)
Leonardo da Vinci (EBF)
Medieval Crusades (EBF)
Medieval Guilds (EBF)
Medieval Knights (EBF)
Medieval Manors (EBF)
Renaissance (EBF)
Roman Wall (Coronet)

Tapes

Caesar Meets Ariovistus (EMC)
Death of Pliny the Elder (EMC)
Interview on Olympus (EMC)
Wrath of Juno (EMC)

    Materials for distribution were made available
for the workshop by the following:

    American Optical Company, Instrument Division,
Buffalo 15, N.Y.
    Audio Devices, Inc., 444 Madison Avenue, New
York 22, N.Y.
    Bell Sound Division, 555 Marion Road, Columbus
7, Ohio
    C. Beseler, 219 S. 18th Street, East Orange,
N.Y.
    Jack Coffey Company, 710 Seventeenth Street,
North Chicago, Ill.
    Da-Lite Screen Company, Warsaw, Ind.

Dept. of A-V Instruction, NEA, 1201 16th Street, N.W., Washington 6, D.C.

DuKane Corporation, St. Charles, Ill.

Educational Development Laboratories, 75 Prospect Avenue, Huntington, N.Y.

Graflex, Inc., General Precision Equipment Corporation, Rochester 3, N.Y.

Keystone View Company, Meadville, Pa.

Merrill Lee Company, 3049 Grand Blvd., Detroit 2, Mich.

LaBelle Industries, Inc., Oconomowoc, Wis.

Levelor Lorentzen, Inc., 720 Monroe Street, Hoboken, N.J.

Newmade Products Corp., 250 W. 57th Street, New York 19, N.Y.

Plastic Products Inc., 1822 East Franklin St., Richmond 23, Va.

Radio Corporation of America, Camden, N.J.

Radiant Screen Company, 2627 W. Roosevelt Road, Chicago 8, Ill.

Reeves Soundcraft, Great Pasture Road, Danbury, Conn.

Revere Camera Company, 320 E. 21st Street, Chicago 17, Ill.

Standard Projector and Equipment Company, Inc., 7106 Touhy Ave., Chicago 48, Ill.

Teaching Tools, 6327 Santa Monica Blvd., Los Angeles 38, Calif.

V-M Corporation, Benton Harbor, Mich.

Webster Electric, Racine, Wis.

Filmstrip distributors whose materials were used at the workshop were the following:

Basic Skills, Inc., 1355 Inverness Drive, Pasadena 3, Calif.

(EBF) Encyclopedia Britannica Films, 1150 Wilmette Ave., Wilmette, Ill.

Eye Gate House, Inc., 146-01 Archer Avenue, Jamaica 35, N.Y.

Educational & Recreational Guides, Inc., 10 Brainerd Road, Summit, N.J.

Jam Handy Organization, 2821 East Grand Boulevard, Detroit 11, Mich.

Museum Extension Service, 10 E. 43rd Street,

New York 17, N.Y.
    Roa's Films, Inc., 1696 N. Astor Street, Milwaukee 2, Wis.
    (SVE) Society for Visual Education, Inc., 1345 Diversey Parkway, Chicago 14, Ill.
    Richard Walker, Bronxville, N.Y.

Movie film distributors whose materials were used at the workshop were the following:

    Coronet Films, 65 E. So. Water Street, Chicago 1, Ill.
    (EBF) Encyclopedia Britannica Films, 202 E. 44th Street, New York 17, N.Y.
    Eastman Kodak, 343 State Street, Rochester 4, N.Y.
    Eternal Films, 1790 Broadway Ave., New York 19, N.Y.
    International Films, Inc., 57 E. Jackson Blvd., Chicago 4, Ill.
    (NET) National Educational Television Film Service, Audio-Visual Center, Indiana University, Bloomington, Ind.

Slides were shown by courtesy of the following:

    Jacronda, 5449 Hunter Street, Philadelphia 31, Pa.
    Rev. Raymond V. Schoder, S.J., West Baden College, West Baden, Ind.
    Sister Winifred Mary, O.P., Rosary College, River Forest, Ill.

Local distributors who furnished equipment for the workshop were:

    American Optical Company, Mr. George Frid, 7961 Eastern Ave., Silver Spring, Md.
    Electronics Language Laboratory, 1818 M. Street, N.W., Washington, D.C.
    Wilson Gill, Inc., No. 1 Thomas Circle, Washington 5, D.C.

Miscellaneous materials were made available by the following:

Data Guide, 40-05 149th Place, Flushing 54, N.Y.

Folkways Records & Service Corp., 117 West 46th Street, New York, N.Y.

Donald Honz, <u>Stimuli</u>, 1124 Belknap Street, Apt. B., Superior, Wis.

Language Learning Aids, Box 850, Boulder, Colo.

Nystrom Maps, 3333 Elston Avenue, Chicago 18, Ill.

Viewlex Projectors, 35-01 Queens Blvd., Long Island City, N.Y.

PART III

APPENDICES

APPENDIX A

OUTLINES OF THE EVENING LECTURES ON SELECTED ASPECTS OF ROMAN CIVILIZATION

by

Martin R. P. McGuire

I. THE ROMAN CONSTITUTION: ITS MAIN FEATURES AND ITS FUNCTIONING IN THE CICERONIAN AGE (c. 70-43 B.C.)

"Our Republic was not made by the genius of one man, but of many, nor in the life of one, but through many centuries and generations." (Cato ap. Cic. De rep. 2.1.2)

The Roman Res Publica better called a "Commonwealth" than a "Republic" in our sense

The Roman constitution an unwritten one

The three great organs of government: the magistrates, the Senate, and the assemblies

Collegiality a characteristic feature of Roman magistracy -- magistrates not paid in our sense

Imperium and potestas

The Senate in theory an advisory body but one enjoying great prestige -- the Senatus consultum ultimum

The assemblies in theory the possessors of sovereignty, but in practice controlled by the magistrates and the Senate -- the impossibility of asking for the floor in a Roman assembly

The Tribunate a unique kind of office -- its changing interests as the plebeian element in the Roman nobilitas based on office became more prominent

The unit system of voting in Roman assemblies

Roman citizens and their rights: public rights -- ius suffragii, ius honorum, ius provocationis, and private rights -- ius commercii and ius conubii

The important role of mos maiorum in Roman

public as well as private life -- its breakdown in the
Late Republic

The rise of an extreme individualism and ruthless
imperialism in the second century B.C.

The Gracchan crisis the first in a series of
crises culminating in the collapse of the Republican
system of government in the age of Cicero

The conflict between the Optimates and Populares
largely dominated by self-interest at the expense of
the public welfare

The revolt against Rome in Italy and outside Italy
occasioned by injustice and the rise of the extraordinary commands

The failure of the Senate to assume responsibility
for veterans and its loss of control over ambitious
generals

A succession of great generals the real masters
of the state -- Marius, Sulla, Pompey, Caesar

The repudiation of Sulla's reactionary constitution and the breakdown of senatorial government in the
60's and 50's of the first century B.C.

Civil war and the dictatorship of Caesar

Cicero a man of peace and a champion of constitu-
tional government thwarted in his efforts and ultimately a victim of the political violence and anarchy of his
age

The failure of the Romans to develop a system of
representative government

Italy and the provinces ruled by a city-state

The Quirites Romani of Cicero's Orations the
faex Romuli of his Letters -- the degeneration of the
Roman citizenry in the second and first century B.C.
and its causes

Roman courts and court procedure in the age of
Cicero

The Praetor and his handling of civil cases

The Praetor's edict -- the importance especially
of the edict of the praetor urbanus

The contribution of the iuris consulti to the
development of Roman law

The quaestiones established to handle criminal
cases

The presiding officer (usually a praetor) and the
judges (iudices)

In the absence of a public prosecutor under the

Roman system, charges made in criminal cases by an individual <u>accusator</u>

SELECT BIBLIOGRAPHY

A. E. R. Boak, <u>A History of Rome to 565 A.D.</u> (4th ed. New York 1955) 171-260.

F. B. Marsh, <u>A History of the Roman World from 146 to 30 B.C.</u> (2nd ed. revised London 1953) 1-228, 245-260, 312-339.

F. R. Cowell, <u>Cicero and the Roman Republic</u> (New York 1948), especially the Isotype Charts following p. 66, and p. 210.

Cambridge Ancient History IX (London and New York 1932): ch. 1, "Tiberius Gracchus," ch. 2, "Gaius Gracchus," ch. 3, "The Wars of the Age of Marius" (especially 131-138), ch. 4, "The Enfranchisement of Italy," ch. 6, "Sulla," ch. 7, "The Breakdown of the Sullan System and the Rise of Pompey," ch. 10, "The Provinces and Their Government," ch. 11, "Rome in the Absence of Pompey," ch. 12, "The First Triumvirate," ch. 15, "From the Conference of Luca to the Rubicon," ch. 17, "Caesar's Dictatorship," ch. 21, "The Development of Law under the Republic"; CAH X (1934), ch. 1, "The Avenging of Caesar," ch. 2, "The Triumvirs".

F. F. Abbott, <u>A History and Description of Roman Political Institutions</u> (3rd ed. Boston 1910) 95-149, 150-265, 400-412 (on the Roman judicial system).

L. R. Taylor, <u>Party Politics in the Age of Caesar</u> (Berkeley 1949; Sather Lectures Vol. 22).

Oxford Classical Dictionary, pertinent articles, e.g.: "Magistracy, Roman," "Comitia," "Consul," "Praetor," etc., "Law and Procedure, Roman" (excellent), "Province," "Senatus," "Rome (History)" (especially IV. "The Fall of the Republic [133-31 B.C.]," 773-774).

II. THE PRINCIPATE: THE MAIN FEATURES OF THE NEW FORM OF GOVERNMENT INAUGURATED BY AUGUSTUS

Octavian sole master of the ancient world after

Actium

His assumption of the responsibility of reorgan-
izing the Roman state and of establishing a strong administration for a vast empire

The Principate established by stages and as far as
possible within the framework of traditional offices or
precedents

The imperium maius and the tribunicia potestas
the twin pillars of the Principate

The titles and powers of the princeps as reflected
in typical inscriptions of his age, e.g.:

Imp. Caesar divi f.
Augustus
pontifex maximus
imp. XII cos. XI trib. pot. XIV
Aegupto in potestátem,
populi Románi redáctá
Soli dónum dedit

(CIL VI 701, 702;
Dessau ILS 91)

The old magistracies and the new offices created
by Augustus -- the curatores, praefectus praetorio,
praefectus annonae, and praefectus Aegypti

The new careers opened up to the Equestrian as
well as to the Senatorial Order

The reorganization of the government of the city
of Rome: the regiones and vici, the cohortes urbanae
and cohortes vigilum, the praefectus urbi

The division of the government of the provinces
between the princeps and the Senate: the imperial
legati and procuratores -- the special status of
Egypt

The Senate and the assemblies actually controlled
by the princeps -- the disappearance of the old assemblies after Tiberius

The reorganization of the financial administration
of the state -- the further centralization carried out
by later emperors

The reorganization of the military forces of the
state -- the legions, the auxiliaries, the praetorian
guard, the fleets, the period of service and the
provisions for veterans

The foreign policy of Augustus: his failure to

make the Elbe his northern frontier, the establishment
of protectorates in the East -- the Augustan peace

Augustus pontifex maximus and his revival of
public cults and rebuilding of temples -- Duo et
octaginta templa deum in urbe ... refeci (Res gestae
20)

The imperial cult, its nature and significance in
the history of the Empire

The attempts of Augustus to establish a successor
of his choice

The Principate in theory a magistracy, but in
practice a military dictatorship

The evolution of the Principate into an undis-
guised autocracy in the third century

The lack of a hereditary principle and the frequent
struggles for the imperial office

The great achievement of Augustus as the architect of the Roman Empire and the significance of his
work in universal history

SELECT BIBLIOGRAPHY

A. E. R. Boak, A History of Rome 263-287.

T. R. Holmes, The Architect of the Roman Empire II
    (Oxford 1931).

E. T. Salmon, A History of the Roman World from
    30 B.C. to A.D. 138 (3rd ed. revised London
    1957).

M. Hammond, The Augustan Principate (Cambridge
    [Mass.] 1933).

CAH X ch. 5, "The Princeps," ch. 6, "Senatus
    Populusque Romanus," ch. 7, "The Imperial
    Administration," ch. 8, "The Army and Navy,"
    ch. 10, "Egypt and the Early Principate,"
    ch. 14, "The Social Policy of Augustus," ch.
    18, "The Achievement of Augustus."

Oxford Classical Dictionary, the pertinent articles.

III. ROMAN SOCIETY: THE CLASSES OF SOCIETY,
CITIZENS AND FOREIGNERS, FREEDMEN, AND
SLAVES

Roman society in the last century of the Republic
and in the Augustan Age -- the all-pervading influence
of Hellenism

The Senatorial nobility -- the old aristocracy of blood and the new nobility based on the holding of high office

The rivalry among Senatorial families and the race for office, power, and wealth

The breakdown of morality in private life and its reflection in corruption in public life and ruthless exploitation of subject peoples

The maintenance of large retinues of clients and slaves and the craze for luxury and display of all kinds

Lucullus, Hortensius, Cicero, and Cato the Younger as typical representatives of the contrasting standards of living in their age

The frequency of enormous debts and bankruptcies -- Catiline's case not isolated

The Equestrian class the dominant financial power in the state

The Equestrians supporters of imperialistic expansion

Their use of wealth to support pliant candidates for office and to shape public policy in their own interests

Their relatively conservative standard of living as exemplified by Crassus and Atticus

Plebeians, slaves, and freedmen -- the meagerness of our knowledge of the common man in this period

The precarious position of the poor citizen or lowly foreigner in a laissez-faire economic system based on slavery

The increasing number of poor freemen and freedmen at Rome dependent on the dole and other forms of public support

The wholesale bribery of the poor voters in various forms

Caesar's colonization program and reduction of recipients of the grain dole from 320,000 to 150,000

The crowded tenements or insulae housing the masses

The plebeian collegia

The enormous increase in the slave population of Rome and Italy in the Late Republic and Early Empire -- the sources of slaves: war captives, piratic kidnapping, breeding of home-born slaves --

400,000 war captives sent to the slave market by
Caesar alone
    The racial and cultural backgrounds of the urban
and rural slaves in this period
    The frequency of manumission and the rise of a
large class of freedmen (liberti)
    All professions except law in the hands of slaves
of Greek or Eastern origin: teachers, physicians,
architects, secretaries, managers of estates, actors
-- Cicero's secretary and literary assistant his
freedman Tiro
    The great influence exercised on the lives and
outlooks of their masters and patrons by cultured
slaves and freedmen'
    The lot of urban slaves much better than that of
rural slaves
    The important role of women of the higher
classes in the Late Republic and their active participation in social and intellectual life
    Typical women of the Ciceronian Age: Junia,
Calpurnia, Servilia, Porcia, Julia, Hortensia, Clodia
(the Lesbia of Catullus), Fulvia, Octavia, and the
women of Cicero's family circle -- Terentia, Tullia,
and Pomponia
    The frequency of divorce and remarriage
    The degrading influence of slavery on the morals
of master and slave
    Cicero and Servius Sulpicius Rufus -- men of high
character in an age of violence and corruption
    The beautiful character of Octavia and the
evidence of the laudatio Turiae
    The preservation of the old Roman ideals by many
Senatorial and Equestrian families in Rome, to say
nothing of the more conservative and old-fashioned
life of the Italian municipalities

SELECT BIBLIOGRAPHY

F. R. Cowell, Cicero and the Roman Republic (New
    York 1948) 219-294.
W. Warde Fowler, Social Life at Rome in the Age of
    Cicero (New York 1909).
G. Boissier, Cicéron et ses amis (18th ed. Paris
    1921).
CAH IX, ch. 19, "Ciceronian Society"; CAH X, ch. 14,

"The Social Policy of Augustus."

F. F. Abbott, The Common People of Ancient Rome
    (New York 1911).

H. Hill, The Roman Middle Class (Oxford 1952).

National Geographic Society, Everyday Life in Ancient
    Times (Washington 1953) 267-355.

M. Johnston, Roman Life (Chicago 1957. Sufficient
    attention is not given to differences in the
    several periods of Roman history.)

J. Carcopino, Daily Life in Ancient Rome. The
    People and the City at the Height of the Empire.
    Edited with Bibliography and Notes by H. T.
    Rowell (New Haven 1940; an excellent work).

W. L. Westermann, The Slave Systems of Greek and
    Roman Antiquity (Philadelphia 1955) 57-84.

R. H. Barrow, Slavery in the Early Roman Empire
    (London 1928).

A. M. Duff, Freedmen in the Early Roman Empire
    (London 1928; reprinted with corrections 1958).

T. Frank, An Economic Survey of Ancient Rome. I
    (Baltimore 1933), especially 300-407.

M. Rostovtzeff, The Social and Economic History of
    the Roman Empire. I (2nd ed. Oxford 1957),
    ch. 2, "Augustus and the Policy of Restoration
    and Reconstruction."

IV. ROMAN RELIGION IN THE AGE OF CICERO AND
AUGUSTUS

Definitions
    Religion denotes those activities that are
        motivated by a persuasive or propitiatory at-
        titude towards the supernatural world.
    Magic denotes those activities that are character-
        ized by a coercive or compulsive attitude
        towards the supernatural world.
    A myth may be defined as a pre-scientific or
        imaginative attempt to explain some phenomenon,
        real or supposed, which excites the curiosity of
        or causes bewilderment or uneasiness in the
        myth-maker.
    The definitions of religion and magic just given
are essentially those of J. M. Cooper, and the
definition of myth is that of H. J. Rose.
    The presence of intellectual, emotional, and

volitional elements in religion and magic

Religion and magic frequently found inextricably intermingled in practice

The chief types of religion: manism, animism, polytheism, and monotheism (sometimes rather henotheism)

The basic role of religion and magic in all aspects of public and private life in Antiquity

Roman religion a compound of Etruscan, Italic, and Roman (Latin) elements

The primitive Roman concept of numina as "powers" -- animism

Religio undoubtedly first used to denote a sense of awe or anxiety

The religion of the state and the religion of the household

The college of pontiffs and the college of augurs -- the pontifex maximus the head of the state religion

The pontiffs the guardians and interpreters of ius divinum and the keepers of the calendar -- the maintenance of the pax deorum

The constant official use of auspicium and the Etruscan disciplina in Roman public life

The quasi-official priesthoods: the flamines, especially those of Jupiter, Mars, and Quirinus, the Vestal College, the Salii or priests of Mars, the Luperci, and the Fratres Arvales

The fetiales or priests connected with the solemn declaration and termination of war

Devotio and evocatio reserved to the pontiffs

The Roman triumph a solemn religious rite of thanksgiving to the gods for victory

The household cult under the control of the pater familias and mater familias

The family worship of Janus, Vesta, and the Lares and Penates

The cult of the dead

Roman religion at first almost exclusively agricultural as revealed by its annual cycle of festivals and religio-magical rites

The adoption of Greek cults -- Ceres, Liber, Apollo, and others -- and the development of anthropo-morphic concepts of divinity in Roman religion from the beginning of the Republic

The collection of old Sibylline oracles also taken

from the Greeks

The cult of Aesculapius introduced in 291 B.C.

Early Roman religion strongly formalistic in character and its moral influence in public life most clearly revealed in the discipline and marked sense of duty which it imposed

The deeper penetration of Roman religion by Greek influences from the early third century on

The introduction of the Oriental cult of the Great Mother from Asia Minor under the stress of the Hannibalic War (205 B.C.)

The Senatus consultum de Bacchanalibus (186 B.C.)

The multiplication of public festivals in the third and second century -- Ludi Apollinares (212), Megalenses (204), Ceriales (202), and Florales (173) Lustrationes, supplicationes, and lectisternia

The spread of rationalism in the upper classes under the impact of Greek philosophy

The employment of religion as a political tool by statesmen -- Caesar the most agnostic of his contemporaries made pontifex maximus in 63 B.C. but a promoter of religion as a tool useful to the state

The decay of the old Roman religion and its priesthoods in the last century of the Republic

The spread of Oriental cults in Rome, especially the cult of Cybele and Isis -- the professional priesthood of the Isis cult

The spread of astrology and other forms of magic and superstition in the upper as well as in the lower classes

The revival of the old Roman religion in the years before Actium and its full restoration under Augustus

Augustus pontifex maximus after the death of Lepidus (12 B.C.) and the title held by all emperors until abandoned by Gratian in 382 A.D.

The religious policy of Augustus as reflected not only in his building program and restoration of priesthoods but also in literature and art

The carmen saeculare of Horace composed for the ludi saeculares of 17 B.C.

The sodales and severi Augustales and their religio-political significance

The vitality of the old Roman religion in rural

areas and its persistence into the early Middle Ages
-- the evidence furnished by Martin of Bracara
(died 580 A.D.)

SELECT BIBLIOGRAPHY

Oxford Classical Dictionary, articles, "Religion,
    Etruscan," and "Religion, Italic," "Isis,"
    "Mysteries," "Ruler-Cult."
H. R. Rose, Ancient Roman Religion (London and New
    York 1950).
CAH VIII, ch. 14, "Roman Religion and the Advent of
    Philosophy," CAH X, ch. 15, "Religious Develop-
    ment from the Close of the Republic to the Death
    of Nero."
C. Bailey, Phases in the Religion of Ancient Rome
    (Berkeley 1932).
F. Altheim, History of Roman Religion (London and
    New York 1937).
W. W. Fowler, The Religious Experience of the
    Roman People (London 1911; reprinted 1922).
P. Fabre, "La religion romaine," in Brillant-
    Aigrain, Histoire des religions. 3 (Paris 1955)
    293-432.
A. Grenier, Les religions étrusque et romaine
    (Paris 1948; "Mana" Series 2, III) 1-233.
A. D. Nock, Conversion. The Old and the New in
    Religion from Alexander the Great to Augustine
    of Hippo (London and New York 1933).
A. K. Michels, "Early Roman Religion," Classical
    Weekly 48 (1955) 25-35 and 41-45.

V. GRECO-ROMAN MYTHOLOGY

A myth, as stated in the last lecture, may be
defined as a pre-scientific or imaginative attempt to
explain some phenomenon, real or supposed, which
excites the curiosity of or causes bewilderment or
uneasiness in the myth-maker. "A myth is the result
of the working of naive imagination upon the facts of
experience." (Rose).

Mythology, as a scholarly discipline, concerned
with the systematic examination of traditional
stories of a given people, or of all peoples, for the
purpose of determining how they arose and to what

extent they were believed, their relations and inter-
relations, and their dates in terms of a relative or
absolute chronology

Mythology popularly employed as a term to denote
the whole body of mythological narratives themselves

The older explanations of myths too dogmatic and
oversimplified

Nature-myths very common and the great
majority of myths aetiological in character

Modern methods of investigating Greek myths --
and those of other peoples for that matter:

1. The determination of the source of the story
and its date

2. The determination of its Achaean, Dorian,
Ionian, or pre-Greek origin

3. The classification of the story as myth
proper, saga, or märchen

Myths proper chiefly concerned with the gods
and their activities and worship or with natural
phenomena, and primarily aetiological in character

Saga concerned with human beings as the main
characters and based on an actual historical event
of some kind

The märchen a story apparently invented and told
solely for amusement

Myth, saga, and märchen often completely
blended, as in the story of the Argonauts and in the
stories of Hercules' exploits

The lack of any early "systematic theology"
among the Greeks -- except the treatment of the gods
in Homer and Hesiod -- corresponding to the systems
found in Egypt and Mesopotamia, and the great
freedom, richness, and diversity of Greek mythology

The Cosmogony of Hesiod and its enormous
influence

The origins of the universe and the final organization of the cosmos under the leadership of the
Olympian Zeus, the chief among the younger gods

Greek religion and mythology markedly anthropo-
morphic from the earliest times known to us -- the
whole universe of the Greeks (sky, earth, the waters,
and the regions under the earth) peopled with greater
and lesser divinities and monsters

The complex problem of the origins of Greek
religion and its relation to Greek mythology

The saga cycles connected with Crete, Thebes, Troy, Athens, and other centers

The wide variations and contradictions in many Greek myths and sagas

The great influence exercised by the myths, sagas, and märchen of Early Greece on Classical Greek character, religion, literature, and art

"Thus the entire humanistic education of the Greeks was welded into unity through the majesty and spiritual force which myths exerted on all stages of the inner development of the individual." (W. Jaeger in G. B. Schwab, Gods and Heroes 16).

The continued influence exercised on the Hellenistic Age

The great interest of the Alexandrian scholars in Greek myths and their learned investigations devoted to them

The mythology presented by Ovid and other Roman writers borrowed and adapted from the Greeks -- the great importance of Ovid

Early Roman religion with its concept of impersonal numina not favorable to the development of a rich native mythology in the Greek sense

The transmission of Greco-Roman mythology to the Middle Ages and modern times

The new influence exercised by the direct contact with Greek literature from the Renaissance on

The permeation of all Western literature, and English literature in particular, by Greco-Roman mythology

SELECT BIBLIOGRAPHY

Compton's Pictured Encyclopedia, article, "Mythology" (an excellent tabular presentation of Greek and Roman Mythology).

Oxford Classical Dictionary, articles, "Mythology" (Rose), "Folk-Tales."

H. J. Rose, A Handbook of Greek Mythology Including Its Extension to Rome (4th ed. London 1950. It contains an excellent introductory chapter on the history and critical study of mythology.)

P. Grimal, Dictionnaire de la mythologie grecque (Paris 1952).

W. R. Halliday, Indo-European Folk-Tales and Greek

Legend (Cambridge [England] 1933).
T. Bulfinch, Mythology. The Age of Fables. The
   Age of Chivalry. Legends of Charlemagne (New
   York 1934; Modern Library. This old work is
   still valuable and attractive to high school
   students.)
H. A. Guerber, Myths of Greece and Rome (New
   York 1921).
F. E. Sabin, Classic Myths That Live Today
   (Boston 1940).
C. M. Gayley, Classic Myths in English Literature
   and Art (Boston 1911).
G. B. Schwab, Gods and Heroes (New York 1946; a
   Pantheon Book).
E. Hamilton, Greek Mythology (a Mentor Book).

VI. ROMAN EDUCATION: THE ROLE OF HOME AND THE ROLE OF THE SCHOOL

Early Roman education "a peasant education
adapted for an aristocracy" (Marrou)
      The central place of mos maiorum in early Roman
history from childhood to the grave
      Early Roman education a family education
strictly practical in character
      The persistent emphasis throughout Roman
history on the home as the center of education up to
full adolescence -- the importance ascribed to the
mater familias as a teacher and molder of character
      The boy's assumption of the toga virilis at about
sixteen and his preparation for public life under the
tutelage of his father or some trusted friend of the
family -- Cicero thus placed by his father under the
care of Q. Mucius Scaevola the Augur
      Military service required and performed under
similar guidance
      Moral and religious training and ideal inculcated
by example and fortified by the mos maiorum
      The strong family traditions, and the influence
of the imagines of ancestors and narratives of their
conspicuous devotion to duty
      The continued emphasis on the practical aspect
of education even after the introduction of Greek
rhetoric and philosophy
      The importance attached to a working knowledge

of law as a preparation for life as a citizen and magis-
trate -- the Twelve Tables a required memory exer-
cise for young school boys

The impact of Hellenism on Rome in the third and
second centuries B.C. and the adoption of the Hellenistic enkyklios paideia -- with some modifications --
at Rome

The Greek athletic program rejected, and also
music and, especially, dancing

The three stages of Roman education in the Late
Republic and Early Empire: primary (the ludus
litterarius), secondary (the school of the grammati-
cus), and higher education (the school of the rhetor)

The protests against the dangers to the national
culture and the rise of grammatici Latini beside the
grammatici Graeci

The Roman ability to assimilate without being
overwhelmed by Greek culture a marked feature of
Roman civilization

The ineffectiveness of legislation against Greek
teachers and the prestige enjoyed by the grammatici
Graeci and especially the rhetores Graeci

Rhetoric the capstone of education and all other
subjects in the curriculum regarded as a foundation
for its pursuit

The role of declamatio -- the suasoriae and
controversiae -- in rhetorical education

The Romans the first people to study a foreign
language, Greek, systematically as a means for
mastering their own -- Greek classics studied along
with Latin classics

Young children of well-to-do and rich families
taught by Greek tutors to speak Greek before knowing
Latin

The educated Roman bilingual in the Late
Republic and first two centuries of the Empire -- not
all as well versed in Greek as Cicero

Some attention given to the academic education of
girls at Rome

The custom of studying rhetoric and philosophy
abroad -- Athens, Rhodes, Pergamum, Alexandria --
in the Late Republic and under the Early Empire --
the student days of Caesar and Cicero at Rhodes and
of Cicero's son Marcus at Athens

Forensic oratory and jurisprudence, however,

studied chiefly by a kind of apprenticeship as in
earlier times

Secondary and higher education under the Late
Republic and Early Empire broad in scope but superficial in character

Science, scholarship, and the serious study of
philosophy left largely to the Greeks

The cultural ideal of urbanitas and humanitas

The breakdown of home training in the Late
Republic and the neglect of solid character training in
the new education furnished by the schools of the grammarian and rhetor

Philosophy as a way of life -- conversion to
philosophy

The good and bad influence of Greek philosophy on
Roman students -- Cicero and Caelius as typical
representatives of the new education in its various
aspects -- Caelius perhaps more typical than Cicero
in this respect

Education under the Republic and at the beginning
of the Principate maintained by private means and not
by the state

The extent of literacy much greater than one might
have reason to believe under the circumstances

SELECT BIBLIOGRAPHY

Oxford Classical Dictionary, article, "Education."

H. I. Marrou, A History of Education in Antiquity.
     English trans. by G. Lamb (New York 1956) 226-
     313 (the basic treatment).

A. Gwynn, Roman Education from Cicero to
     Quintilian (Oxford 1926).

M. L. Clarke, Rhetoric at Rome: A Historical
     Survey (London 1953).

J. Carcopino, Daily Life in Ancient Rome (New
     Haven 1940) 101-121.

Johnston, Roman Life 148-157 (inadequate. Marrou
     should be used in its place).

F. F. Abbott, "The Career of a Roman Student,"
     [on Cicero's son Marcus] in his Society and
     Politics in Ancient Rome (New York 1909) 190-
     214.

D. L. Clark, Rhetoric in Greco-Roman Education
     (New York 1957).

VII. ROMAN AMUSEMENTS, WITH EMPHASIS ON PUBLIC ENTERTAINMENTS

No national game in our sense developed by the Romans

Riding, fencing, swimming, wrestling, and boxing cultivated as a preparation for military training

The Campus Martius the chief athletic field of Rome

Games of chance, including much betting, very common -- Roman dice marked like ours but three used in games rather than two

The widespread development of public baths under the Empire and their great popularity -- the more elaborate baths in their appointments to be compared to our clubs or social centers -- the baths of Caracalla and Diocletian among the most imposing ruins of Antiquity

The extravagant banquets of ostentatious nobles and social climbers in Roman society in the Late Republic and Early Empire -- modern parallels

The craze for public entertainments in the Late Republic and under the Empire at Rome and elsewhere and the heavy drain on private wealth and public revenue -- the demand for bread and circuses (panem et circenses)

The term ludi employed to cover all such spectacles, which were religious in origin and regarded as religious rites -- their gradual secularization

The Ludi Romani, founded in 366 B.C. and lasting eventually from Sept. 4 to 19

The Ludi Plebei, founded about 220 and held from Nov. 4 to 17

The Ludi Apollinares, founded in 208 B.C. and held from July 6 to 13

The Ludi Ceriales, founded 202 B.C. and held from April 12 to 19

The Ludi Megalenses, founded in 191 and held from April 4 to 10

The Ludi Florales, established definitely in 173 B.C. and held from April 28 to May 3

The Ludi Victoriae Sullanae founded under Sulla and held from Oct. 26 to Nov. 1

The Ludi Victoriae Caesaris, held from July 20 to 30

The Ludi Fortunae Reducis founded by Augustus in 11 B.C. and held from Oct. 3 to 12

The continued quasi-religious celebration of the Lupercalia, Parilia, Cerialia, Vinalia, Robigalia, Saturnalia, among others

Special holidays and games decreed by Caesar and especially by the successors of Augustus -- 159 days marked as holidays in the Roman calendar in the reign of Claudius, 93 of these being devoted to games supported out of the public treasury; 175 days of games out of 200 public holidays in the third century A.D.

Trajan's victory over the Dacians celebrated with public entertainments lasting 126 days in 107 A.D.

The decline of comedy of the Plautine and Terentian type in the second century B.C. and its replacement at the games by the fabula reciniata (mime and pantomime) -- the immense popularity of mimes and pantomimes under the Empire and their notoriously indecent character

Acting among the Romans an infamous profession

Classical tragedies and comedies, however, still performed under the Empire and the cantica of comedies familiar to all

The first stone theater erected at Rome by Pompey in 55 B.C. (capable of holding 27,000 people), the theater of Balbus built in 13 B.C. (capacity 7500), and the theater of Marcellus completed by Augustus in 11 B.C. (capacity 14,000) -- the theaters at Pompeii, Arausio (Orange), and elsewhere

The chariot races and the gladiatorial games the most popular of all public entertainments in the Late Republic and under the Empire

The ludi circenses originally religious in character and intended by a kind of sympathetic magic to promote the orderly movement of the seasons

The Circus Maximus, going back to the early Republic, in the Vallis Murcia, the Circus Flaminius, built in 221 B.C., on the site of the present Palazzo Caetani, the Circus Gai et Neronis or Vaticanus, and the Circus of Maxentius, dedicated in 309 A.D., on the Via Appia -- circuses in other cities throughout the Empire

The Circus Maximus, under the Empire, capable of accommodating 255,000 persons, and richly

equipped and decorated -- the races run in seven laps
totalling 2.7 miles, the chariots usually drawn by four
horses, but sometimes by two, three, or six, or even
ten, the factions and their colors, the popularity of the
charioteers and horses as revealed by inscriptions and
writers, gambling on the races

The employment of the circuses for displays of
various kinds, and especially for venationes

The gladiatorial games originally connected,
apparently, with funeral rites in Etruria and Campania

The gladiators first introduced at Rome in 264
B.C.

Gladiators usually prisoners of war, slaves, or
condemned criminals -- the gladiatorial ludi and their
strict programs of training -- Capua

The fighting by pairs most usual under the
Republic and the number killed in such combats very
small

The gladiatorial combats first held in the Forum
or the circuses and then in buildings especially
constructed for them, the amphitheaters -- the amphi-
theater of Staurus (29 B.C.), the Colosseum completed in 80 A.D., and the many examples throughout
the Roman World -- the well-preserved one at Arles

The gladiatorial combats in pairs and in organized
battles or seafights under the Empire -- 5000 pairs of
gladiators exhibited by Trajan in one triumph

The first seafight put on by Caesar in 46 B.C.;
19,000 participants in the seafight staged on the
Fucine Lake by the Emperor Claudius in 52 A.D.

The venationes and the enormous slaughter of
wild beasts -- 5000 wild and 4000 domestic animals
killed in one day at the inauguration of the Colosseum
by Titus, and 11,000 animals killed in the celebration
of the Dacian triumph of Trajan in 107 A.D.

The failure of Nero and others to replace the
gladiatorial combats by athletic games and poetical
and musical competitions of the Greek type

The brutalizing effect of all this slaughter on the
spectators

The Christians often found among those condemned ad bestias at Rome, Carthage, Lyons, and
elsewhere -- no actual evidence, however, of the
martyrdom of Christians in the Colosseum, although it
is probable that Christians were martyred there

The final abolition of gladiatorial combats by an
edict of the Emperor Honorius in 404 A.D. -- the
story of the monk Telemachus

SELECT BIBLIOGRAPHY

Oxford Classical Dictionary, pertinent articles.
Johnston, Roman Life 238-303.
W. Warde Fowler, Social Life at Rome in the Age of
    Cicero 285-318.
Carcopino, Daily Life in Ancient Rome 202-263
    (excellent).
L. Friedländer, Roman Life and Manners under the
    Early Empire. English trans. (4 vols. London
    and New York 1908-1913) II 1-164, and IV 148-
    270.
H. Leclercq, "Amphitheâtre," Dictionnaire d'arché-
    ologie chrétienne et de liturgie I.2 (Paris 1924)
    1648-1682.

VIII. THE LIFE OF THE EARLY CHRISTIANS AS REVEALED IN INSCRIPTIONS AND EARLY CHRISTIAN LITERATURE

The permeation of all phases of public and private
life by paganism

Participation in the imperial cult an act and
symbol of civic loyalty

The moral, religious, and political difficulties
facing Jews and Christians in their pagan milieu

The Jews despised and ridiculed but recognized as
a special ethnic group and not required to participate
in the religion of the State

Christianity by the time of Trajan a religio
illicita and persecuted either intensively and systematically, or sporadically on a local basis, to the time
of Constantine

The early Christians drawn almost entirely from
the masses and the Senatorial aristocracy before the
Peace of the Church

The small number of converts from the middle
class and municipal aristocracy and the cause

The Christians regarded as enemies of the
national traditions

The pagan schools and their role in promoting

pagan culture and emperor worship

The full meaning of Philippians 3.20, "Our commonwealth is in heaven," only adequately understood when examined against its background

The condition and attitude of the Christians at the end of the second century as revealed in the Letter to Diognetus:

> To say it briefly: what the soul is in the body, that the Christians are in the world. The soul is disseminated through all the members of the body, and the Christians through all the cities of the world. The soul dwells in the body, but it is not of the body; and the Christians dwell in the world, but they are not of the world. The soul, invisible, is kept shut up in the visible body; the Christians know that they are in the world, but their worship of God remains invisible. The flesh hates and wars on the soul, though suffering no injury from it, because it is hindered from enjoying sensual pleasures; and the world, though suffering no injury from them, hates Christians because they oppose its pleasures. The soul loves the flesh that hates it, and its members. The Christians love those that hate them. The soul is locked up in the body, but it holds the body together. The Christians are held in the world, as it were, in a prison, but they themselves hold the world together. The soul dwells immortal in a mortal tenement; the Christians live amid perishable things, looking forward to imperishableness in heaven. Treated harshly in respect to food and drink, the soul is made better. The Christians, though punished daily, increase the more. In this position has God placed them, and it is not lawful for them to renounce it.

(For editions of the Letter to Diognetus, see Quasten, I 252.)

The practice of Christian charity in the Early Church one of its most distinguishing features and one that perhaps impressed pagans most

The Church and slavery -- the recognition of the

slave as a creature of God, endowed with a soul and possessing sacred rights as a person

The Christian community at Rome Greek-speaking at first -- as noted in my lecture on the origin of Christian Latin

The catacombs underground cemeteries outside the City -- known to the Roman authorities and protected by Roman law even in time of persecution

About three-fourths of all burials in the catacombs made after 313 A.D.

Total length of the galleries of the catacombs some 60 miles and total burials from 150-400 A.D. about 500,000

Total Christian population of Rome c. 200 A.D. not more than 10,000, and in 313 about 75,000

The ornamentation of the tombs of the martyrs in the 4th century -- the inscriptions of Pope Damasus

The art of the catacombs of great importance for the history of Christian doctrine, especially for the evidence furnished on Baptism and the Eucharist

The precise meaning of <u>coemeterium</u>, <u>depositio</u>, <u>decessit</u>, <u>dies natalis</u>, <u>patria</u>, etc.

Christian symbolism: the fish, the anchor, the ship alone or with four rowers, the vase with and without doves, the praying figure, the palm, the crown, the shepherd carrying a sheep

Some Typical Christian Inscriptions

1.   Asellus et Lea Prisco Patri bene
merenti in pace
qui bixit annis LXIII mensibus III
✖ in signo ✖ dies n. XII
V. kal. Oct. d̄. Basso et Ablavio
Conss.

(331 A.D. De Rossi 39; Diehl[1], Pl. 32, 11; Diehl[2] 1545)

2.   Successae filiae dul
cissimae parentes q. v. an
nos duos m. XI d. II, b. m. in pace
Dp. XVIII kal. Sept. Nicriniano ... conss.

(350 A.D. De Rossi 110; Diehl[1], Pl. 32, 22; Diehl[3] 2628)

3.   Hic iacet Muscula quae et Galatea
quae vix. ann. duob. mens. duob. et d. XVII.
Dep. XV kal. Aug. Gratiano Aug II et
Probo conss. in pace ✖

(371 A.D. De Rossi 371; Diehl[1], Pl. 33, 13; Diehl[2] 3253A)

4.   Laurentia que vi
xit annos ✕Ꝿ mises V zi. XIII

(mises = menses, and zi = dies)

(392 A.D. De Rossi 400; Diehl[1], Pl. 34, 2)

5.   +Hic requiescit in pace Iulianus a̅r̅g̅t̅. qui visit
Annus plus Minus XLV depositus est sub XVII kal. Nobembris
p̅c̅ Basili V̅C̅ anno ✕Ꝿ

(557 A.D. De Rossi 1094; Diehl[1], Pl. 35, 21; Diehl 696)

6.

Quiescit in pa[ce P]raetextata, virgo sacra, deposita d. VII
id. Aug. cons. R[usti]ci et Olybri

(464 A.D. De Rossi 813; Diehl[2] 1708)

7.   Benemerenti in pace Libera
                        que bixit an. Ç II
    neofita dep. die III nonas Maias con. Gratiano et Equitio

(375 A.D. De Rossi 243; Diehl[2] 2007)

8.   Ic positus est Silbanus marmorarius
        q. vi. an. XXX et fecit cum uxxore an. III
            et mensis III depositus IIII kal. Iulias

(Diehl[2] 656)

9.   Cornelius martyr ep.

(Diehl[2] 956 a. Pope Cornelius, 251-253 A.D. This is the
first papal inscription in Latin).

10.   Dalmatio filio dulcissimo
            totius ingeniositatis ac sapienti
            ae puero quem plenis septem an
            nis perfrui patri infelici non licu
            it qui studens litteras Graecas non
            monstratas sibi Latinas adripuit et in
        triduo ereptus est rebus humanis IIII d. fer
        atus VIII kal. Apr. Dalmatius pater fec.

(Diehl[2] 742; Silvagni 1978; CIL VI 33929)

For the metrical inscription composed by Pope Damasus in
honor of St. Agnes and cut in the Philocalian letters, see
Diehl[1], Pl. 36; A. Ferrua, S.J., Epigrammata Damasiana
(Rome 1942) 176, Pl. 37.

SELECT BIBLIOGRAPHY

Bihlmeyer-Tüchle, Christian Antiquity. Engl. trans.
    by V. E. Mills, O.F.M. (Westminster, Md.,
    1958).

Fliche-Martin, edd., Histoire de l'Eglise ... English
    translation of Vols. I-III by E. C. Messenger
    under the following titles: I, The Primitive
    Church (New York 1942); Vol. II, Part I, The
    Church and the Arian Crisis (1952); Vol. II,
    Part 2, The Life of the Church in the Fourth
    Century (1952).

J. Quasten, Patrology (2 vols. Utrecht, and West-
    minster, Md., 1950-1953).

I. Giordani, The Social.Message of the Early Church
    Fathers. Engl. trans. by A. L. Zizzamia
    (Paterson, N.J., 1944).

O. Marucchi, Manual of Christian Archeology. Engl.
    trans. by H. Vecchierello, O.F.M. (Paterson,
    N.J., 1935; reprinted 1949).

L. Hertling, S.J., and E. Kirschbaum, S.J., The
    Roman Catacombs and Their Martyrs. Engl.
    trans. by M. J. Costelloe, S.J. (Milwaukee
    1956).

F. van der Meer and C. Mohrmann, Atlas of the
    Early Christian World. Engl. trans. by M. F.
    Hedlund and H. H. Rowley (London 1958).

H. Delehaye, S.J., Les origines du culte des
    martyrs (2nd ed. revised Brussels 1933).

J. M. C. Toynbee and J. W. Perkins, The Shrine of
    St. Peter and the Vatican Excavations. (New
    York 1957; Pantheon Books).

C. R. Morey, Early Christian Art. An Outline of the
    Evolution of Style and Iconography in Sculpture
    and Painting from Antiquity to the Eighth Century
    (new ed. Princeton 1953).

A. Grabar, Byzantine Painting (Geneva 1953; Skira
    Series).

E. Diehl, Inscriptiones Latinae (Bonn 1912; = Diehl[1]).

E. Diehl, Inscriptiones Latinae Christianae Veteres
    (3 vols. Berlin 1925-1931; = Diehl[2]).

G. B. DeRossi, Inscriptiones Christianae Urbis Romae
    septimo saeculo antiquiores. I (Rome 1857).

A. Silvagni, Inscriptiones Christianae Urbis Romae
    septimo saeculo antiquiores. NS. I. (Rome 1922).

APPENDIX B

SUGGESTED SYLLABUS MATERIAL FOR HIGH SCHOOL COURSE IN LATIN -- FOUR YEARS

First Year

Vocabulary	Grammar	Composition	Translation	Background
300-50 words from standard list, e.g., College Board, New York State Regents	Five declensions, all cases Four conjugations, all tenses and moods, both voices; deponents -- io verbs irregular verbs, especially sum, eo, possum Adjectives, formation and agreement Adverbs Comparison of adjectives & adverbs Pronouns: personal, reflexive, demonstrative, relative, interrogative, intensive Numerals Infinitives; participles Indirect discourse Independent subjunctive and subjunctive of purpose Ablatives -- 8 or 10 common uses Accusative: time, motion, with certain prepositions; subject of infinitive; double Dative -- indirect object; special verbs Genitive: possessive, objective and subjective	Simple sentences illustrating points of grammar taught; also some connected sentences	Reading of simple material based upon or adapted from the Classical writers, e.g., Ovid, Livy, Seneca; also selections from the Liturgy The Labors of Hercules; Ritchie's Ulysses; Adapted selections from Caesar	Roman family life and public life; home, education, religion, mythology. General ideas on the major contributions of Rome to civilization

500-700 words from standard list. Idioms and special phrases for Caesar	All of above. Other uses of ablatives Genitive -- other uses Dative -- agent, purpose, reference, possession, with special verbs Gerund and gerundive Periphrastics Supine -- with other forms of purpose Subjunctive -- all normal uses	Sentences and passages illustrating the points of grammar taught, especially: Indirect statement Indirect question Purpose and result clauses Clauses of time, cause, circumstance, concession, etc. Cases governed by special verbs and adjectives, etc.	Argonauts Stories from Roman history: selections from Livy, Nepos, Eutropius Caesar, De bello Gallico. Selections to be largely determined by the text used: Helvetian campaign, Ariovistus, campaign against Belgae; Vercingetorix, etc.	Appreciation of Roman civilization: Julius Caesar, the man, the author, the general, the statesman

Third Year

700 words; idioms and special phrases for Cicero	All of above Conditional sentences Clauses of characteristic Rhetorical figures	Many sentences drilling the rules of syntax; all of the above plus the special third year constructions; Ciceronian style to be stressed	In Catilinam (I and one other) De imperio Pompeii Pro Archia Selections from Verrines, Philippics, Letters; also selections from Sallust, Pliny, and Augustine	Roman life in the time of Cicero, especially government, geography, literary history

Fourth Year

As above plus special poetry list	Review of above as met Grammar peculiar to poetry: alternate endings; short forms; figures; significant word order; verse scansion	Composition is optional in a Vergil course	Aeneid I, II, IV, and VI. Selections from other books and from other poets, e.g., Catullus, Horace, Ovid, Prudentius, Christian Latin Hymns	Roman history; Latin literature, especially the Latin epic; study of the Aeneid: genre, pattern, influence, etc. Life of Vergil

APPENDIX C

A NEW PRONOUNCEMENT FROM ROME ON THE STUDY OF LATIN*

In 1958, the Sacred Congregation of Seminaries and Universities issued a Letter to local Ordinaries on the proper study of Latin. It is published in the Acta Apostolicae Sedis, L (1958), 292-295. While the document is primarily concerned with the Latin curriculum, and especially with the methods of teaching Latin, in seminaries, it contains much that applies to Latin and the teaching of Latin in Catholic secondary schools and colleges in general. Before discussing the document further, however, it will be well to present its full text in English translation.

The Sacred Congregation of Seminaries and Universities

Letter to Their Excellencies, the Local Ordinaries, on the Proper Study of Latin

"We consider that, in doing all in your power to give a sound training to young seminarians, you are fully aware how much the Church insists by her precepts that those aspiring to the Priesthood should be carefully imbued with a knowledge of the humanities in general, but especially with a good knowledge of Latin. We know very well that Latin is signally proper to the priest, for it is the language which the Church requires him to use when as the vicegerent of Christ before God he is performing his sacred functions. There can be no doubt whatever, therefore, that, by virtue of the nature of his very office itself, he should

*This translation was made by Martin R. P. McGuire, Head of the Department of Greek and Latin and member of the Committee on Affiliation, as Affiliation Document SC 39:59, and copies are available through the Committee at The Catholic University of America.

not merely know Latin, but should know it as perfectly
as possible.

"In our time, however, the opinion has become
widespread that ecclesiastics are no longer so well
trained in those noble studies through which their
predecessors in the past won for themselves the admiration of all. The observation is now often made
and heard in various places that recently ordained
priests are so deficient in Latin that they are not only
unable to speak the language with any facility or write
it correctly, but they cannot understand even the
easiest Latin author. The reason for this decline will
be evident to anyone who examines, however cursori-
ly, our young students who are trained at the present
time. It must be admitted frankly that even in our own
seminaries there has been a marked decline in the
study of Latin, and in our days these institutions have
often lost the splendid reputation they once enjoyed for
their ability to combine so successfully the cultivation
of letters and the love of goodness and virtue -- an
achievement which made them such authoritative
examples to others. Unfortunately, our age seems to
esteem and avidly desire more than all else the
material advantages and comforts of life and, in a
spirit of contemptuousness, to despise the love and
study of arts and literature.

"Let no one think that we are exaggerating when
we complain of the decline of Latin in our seminaries.
It will be sufficient to cite a few examples from the
evidence which this Sacred Congregation has in its
possession. The Apostolic Visitors who recently
made a thorough investigation of the program of
studies in the Seminaries of the various countries have
furnished us with very depressing information on this
score. In fact, some were so disturbed by the increasing decline, that on their own initiative they
called our attention to this matter of such grave importance. These men are worthy of trust because of
their very positions, all without exception occupying
high offices: rectors of universities, heads and
professors of seminaries, and also certain laymen of
great influence and zealously interested in the welfare
of the Church.

"But we have been moved most by the representation of numerous bishops, who at length and in almost

identical terms warn of the damage that the Church
will suffer unless timely and efficacious remedies are
applied. In their complaint on the sad condition of
Latin, they maintain that the ignorance of Latin must
be regarded as chiefly responsible for the fact that the
students of our seminaries seem less interested in
theology and philosophy or study these disciplines only
in a superficial manner. For, unless seminarians
really know Latin well (as the bishops rightly emphasize), they have no access to the writings of the Holy
Fathers, the definitions and decrees of the Councils,
Papal documents, opinions of theologians, in a word,
to the great and rich mass of writings which constitute
the whole Tradition of the Church.

"Therefore, this Sacred Congregation has not
hesitated to take cognizance of such numerous and
important appeals which have come to it from everywhere, and, with full confidence that this will be useful and welcome to all, it has decided to assemble in a
brochure a number of splendid documents pertaining
to this matter which have been issued by the Sovereign
Pontiffs since the middle of the last century. Any one
who reads this brochure will easily see the great
force of the arguments presented in favor of the careful and diligent study of Latin on the part of our youth.
We have brought in the Sovereign Pontiffs as our
speakers, so that all concerned may see without any
uncertainty what must be done, and so that there may
not be any delay in putting into effect most zealously
what the Church herself commands through the voices
of the Popes. [1]

"For the fuller attainment of our purpose, it will
be useful to call attention to the remedies to be employed for curing the evil. Those selected, it will be
noted, are few in number, but they are ones which are
to be regarded as especially efficacious.

"I. Without question, for giving Latin its old
strength and prestige, it is necessary first of all to
select teachers carefully. It is obvious that no progress in the study of Latin can be hoped for as long as
unqualified teachers are assigned to the work of instruction. The Apostolic Visitors are unanimous in
affirming that the deplorable situation in respect to
Latin has arisen repeatedly through the fact that unqualified teachers are set to teach that language.

Ordinaries, therefore, should see to it that students
are placed in the hands of competent teachers only,
and particularly of those who have been solidly and
carefully trained in their discipline at the university
level and who have acquired skill in the art of teaching. If teachers of this kind are lacking, every effort
must be made to prepare them.

"II. In order that Latin may be more easily and
thoroughly mastered, the young seminarians must become well grounded, from the beginning of their
literary studies, in the elements of this language. But
a right method of instruction must be chosen and followed, whereby this discipline will be so taught that
they will study it and love it, and through their love of
it learn it well.

"Some teachers follow a forbidding system, de-
voting too much time and care to philological investigations and cramming the minds of their pupils with
learned and almost endless lucubrations. Is it any
wonder that young students exhibit indifference and
dislike when they are exposed to such a mass and
weight of learning? Others, on the contrary, like to
adopt certain modern methods of teaching, and think
that their pupils, when they have mastered a modicum
of rules covering writing and speaking, should plunge
as soon as possible into the reading of the great Latin
authors. The result is that the learners, who are not
yet instructed in the basic elements, are prevented by
all kinds of difficulties from being able to get a correct
understanding of what they read. Hence, boys are
made weary of their vain and profitless efforts and become so discouraged that they despair of ever being
able to learn Latin.

"Since whatever exceeds due measure is always
harmful, we ought to follow the mean. Accordingly,
the appropriate and effective form of Latin training
will be that which -- with sufficient attention being
given to the inculcation of the rules of grammar and
to elementary Latin composition -- will lead gradually through frequent exercises to the overcoming of
difficulties and the correct understanding of Latin
authors.

"What authors are to be chosen? We ought not
rest content with the great Classical authors alone,
but we ought to esteem highly all writers of Latin who

by the purity of their vocabulary, by their polished
diction, and by their whole style deserve a place close
beside the masters of the golden age. For Latin never
fell so low as not to have at times outstanding representatives equally distinguished for their style and
their learning. Therefore, let the pupils draw examples and inspiration from good Latin writers of all
periods. In this way they will discover a well established truth, namely, that Latin is not a kind of
dead or lifeless thing covered with the dust of ages,
and hence completely useless for life in our time, but
rather an instrument and vehicle of wisdom and culture
which, under the leadership and tutelage of the Church,
has developed and shaped our secular civilization.
Latin, therefore, rightly retains its strength and effectiveness even at the present time.

"III. Finally, it remains for us to recommend
strongly that pupils be given adequate opportunity to
learn Latin. To know its rules and to become proficient in its use requires much time and labor, for
there are many difficulties to overcome. Accordingly,
what can be said in favor of those programs of study
-- in force in certain seminaries -- under which so
few hours in the curriculum are assigned to Latin?
Some offer the excuse that they must yield to grave
necessity, for they say that, unless their pupils follow
the program of studies prescribed by the government,
they cannot acquire academic degrees that are publicly
recognized. This excuse, however, cannot be accepted. The Church, in the education of its candidates
for the priesthood, has and pursues its own special
purpose. Therefore, it follows its own laws, which it
cannot abrogate in any way. Furthermore, it is well
known that there are seminaries in which young students do learn Latin and at the same time earn academic degrees.

"We have thought it necessary to address this
communication to you. Its contents would seem, certainly, to be of such importance and authority as to
merit your most serious care and solicitude. We are
fully confident that in your seminary everything will
be arranged to bring about prompt conformance to
these rules and exhortations.

"Relying on this hope, we send you our best
wishes and greet you cordially in the Lord.

"Given at Rome, in the Palace of St. Callistus, on the Feast of Christ the King, October 27, 1957.

J. Cardinal Pizzardo, Prefect
C. Confalonieri, Secretary"

---

[1] To furnish their Excellencies the Ordinaries with fuller arguments respecting the study and use of Latin, the Sacred Congregation of Universities and Seminaries has sent them two brochures: I. Summorum Pontificum cum de humanioribus litteris tum praesertim de Latina Lingua documenta praecipua; II. Il Latino lingua viva nella Chiesa. In this second brochure, a number of distinguished men present clear and learned arguments on the importance of Latin.

The following Papal pronouncements on Latin have been assembled and are presented together: Pius IX, Encyclical Singulari quidem, March 17, 1856 (Enchiridion Clericorum, n. 338); Leo XIII, Letter Plane quidem, May 20, 1885, (Ench. Cler., nn. 461-465); Encyclical Depuis le jour, Sept. 8, 1899 (Ench. Cler., nn. 593-596; Pius X, Letter of S.C. of Studies Vehementes sane, July 1, 1908 (Ench. Cler., nn. 820-822); Letter Sollicitis Nobis, Dec. 8, 1910 (Ench. Cler., n. 849); Letter Votre lettre, July 10, 1912 (Ench. Cler., n. 861); Benedict XV, Letter of S.C. of Seminaries and Universities Vixdum Sacra Congregatio, Oct. 9, 1921 (Ench. Cler., n. 1125); Pius XI, Ap. Letter Officiorum omnium Aug. 1, 1922 (Ench. Cler., n. 1154); Ap. Letter Unigenitus Dei Filius, March 19, 1924 (Ench. Cler., n. 1189); M. P. Latinarum litterarum, Oct. 20, 1924 (Ench. Cler., nn. 1200-1202); Pius XII Encyclical Mediator Dei, Nov. 20, 1947 (A.A.S. 39 1947, 544s.); Address Magis quam Sept. 23, 1951 (A.A.S. 43 1951, 737); Address C'est une grande joie, Sept. 5, 1957 (A.A.S. 49 1957, 845-849).

Translator's note. The brochure Summorum Pontificum... was published by the Sacred Congregation of Seminaries and Universities, Rome, 1957, pp. 15. The brochure Il Latino... was published by the same Congregation, ibid., 1957, pp. 39. Among other selections, it contains a passage on "Latin the Liturgical Language," taken from Cardinal Gibbons,

Faith of Our Fathers.

The first part of the Letter expresses the deep
concern of Rome over the decline of Latin among
candidates for the priesthood as reported by the
Apostolic Visitors and by many bishops on their own
initiative. It is emphasized that a good knowledge of
Latin is absolutely essential for the priest, not only
for carrying out his sacred functions, but also to enable him to read firsthand the works of the Fathers,
papal documents, conciliar decrees, and theological
and ecclesiastical writings in general. The lack of a
sound knowledge of Latin, furthermore, has already
impaired the proper study of philosophy and theology.
The first part of the Letter closes with a strong
recommendation to read the accompanying brochures
prepared by the Sacred Congregation of Seminaries
and Universities which contain a series of papal pronouncements on the value and necessity of Latin for
the Church herself and a collection of appreciations of
Latin as the foundation and unifying element of
Western civilization.

The rest of the letter deals specifically with ways
and means for combating the present decline in the
knowledge of Latin among seminarians and priests.
This section of the document gets to the heart of the
matter and deserves the most careful study on the
part of high school and college teachers and administrators as well as on that of professors and heads of
seminaries. The remedies and recommendations are
presented in three main sections. Accordingly, they
will be presented here and discussed in the same
order.

1. Competent teachers are the prime need.
Nothing can be done unless Latin teachers are really
competent to teach their subject. Poor teaching was
reported unanimously as the chief cause for the poor
knowledge of Latin exhibited by seminarians and
newly ordained priests. It is significant that the
Letter stresses a long and thorough training culminating in university studies as the indispensable
preparation for Latin teachers. The Letter clearly
indicates that even teachers of Beginning Latin should
have this kind of solid training. The writer of this
article welcomes this recommendation most heartily.

On the basis of long experience, he has become con-
vinced that Elementary and Intermediate Latin and
Greek should be taught by exceptionally well-trained
and experienced teachers. Strictly speaking, a
teacher of Elementary Latin should have completed
six or eight years of Latin at the high school and
college level and obtained a Master's degree in
Classics at a good graduate school before entering the
classroom. Such a teacher, as the Letter also emphasizes, should have skill in the art of teaching.

   II. The Letter stresses the need of employing a
sound method in Latin instruction and advocates the
golden mean in this matter. The student should not be
overburdened with needless philological erudition of
various kinds. On the other hand, the teacher, under
the influence of "modern" methods, should not skim
over or neglect the rudiments of grammar and attempt
to begin reading Latin authors too soon. Students with
inadequate preparation are inevitably faced with
serious difficulties in trying to comprehend a Latin
writer and soon become frustrated and discouraged.
"The right and effective form of training will be that
which -- with sufficient attention being given to the
inculcation of the rules of grammar and to elementary
Latin composition -- will lead through frequent
exercises to the overcoming of difficulties and the
correct understanding of Latin authors."

   Throughout this section the Letter stresses the
necessity of mastering the elements as an indispensable foundation for all subsequent work in Latin.
It is clear that declensions, conjugations, and the
elements of syntax must be learned and fixed in the
mind by frequent oral and written exercises before
much, if any, connected reading of a Latin author is
attempted. While modern devices may be employed
in Latin instruction, the fact remains that no one will
ever learn to read Latin with facility and accuracy
unless he has acquired a solid foundation in grammar.
It is regrettable that what is so obvious needs to be
formally stressed.

   What Latin authors should be read? The Letter
assumes that Classical authors will be read, but
recommends that authors who have written "good"
Latin from antiquity to modern times be also included
for reading. Students must be made to realize by

concrete examples   that Latin has always been and
continues to be a vital element in our civilization.   It
is interesting to note that the Letter itself is written
in a fine, clear Classical style, but is not narrowly
Ciceronian in its vocabulary.   Throughout this section
emphasis is placed on the writing and speaking of
Latin as well as on the reading of Latin authors, as is
understandable in a document primarily concerned
with Latin instruction   in seminaries.

III.   It is strongly recommended that adequate
time be assigned for Latin instruction.   "To know the
rules of Latin and to become proficient in its use
requires much time and labor, for there are many
difficulties to overcome."   The hours of Latin instruction must not be reduced on the ground that the program of studies must be adjusted to meet the requirements of the state if degrees or diplomas of the institution are to be officially accepted and recognized.
The Church must insist on its prior rights at least
as regards its seminary curriculum.   A good
knowledge of Latin is indispensable for the priesthood, and training in Latin must not be sacrificed.

This Letter, as was observed at the outset, is
addressed to local ordinaries, and is primarily
concerned with the study of Latin especially in minor
seminaries.   However, as stated at the outset also,
it contains much that applies to secondary schools and
colleges.   It will suffice to highlight a few points.

1.   Catholic secondary school and college administrators might do a little pondering on the place
of Latin in Catholic education.   Latin is not merely
another foreign language to be equated as a required
subject or as an elective on the same level with
French, German, Spanish, or Russian.   Latin has
been a great unifying element in Western civilization
and has been, since the fourth century A.D., the
official and liturgical language of the Western Church.
The matter may be put as simply as this: as long as
Latin remains the official language of the Church,
and, especially, of the Liturgy, Latin must have an
essential place in Catholic education in general and
should be studied by every Catholic capable of
learning it, if he wishes to be regarded as a truly
educated Catholic in the strict sense of the term.
The wholesale dropping of Latin in our Catholic high

schools and colleges is an interesting phenomenon to
the social historian. It reveals to what extent Catholic
education in this country, though freer than anywhere
else in the world, can be and has been influenced by
its secular environment. In dropping Latin we are
cutting at the very roots of our cultural tradition. The
study of Classical, Patristic, and Mediaeval Latin
literature in translation is to be encouraged, but it
is no real substitute for Latin literature in the original
and should not be thought of or presented as such. It
may be observed, too, that poor training, or the lack
of required training, in Latin, in Catholic schools and
colleges is having the practical result that an increasing number of young men who wish to become priests
discover that lack of Latin is a formidable obstacle.
The writer does not share the opinion of Father
Abbott in his very timely and valuable article in
America (January 10, 1959, p. 422) that special
courses in Latin for men with delayed vocations or in
seminaries are satisfactory. These are essentially
"cram courses" which are not equivalent to a regular
program of sound instruction spread over a normal
period of time.

2. The writer would like to emphasize as
strongly as possible what is said in the Letter about
the necessity of competent teachers of Beginning
Latin. Too many teachers of Latin in our high
schools are simply not trained to teach Latin, and the
results of poor teaching are only too evident. Poorly
trained teachers are necessarily the slaves of textbooks, translations, and keys, and the results are
deplorable. Under such teaching a student may be
exposed to Latin for four years and, of course,
receive no satisfactory training in the language. As
indicated earlier, the teacher of Beginning Latin
should have had good training in Latin for six or
eight years in high school and college, and should
have received an M.A. in Classics, as a preparation
for intelligent and effective teaching of Elementary
and Intermediate Latin.

3. A great Classical scholar of the nineteenth
century once said that if one can find nothing else to
talk about he can always talk about method. For
some years, methods in Latin instruction have been
and continue to be discussed ad nauseam, and useful

helps for instruction tend to be regarded as magic
lamps, as rapid, complete -- and painless -- solutions
for all our difficulties. As a historian, the writer
would be the last to disparage the use of audio-visual
materials, the building of Roman homes and bridges,
the holding of Roman suppers in full toga, and the
rest, but this is not Latin. When all the pictures
fade, and the models are put on the shelves, there are
the same old declensions, conjugations, and basic
rules of syntax to be mastered, along with steadily increasing vocabulary, if one wishes really to know and
read Latin with accuracy. Furthermore, no adequate
substitute has yet been found for constant drill and
written exercises, and especially Latin composition,
as a means of fixing forms and rules of syntax and of
showing concretely the differences between English and
Latin idiom. Without such training, a student will
never learn to read and comprehend Latin accurately.
To the writer, half comprehension, or even four-
fifths comprehension, is not enough, when the meaning
of a significant passage is involved. It is rightly
recommended that reading should be begun as soon as
students have the necessary preparation in grammar,
and not before.

4. It is especially important to note that the
Classics are not to be put aside, but are to continue
to form the basis of instruction on the grammatical
side. Reading of non-Classical authors is recommended provided that they represent "good" Latin.
There is no justification for a present tendency to
introduce grammatical constructions from Late or
Mediaeval Latin into elementary instruction. The
usages of Classical Latin are clearly regarded as
basic at this stage. The role of Classical Latin in
instruction is also emphasized in the Apostolic
Constitution, Sedes Sapientiae, issued by Pius XII
(May 31, 1956), Art. 43, 3.2: "In accord with the
oft-repeated desire of the Holy See, diligent care
must be used in concentrating on the study and use of
Latin both because of its power in training minds and
also because it is the language of the Church. Students should be versed in Classical and Christian
Latin literature at least to the extent that they can
read scholarly texts with ease and, when the time
comes, may be able to use the sources of

ecclesiastical traditions fruitfully."

   5. On the basis of what has already been said,
Latin should have an essential place in the Catholic
secondary school and college curriculum. Granted
that the curriculum has become crowded to take care
of subjects that would seem to be necessary, there
remains the basic question of religious, cultural, and
practical values and their order of importance. In
the light of a truly Catholic philosophy of education, is
it right that Latin has been so neglected in our
curricula during the past twenty years, especially,
and that the study of Latin is at such a low ebb in so
many schools that pride themselves on being Catholic
even to an exemplary degree?

APPENDIX D

PARTICIPANTS IN THE WORKSHOP ON TEACHING LATIN IN THE MODERN WORLD

June 12 to June 23, 1959

Name	Representative of
Rev. Alban J. Alblinger, O.S.B.	St. Bede Academy, Peru, Ill.
Rev. William J. Bamber, C.M.	St. Joseph's College, Princeton, N.J.
Rev. Peter E. Barauskis, M.I.C.	Marianapolis Preparatory School, Thompson, Conn.
Sr. Marie Francis Barchie, R.S.M.	Sisters of Mercy, Pittsburgh, Pa.
Rev. Emmett A. Barrett, O.F.M.	Siena College, Loudonville, N.Y.
Sr. Theresa M. Bernhart, C.D.P.	Sisters of Divine Providence, Allison Park, Pa.
Sr. Mary Carmela Blust, R.S.M.	St. Mary High School, Bay City, Mich.
Sr. M. Clare Adelle Bolzenthal, O.S.F.	Holy Family Convent, Manitowoc, Wis.
Francis G. Borosko	Ursuline High School, Youngstown, O.
Sr. M. Immaculata Boyle, O.P.	Caldwell College, Caldwell, N.J.
Sr. Mary Benedetta Bray, O.P.	SS. Peter and Paul High School, Saginaw, Mich.
Sr. M. Josephine Brennan	Marywood College, Scranton, Pa.
Sr. M. Dolora Brogan, C.S.A.	St. Mary's Springs Academy, Fond du Lac, Wis.
Sr. M. Vincentia Brown, O.S.F.	College of St. Francis, Joliet, Ill.
Sr. M. Padraic Burke, I.H.M.	Marywood College, Scranton, Pa.
Sr. Ann Edmund Carey	St. Joseph's College for Women, Brooklyn, N.Y.

258

Sr. Charlotte Carl — Magnificat High School, Rocky River, O.

Bro. T. Ronald Char-shaf, F.S.C. — Bishop Armstrong High School, Sacramento, Cal.

Rev. Jeremy Chodacki, O.F.M.Conv. — St. Hyacinth College and Seminary, Granby, Mass.

Rev. Ralph F. Christ-man, M.M. — Maryknoll Junior Semi-nary, Clarks Summit, Pa.

Rev. Richard F. Clavelle, O.S.B. — St. Anselm's College, Manchester, N.H.

Rev. Benignus J. Cloonan, T.O.R. — St. Francis College, Loretto, Pa.

Bro. Godwin John Condon, F.S.C. — South Hills Catholic High School, Pittsburgh, Pa.

Bro. Christopher W. Conlon, S.M. — Cathedral Latin School, Cleveland, O.

Sr. Michael Eucharia Connor, S.C. — Marylawn of the Oranges, South Orange, N.J.

Marietta C. Conroy — Academy of Our Lady of Mercy, Milford, Conn.

Sr. Mary Lurana Cranny, B.V.M. — St. Mary High School, Chicago, Ill.

Rev. John Curran, S.M. — The Society of Mary, Washington Province, Penndel P.O., Pa.

Rev. James D. Daley — Diocese of Albany, N.Y.

Rev. Paul J. Day, C.M. — St. Joseph's College, Princeton, N.J.

Rev. Joseph D. Dillon — St. Francis De Sales Seminary, Oklahoma City, Okla.

Sr. Mary Armelia Doda, F.S.S.J. — Franciscan Sisters of St. Joseph, Hamburg, N.Y.

Sr. Mary Eileen Doherty — Cathedral High School, Trenton, N.J.

Sr. Maria Assumpta Dooley, S.S.J. — St. Mary's Central Catholic High School, Milford, Mass.

Sr. St. David of Mary Dwyer, C.N.D. — Waterbury Catholic High School, Waterbury, Conn.

Rev. Francis T. Ennis — School of St. Philip Neri,

Rev. Mark C. Ernstmann	Boston, Mass. Sacred Heart House of Studies, Springfield, Mo.
Sr. Marie Liguori Ewald, I.H.M.	Marygrove College, Detroit, Mich.
Sr. Mary Ethel Feehan, R.S.M.	Mercy High School, Chicago, Ill.
Rev. John P. Finnegan	Quigley Preparatory Seminary, Chicago, Ill.
Rev. Raymond J. Firmin	Maryhill Seminary, Pineville, La.
Sr. St. Eileen Margaret Fitzgerald, C.N.D.	St. Jean Baptiste High School, New York, N.Y.
Rev. Vincent A. Fitzpatrick	St. Joseph's Preparatory Seminary, Holy Trinity, Ala.
Rev. Charles J. Flood, S.C.J.	Kilroe Seminary of the Sacred Heart, Honesdale, Pa.
Bro. Borromeo Flynn, C.F.X.	Xaverian High School, Brooklyn, N.Y.
Sr. Mary Grace Flynn	Mount de Chantal Visitation Academy, Wheeling, W. Va.
Rev. William J. Foley	Sacred Heart Seminary, Detroit, Mich.
Bro. D. Benedict Gilroy, F.S.C.	Central Catholic High School, Pittsburgh, Pa.
Sr. Marie Dominic Gitre	Sisters Servants of the Immaculate Heart of Mary, Monroe, Mich.
Rev. John J. Gonchar, O.F.M.	Franciscan Fathers, Easton, Pa.
Rev. John P. Grady	Maryknoll Junior Seminary, Clarks Summit, Pa.
Sr. M. Euphemia Grunloh, O.S.F.	Sacred Heart High School, Joliet, Ill.
Sr. Mary Octavia Gutman, C.PP.S.	Precious Blood High School, Dayton, O.
Sr. M. Eileen Hagarman, C.D.P.	Sisters of Divine Providence, Allison Park, Pa.
Sr. Mary Berchmans Hannan	Georgetown Visitation Preparatory School,

Sr. Ellen Claire Hare, S.N.D.
Washington, D.C.

Sr. Mary Francis Holloway, C.S.J.
Notre Dame High School, Moylan, Pa.

Bro. Edmund Holmes, O.S.F.
Regis College, Weston, Mass.

Rev. Augustine S. Horn, O.S.B.
St. Francis College, Brooklyn, N.Y.

Sr. M. Macrina Hvizdos
St. Gregory's College, Shawnee, Okla.

St. Peter High School, Pittsburgh, Pa.

Rev. Paul F. Izzo, S.J.
Holy Cross College, Worcester, Mass.

Rev. Claude M. Jarmakiewicz, O.F.M.Conv.
Bishop Ryan High School, Buffalo, N.Y.

Sr. Mary Vivien Jennings, O.P.
Lacordaire School, Upper Montclair, N.J.

Mother Ellen Marie Keane, R.S.H.M.
St. Bridget's School, Richmond, Va.

Sr. M. Madeleva Kelleher, I.H.M.
Marywood Seminary, Scranton, Pa.

Mother Margaret Mary Kelleher, O.S.U.
Ursuline Academy, Bethesda, Md.

Sr. St. Mary Cornelius Kelliher
Congregation of Notre Dame, Bronx, N.Y.

Rev. Edward R. Kelly, O.P.
Dowling High School, Des Moines, Iowa

Sr. Marie Gertrude Kelly, S.N.D.
Maryvale-Trinity College Preparatory School, Brooklandville, Md.

Sr. Margaret Vincent Kennedy, O.P.
Pope Pius XII Diocesan High School, Passaic, N.J.

Sr. M. Ann Virginia Kenny, O.P.
Mount St. Mary, Newburgh, N.Y.

Sr. Marie Lillian Kerwin
Sisters Servants of the Immaculate Heart of Mary, Monroe, Mich.

Sr. M. Walburga Killmeier, O.S.U.
St. Joseph High School, Jackson, Miss.

Sr. M. Remigia Kostick
Sisters of St. Francis, Sylvania, O.

Sr. M. Kathryn Clare Krabbe, C.S.C.
St. Mary's College, Notre Dame, Ind.

Rev. Clement J. Kuhns,   St. Joseph's College,
   C.PP.S.   Rensselaer, Ind.
Sr. Mary Philip Kwolek,   Felician Sisters, Cora-
   C.S.S.F.   opolis, Pa.
Mother M. Immaculee   Marymount School,
   Landry, R.S.H.M.   Arlington, Va.
Rev. Bartholomew R.   Carmelite Fathers,
   Larkin, O.Carm.   Washington, D.C.
Sr. Mary Roberta   Siena High School, Chicago,
   Lenihan, R.S.M.   Ill.
Sr. Mary Carmelita   Ursuline High School,
   Lorenzo, O.S.U.   Youngstown, Ohio
Rev. Giles E. Laughlin   Carmelite Fathers,
                        Chicago, Ill.
Rev. James T. Lowery,   La Salette Seminary,
   M.S.   Hartford, Conn.
Rev. Leo R. Lynch   St. Paul Seminary,
                        Saginaw, Mich.
Sr. Ramona Lynch,   Cathedral Preparatory
   S.S.J.   School, Erie, Pa.
Sr. M. Francis Raphael   St. Andrew's High School,
   McCarthy   Pasadena, Cal.
Rev. Michael J. McCaul Epiphany Apostolic College,
                        Newburgh, N.Y.
Sr. Anne Raymond   Notre Dame High School,
   McCormick, S.N.D.   Moylan, Pa.
Rev. Henry J. McIntyre, Merrimack College, North
   O.S.A.   Andover, Mass.
Rev. Vincent McKiernan, St. Peter's College,
   C.S.P.   Baltimore, Md.
Sr. Maria Berchmans   Central Catholic High
   Madden, H.H.M.   School, Canton, O.
Bro. Albertus Mahoney,   Xaverian College, Silver
   C.F.X.   Spring, Md.
Rev. Henry Maibusch,   Austin Catholic Preparatory
   O.S.A.   School, Detroit, Mich.
Mother Mary Augusta   Ursuline Academy,
   Malone, O.S.U.   Bethesda, Md.
Sr. Gertrude-du-Divin-   The Sisters of the Assump-
   Coeur Marchessault,   tion B.V.M., Lowell,
   A.S.V.   Mass.
Sr. Mary Madeline   St. Teresa's Academy,
   Marlborough, C.S.J.   Kansas City, Mo.
Sr. Esther Meehan   Seton High School, Balti-
                        more, Md.

Sr. M. Venard Metro — Sisters of St. Francis, Sylvania, Ohio

Rev. Andrew T. Metzger, O.S.B. — St. Leo Abbey, St. Leo, Fla.

Rev. Joseph C. Miller, O.S.C. — Crosier Seminary, Onamia, Minn.

Sr. M. Seraphia Miller, C.PP.S. — Regina High School, Norwood, O.

Sr. M. Praxedes Morus — The Bernardine Sisters of St. Francis, Villanova, Pa.

Sr. Gerard Majella Mulroy — St. Mary Convent, Monroe, Mich.

Rev. Martin J. Murphy, C.Ss.R. — St. Mary's College, North East, Pa.

Sr. Mary Amabilis Niemcewicz — Our Lady of the Angels Academy, Enfield, Conn.

Sr. Jerome Nossell — Seton High School, Baltimore, Md.

Sr. Patricia Ann O'Brien — Seton High School, Baltimore, Md.

Miroslaus L. Ochrymowycz — St. Mary's College, Winona, Minn.

Bro. C. Eugene O'Gara, F.S.C. — St. Mary's High School, Waltham, Mass.

Sr. Eleanor O'Gorman — Seton High School, Baltimore, Md.

Sr. M. Michael O'Grady — Sacred Heart Junior College and Academy, Belmont, N.C.

Mother Marie Jeanine O'Leary, R.S.H.M. — Marymount Secondary School, Tarrytown, N.Y.

Sr. Marie Vianney O'Reilly, C.S.J. — St. Joseph's Academy, St. Louis, Mo.

Sr. Marietta Perotta, S.S.J. — Villa Maria Academy, Erie, Pa.

Rev. Roy A. Persich, C.M. — St. Mary's Seminary, Perryville, Mo.

Rev. Owen J. Pollard, O.F.M.Conv. — O.L.C. Seminary, Carey, O.

Rev. Martin A. Power, O.F.M.Conv. — St. Francis Seminary, Staten Island, N.Y.

Sr. Marie Michele Powers, O.P. — Sacred Heart School, Camden, N.J.

Sr. Eleanor Louis — Saint Mary's Academy,

Proctor, S.S.J.	Philadelphia, Pa.
Rev. John H. Ramsey	Villa Madonna College, Covington, Ky.
Sr. Mary Evelyn Reynard, S.S.J.	St. Bernard High School, Bradford, Pa.
Rev. Peter F. Rudden, S.A.	Friars of the Atonement, Montour Falls, N.Y.
Sr. M. Thomas More Ruffing	Sisters of St. Francis, Sylvania, O.
Rev. Charles J. Rukus, M.S.	La Salette Seminary, Altamont, N.Y.
Rev. John P. Sankovitz	Nazareth Hall Preparatory Seminary, St. Paul, Minn.
Sr. Mary Conrad Schnitzmeier, C.PP.S.	St. Mary's Junior College, O'Fallon, Mo.
Sr. M. Celeste Schultz, C.S.A.	Sacred Heart High School, Yonkers, N.Y.
Sr. Ruth Julie Schutzenhoffer, S.N.D.	Maryvale-Trinity College Preparatory School, Brooklandville, Md.
Sr. Leonie Shanley, S.S.J.	Villa Maria Academy, Erie, Pa.
Sr. John Marie Sheehan	Holy Trinity High School, Trinidad, Colo.
Rev. William H. Sheridan	Quigley Preparatory Seminary, Chicago, Ill.
Sr. Bonita M. Simon	Third Franciscan Order, Syracuse, N.Y.
Mother Mary Aelred Sinclair	Rosemont College, Rosemont, Pa.
Sr. St. John of Mercy Slattery, C.N.D.	Notre Dame Academy, Waterbury, Conn.
Sr. Mary Immaculate Smith, O.S.P.	St. Frances Academy, Baltimore, Md.
Rev. John A. Sokolski, O.M.I.	St. Anthony's Junior Seminary, San Antonio, Texas
Noreen Theresa Stack	Immaculata High School, Washington, D.C.
Anthony T. Stevens	North High School, Youngstown, Ohio
Sr. Mary Serafia Strot, O.S.F.	Charleston Catholic High School, Charleston,

Sr. Mary Josephine Suelzer — W. Va.
St. Mary-of-the-Woods College, St. Mary-of-the Woods, Ind.

Sr. Bernadette Marie Sweeney, A.S.V. — Sisters of the Assumption B.V.M., Petersham, Mass.

Rev. John M. Sweeney — Quigley Preparatory Seminary, Chicago, Ill.

Sr. Mary Regina Sweeney, S.N.D. de N. — Trinity Preparatory School, Ilchester, Md.

Rev. Ladislas I. Szymanski, O.F.M. — Duns Scotus College, Detroit, Mich.

Sr. Rita Teresa Tavernason, C.S.T. — Carmelite Sisters of St. Therese, Oklahoma City, Okla.

Sr. M. Helen Ruth Taylor, O.P. — Sisters of St. Dominic, Caldwell, N.J.

Sr. Mary Catherine Tronolone, O.S.F. — Order of St. Francis, Stella Niagara, N.Y.

Sr. Mary Stanislaus Unferfate, O.S.U. — Ursuline College, Cleveland, O.

Rev. Thomas J. Vail — Mater Christi Minor Seminary, Albany, N.Y.

Sr. St. Eleanor of Mary Verrastro, C.N.D. — Stamford Catholic High School, Stamford, Conn.

Sr. Mary Bernard Volk, O.S.U. — Ursuline High School, Youngstown, Ohio

Sr. Catherine Clare Walsh, S.N.D. de N. — Academy of Notre Dame, Villanova, Pa.

Sr. M. St. Corneille Warren, B.V.M. — Sisters of Charity, B.V.M., Dubuque, Ia.

William T. Wiesner, C.M. — St. Mary's Seminary, Perryville, Mo.

Rev. Edward M. Wilson — Gannon College, Erie, Pa.

Rev. Karl M. Wittman — Nazareth Hall Preparatory Seminary, St. Paul, Minn.

Rev. Marvin R. Woelffer, O.F.M. — St. Anthony Seminary, Santa Barbara, Cal.

Sr. M. Rose Angela Woolley, O.S.F. — The Catholic High School, Baltimore, Md.

Rev. Elmer P. Wurth, M.M. — Maryknoll Seminary College, Glen Ellyn, Ill.

Sr. Mary Franciline   Towson Catholic High
    Young, O.S.F.   School, Towson, Md.
Sr. Mary Stephen Zack,   Sisters of St. Joseph,
    S.S.J.   Erie, Pa.